_____

STUDIES IN ENGLISH LITERATURE

Volume XCIII

THE
MARLOVIAN
WORLD PICTURE

by

W. L. GODSHALK

University of Cincinnati

1974
MOUTON
THE HAGUE · PARIS

Published with the help of the Charles Phelps Taft Memorial Fund,
University of Cincinnatti.

Printed in The Netherlands by Mouton & Co., Printers, The Hague.

To Herschel Baker, who encouraged my daring

PREFACE

In the following chapters, I have used the term 'Romantic critics', and the term needs some initial clarification. By Romantic critic, I mean one who sees Marlowe as a propagandist for Renaissance aspiration, a purveyor of Elizabethan confidence, and for whom the playwright is a kind of pre-Romantic, perhaps an Elizabethan Keats. Of course, this is a rough-and-ready definition, and I might be hard pressed to apply it strictly to such diverse critics as Una Ellis-Fermor, Paul Kocher, Harry Levin, and Michel Poirier, although they are all basically Romantic in tendency. An off-spring of the Romantic point of view is the recent suggestion that Marlowe was mentally disturbed and wrote plays which are equally insane and disjointed. Wilbur Sanders is perhaps the chief exponent of this view. Refining Sanders' position, Christopher Fanta describes a Marlowe who is divided within himself, and whose plays illustrate his bifurcated psyche. In this strain of criticism, Marlowe is seen not so much as an artist controlling his medium as a man whose uncontrolled neuroses are expressed in his drama.

My own forebears (to whom I owe a great debt) are Roy Battenhouse and Douglas Cole, critics whom Harry Levin has called "neo-orthodox moralists". Were the label not used pejoratively, it might be accepted gladly. But Battenhouse and Cole may with equal justice be called the 'common sense critics' because they try to see Marlowe in a Renaissance, rather than in a Romantic context. From this point of view (to which I subscribe), Marlowe is neither a propagandist nor a psychotic, but a playwright with a strong sense of personal and social evil. He was not creating protagonists with whom he expected us to identify, but, like Swift, he was trying to force his audience to perceive the evils resulting from human pride.

There is a good deal of the intentional fallacy in the present study. But I have derived my ideas of Marlowe's intention from the plays, and if the reader wishes to see my use of Marlowe's name as a metaphor for his work, I am quite agreeable. Nevertheless, the intentional fallacy becomes critically dangerous only when it is arrived at *a priori*, when the critic decides what the author SHOULD HAVE DONE and then complains that the author has not done it. If the author's supposed intention is ascertained from his actual accomplishment, there seems to be no critical harm in assuming (however wrongly) that the author intended the effects which the critic has found.

In the attempt to discern if these effects were also available to a Renaissance audience, I have cited a good deal of sixteenth- and seventeenth-century material which relates to ideas and actions in the plays. I am, in general, not arguing that Marlowe was directly indebted to this material (although he certainly was in some cases). At its most valuable, the parallel gives us a point of comparison, allows us to see how other authors handled similar material and what attitudes they had toward it. Where the parallel was well-known, I am sure that Marlowe wished his audience to make the implied (often ironic) contrast, for the contrast helps the audience to gain perspective on the play.

There is one highly unorthodox aspect of this study: it does not follow a traditional canonical ordering. As far as I am aware, no other recent critical study has avowedly attempted a total rearrangement of the plays. Although scholars are becoming increasingly aware of the tenuous evidence upon which the present order has been built, still it has become 'standard' to see *Dido*, *1* and *2 Tamburlaine* as 'early' plays, and *The Jew of Malta*, *The Massacre at Paris*, and *Edward II* as 'late'. Only *Faustus* seems to be disputed. Defenders of the *status quo* will probably be upset to find *Edward II* yoked with *Dido*, and *The Massacre at Paris* discussed before the Tamburlaine plays. I would not go to the stake for this heresy, but until more definite evidence is forthcoming, the present arrangement of the canon does (I believe) make critical sense.

In the footnotes I have used *Short-Title Catalogue* numbers for the books printed before 1640. Since several of the better known collections have adopted this numbering, the inclusion of the STC numbers should help scholars who wish to check my findings.

The material contained in Chapter II first appeared in *ELH* and is used here with the kind permission of the editors.

The research for and writing of this study were done with the help of grants from the Folger Shakespeare Library and from the Taft Memorial Fund, University of Cincinnati. The basic ideas, however, were formed in the seminar room with the help of my students, and I owe much to their arguments. I also owe a debt to Herschel Baker, who, with a few incisive comments, changed the structure of this entire work. The staffs at the Folger, at the Harvard College Libraries, and at the University Library, Cincinnati, have been very cooperative. My most enormous debt is to the critics and scholars who have already written their books and articles on Marlowe. I regret that not each influence, whether positive or negative, can be recorded in the footnotes.[1]

---

[1] Charles G. Masinton's *Christopher Marlowe's Tragic Vision: A Study in Damnation* (Athens: Ohio University Press, 1972), was published after the present study was completed, and unfortunately could not be used as it merits.

CONTENTS

CONTENTS

I

CONSIDERATIONS AND RECONSIDERATIONS

The interpretation of Marlowe's plays, and consequently his dramatic career, is a much vexed subject. In recent years, some critics have tried to understand and explain why a play such as *Tamburlaine* has been interpreted so divergently.[1] Does the play condemn or glorify its protagonist? Readers seem unable to decide this basic question conclusively, and various reasons have been advanced for their indecision and disagreement. Since drama is the least subjective of the verbal arts, possibly Marlowe is not attempting to direct audience response; perhaps he is merely presenting the imitation of an action without enlisting our sympathies for any one character or system of ideas. This answer postulates a conscious objectivity on the part of the playwright, whose feelings are not engaged one way or the other by the dramatic characters he has created. The reader or playgoer, without guidance from the author, must decide for himself what he will admire or detest.

A variation of this answer suggests that the playwright lacks sufficient ethical direction. In discussing Marlowe's *Massacre at Paris*, for example, Wilbur Sanders senses an "equivocation at the moral heart" of the play:

This kind of moral ambiguity is a problem in other plays of Marlowe's besides this one. What else accounts for the rival interpretations of

---

[1] See, e.g., Irving Ribner, "Marlowe and the Critics", *TDR*, 8:4 (1964), 224. Cf. Ronald S. Crane, *The Languages of Criticism and the Structure of Poetry* (Toronto: University of Toronto Press, 1953), pp. 3-13, and Mildred Hartsock, "The Complexity of *Julius Caesar*", *PMLA*, 81 (1966), 56-58.

Tamburlaine – as a Christian fable against presumption, or as a humanist manifesto of the free spirit? Isn't there an analogous problem with the damnation of Faustus, the problem of deciding where precisely Marlowe stands? *The Massacre* is a useful focus for these perplexities, because it articulates the possibility, which cannot be dismissed out of hand, that perhaps he stands precisely nowhere.[2]

For Sanders, this ambiguity is reprehensible, though Keats might have called it negative capability and praised it as the crowning quality of a great dramatist.

We are indeed faced in our study of Marlowe with a spectrum of rival and incompatible interpretations. But we must not believe, as some critics do,[3] that only Marlovian criticism is plagued with such interpretive uncertainty. We may just as easily find diverse interpretations of Homer's *Odyssey*, Virgil's *Aeneid*, Shakespeare's *Hamlet*, or even the play we saw, or the novel we read, last weekend. These interpretations may be totally different, arriving at diametrically opposite conclusions about the purpose of the artist as well as the meaning of his work.

From the variety of critical interpretation, we may only conclude that Marlowe's plays are like other pieces of complex art which elicit varying responses from different sensibilities, not that Marlowe had or tried to have no attitude toward his creations, or that he had no moral direction. Audience reaction is conditioned by the many factors that psychologists and sociologists have taught us to recognize; and we must never accept the postulate that each member of an audience reacted in the same or similar manner; saw the same things; or caught the same emphases. Our experience tells us that this idea is wrong. Though responses to literature are conditioned by the general outlook of the age,

---

[2] Wilbur Sanders, *The Dramatist and the Received Idea: Studies in the Plays of Marlowe & Shakespeare* (Cambridge, England: Cambridge University Press, 1968), p. 35. Cf. Christopher G. Fanta, *Marlowe's "Agonists": An Approach to the Ambiguity of His Plays* (Cambridge, Mass.: Harvard University Press, 1970), p. 7: "the forms of the plays give expression to a duality of outlook, and equally to a gradually developed pessimism, that characterized Marlowe's mind."
[3] E.g., Ribner, p. 224.

still variety rather than uniformity must be the expectation. Marlowe's first audience must have been far from uniform in its reaction to the character of Tamburlaine. As Geffrey Whitney observed, "men ... in myndes do differ still [i.e., always]: ... So varried they, in their opinions all."[4] Human responses, even in the Renaissance, were varied and complex – no matter what the Tribe of Tillyard may believe.

Nevertheless, it is instructive to know some of the possible ways an Elizabethan may have reacted to the figure of Marlowe's Tamburlaine and his dramatic compeers. Let us take Sir Richard Barckley's comments on Renaissance soldiers as a point of departure. Soldiers, he tells us, take great "paines ... to embrue their hands in the bloud of them for whose preseruation Christ was contented to shed his own bloud".

And what be the frutes of these mens profession? Beside their owne miseries which are many, is the effusion of their owne bloud, and that of infinite numbers of innocents, men, women, and children; burning and sacking of goodly cities and townes, spoyling and ryfling mens goods, wasting territories and fields; rapes vpon matrones and virgines; prophaning Temples and sacred places; making men captiues and slaues, and to end in one word, all manner of impieties and outrages that men can commit.[5]

Barckley concludes that "so farre are these men from happines, that if any estate be more vnhappie then others, these seeme to challenge the vantgard".[6] We may surmise what his attitude toward Tamburlaine would have been, but if we generalized from his statement, we would be in error.

As far as we can determine, the attitude of the Elizabethan military to Tamburlaine would have varied significantly from Barckley's. Returning from action against Spain, a contemporary soldier might very well have excused Tamburlaine's inhumane acts as perfectly legitimate in wartime. This may well have been

[4] Geffrey Whitney, *A Choice of Emblemes* (1586; rpt. New York: Benjamin Blom, 1967), p. 46.

[5] Sir Richard Barckley, *A Discovrse of the Felicitie of Man* (London, 1598), p. 370 (STC 1381). See E. E. Reynolds, *Thomas More and Erasmus* (London: Burns and Oates, 1965), p. 125, for Colet's similar comments.

[6] Barckley, p. 381.

the reaction of a man like Geffrey Gates who, in 1579, published a book defending English militarism, "Wherein is eloquently shewed the due commendation of Martiall prowesse, and plainly how necessary the exercise of Armes is for this our age." In conclusion he writes:

the man, the people, or nation that fauour not the renowme and main-tenance of Military prowess, nor imbrase the high value of Armes, the same are enemies of all vertues, neyther haue they respect to godlinesse: but all to their owne bellies, as the swine .... In deede it is not a matter that doth properly apperteine to base & seruile mindes, but doth belong to the noble and ambitious courages. Let them therfore that are truely noble, loue Armes, and let them that chalenge, or loue the name of honour, vertue, honestie, or worthines, put their hands to the vse and aduancement of warlike knowledge and actiuitie; yea, the more noble, the more prudent, and honorable that men will be esteemed, so much the more friendly to Armes ought they to be, and the like delightfull in the practise and vse of the same.[7]

Gates' attitude toward Tamburlaine may be as confidently guessed at as Sir Richard Barckley's. Coming to the theater from his study, Sir Richard may well have been disgusted by Tamburlaine's cruelty; coming from the battlefield, Gates may have applauded roundly. Or, depending on the individual, the reverse may easily have been true. From that most warlike of Elizabethan scholars, Gabriel Harvey, we would expect a warm endorsement of Tam-burlaine's will to power.[8]

These paragraphs of conjecture and dubiety are not a sly hint that background studies are utterly valueless in understanding a work of art from a former century; this kind of study may help us to see the possibilities confronting the artist and to interpret the choices that he made. It can show us the way certain segments of the audience may have reacted and prove that our present interpretations were not completely impossible for a Renaissance

[7] Geffrey Gates, *The Defence of Militarie Profession* (London, 1579), p. 56 (STC 11683).
[8] In the margin of *Historiarum et Chronicorum totius Mundi epitome*, p. 256, Harvey writes: "Tamerlane of a lusty stowt Heardman A most ualiant & inuincible Prynce", with obvious admiration. See G. C. Moore Smith, *Gabriel Harvey's Marginalia* (Stratford: Shakespeare Head Press, 1913), p. 109, and Hale Moore, "Gabriel Harvey's References to Marlowe", *SP*, 23 (1926), 337-57.

sensibility. But we cannot argue that the sixteenth-century response to Marlowe's characters and ideas was uniform, simple, and unequivocal. Although this statement may seem transparently axiomatic, it has not been a basic rule in Marlovian criticism.

I am not suggesting that the search for meaning in literature is a futile task; I am simply reminding the reader, of what should be the obvious fact, that he will not find certainties in literature – or in literary criticism – any more than he finds certainties in the universe at large. The role of the critic is not to establish certainty, but to estimate possibility. The critic's business is to help his reader more fully respond to a complex verbal structure, be it poetry or prose. Hopefully the critic in the course of his discussion will suggest some new ways to read old lines, new ways to see what we have seen before as merely conventional action and language. He may be able to describe a hitherto unnoticed verbal pattern, or to give a new understanding to a pattern we have many times observed. But just as the physicist cannot claim that the atomic theory is the ultimate explanation or description of universal matter, so the critic cannot ask us to believe that his interpretation of a work of art is final or inevitable. He only suggests one way of seeing – his 'vision', and in this manner, he, as well as the artist, is a seer. With all due sadness, he realizes – somewhere behind the confident front he presents to his reader – that his vision is partial, limited, and incapable of being fully conveyed by the words which he loves so well to read and to write.

However, the serious student of Marlowe's drama must begin, not with interpretation, but with the consideration of three basic problems. First, we must understand what kind of texts we will have to work with. Second, we must deal with the problem of chronology. For the critic who wishes to describe the development of Marlowe's ideology and dramatic technique, this question is extremely important. Nevertheless, scholarly opinion is widely divided even on the relative position of the plays in the canon, let alone on the absolute date of each play. Third, how do the perplexing details of Marlowe's life fit into the total picture of the man and his work? How are we to explain the apparent discrepancy between the charges of atheism in his personal life and the religious morality of *Doctor Faustus*? How do we reconcile, in our interpretation of the plays, the radical skeptic with the conservative moralist? These are fundamental problems which the critic must consider, or determine to ignore, before he can begin a full-scale criticism of the plays.

Since most twentieth-century criticism relies heavily on a close reading of the text, the critic of Marlowe's plays must tread very carefully and remember that his grounds for imaginative leaps are not very firm. Although it is possible that *The Massacre at Paris* was printed in 1592, the only plays undoubtedly printed during Marlowe's life are the two parts of *Tamburlaine*, and they appeared without an author's name on the titlepage. It was not until sixteen years after his death, in 1609, that the plays were first attributed to him,[9] and perhaps the strongest evidence for Marlowe's authorship is internal – the aspiring protagonist and the verbal parallels with his other plays. But the question of attribution is overshadowed by the problem of text.

In 1590, when Richard Jones printed both parts of *Tamburlaine*, he wrote in his preface to the readers: "I haue (purposely) omitted and left out some fond and friuolous Iestures, digressing (and in my poore opinion) far vnmeet for the matter."[10] These fond and frivolous gestures have never been recovered, and we can only conjecture what their precise nature may have been. If we may judge from *Faustus*, it seems likely that Jones deleted the comic subplot, which analogically echoed the main action. If we have lost a subplot of this nature, one which mirrors and implicitly comments upon the Tamburlaine story, we have lost a valuable key to the interpretation of the play, and should this subplot come to light, all present interpretations might be called in question. Admittedly, this train of reasoning is merely con-

[9] Joseph Wybarne, *The New Age of Old Names* (London, 1609), p. 24, sig. D4^r (STC 26055). See R. W. Dent, "Marlowe, Spenser, Donne, Shakespeare – and Joseph Wybarne", *Renaissance Quarterly*, 22 (1969), 360-62.
[10] The text used throughout, except for *Doctor Faustus*, is *The Works of Christopher Marlowe*, ed. by C. F. Tucker Brooke (Oxford: Oxford University Press, 1910).

jectural. The frivolous gestures were possibly a few more jokes about Mycetes, excised because Jones feared they might be objectionable to extreme royalists. However, we do know from Jones's admission – and this is the major point – that the Tamburlaine plays have been cut.

We are also led to believe that the extant version of *The Massacre at Paris* is shorter than Marlowe's final draft. Although one may detect an incompleteness in reading the play, a comparison of the manuscript version of the soldier's speech (lines 812-23)[11] with the printed version gives proof absolute of cuts in these particular lines; and it has been assumed that the rest of the printed play is a good deal shorter than Marlowe's completed manuscript. In any case, we are here confronted with a complex textual problem which will receive detailed attention at the beginning of Chapter IV.

Turning to the celebrated case of *Doctor Faustus*, we have two different versions of the play, Thomas Bushell's 1604 quarto and John Wright's enlarged edition of 1616. Although Sir Walter Greg cast a good deal of light upon the problems raised by these divergent texts, the critic and editor are still presented with the fact that Greg deemed a reconstructed text necessary in order to approach the original state of the text.[12] Such a reconstruction is guided in part by bibliographical facts, but it depends largely on the literary discrimination of the editor. Which lines seem most Marlovian? The question can only be answered by a critic who has already developed an interpretation of the canon, and thus the text is chosen to fit an interpretation rather than the interpretation to fit the text. The dangers of such a procedure are fully apparent to the textual scholar.

The Marlovian canon is further troubled by the shadow of

[11] The manuscript is at the Folger Shakespeare Library, where I have examined it. See H. J. Oliver (ed.), *Dido Queen of Carthage and The Massacre at Paris* (Cambridge, Mass.: Harvard University Press, 1968), pp. 165-66, for a complete transcription.

[12] See W. W. Greg (ed.), *Marlowe's Doctor Faustus, 1604-1616: Parallel Texts* (Oxford: Clarendon, 1950), and *The Tragical History of the Life and Death of Doctor Faustus: A Conjectural Reconstruction*, ed. by W. W. Greg (Oxford: Clarendon, 1950).

multiple authorship.[13] The titlepage of the 1594 quarto of *Dido* carries the names of both Christopher Marlowe and Thomas Nashe. Although scholars such as McKerrow have endeavored to single out the passages written by Nashe, they have been able to isolate few parallels to his known work.[14] Of course, the discovery of parallels is never conclusive evidence for proving authorship, especially since *Dido* draws heavily on Virgil for plot and often for language. If Nashe did in fact have a hand in the play, the ebullient Nashean style may have been tempered by the Virgilian influence. F. S. Boas has suggested that Nashe's name was added to the titlepage, under Marlowe's and in italics, only as an indication that he prepared the manuscript for the printer.[15] Perhaps Nashe had nothing else to do with planning or writing the play. Although this has been the assumption of most scholars, the alternative that Nashe contributed substantially to the play cannot be entirely dismissed. More evidence must be forthcoming before we will be able to decide conclusively the problem of authorship.

The Jew of Malta raises the question of textual conservation. Although the play has a fairly continuous record of performances from the 1590's to the 1630's, it was not printed until forty years after Marlowe's death. The possibility of non-authorial additions and changes is great, especially since the playwright Thomas Heywood was responsible for publication. Perhaps Heywood himself, it has been suggested, tampered with the play. Examining the text for difficulties which may be attributed to improper revision or textual corruption, J. C. Maxwell finds only three cruxes, and these can be explained without recourse to emendation.[16] His

---

[13] Greg (ed.), *Marlowe's Doctor Faustus*, pp. 133-35, suggests that Samuel Rowley may have written portions of *Faustus*. The suggestion has not gained wide critical acceptance.

[14] Ronald McKerrow (ed.), *The Works of Thomas Nashe* (London: A. H. Bullen, 1904-10), IV, 295, expresses his doubt "whether Nashe had much or any share in the composition", while H. J. Oliver, pp. xxii-xxv, argues for Nashe's hand in the play.

[15] Frederick Boas, *Christopher Marlowe: A Biographical and Critical Study* (Oxford: Clarendon, 1940), p. 50.

[16] J. C. Maxwell, "How Bad Is the Text of *The Jew of Malta?*", *MLR*, 48 (1953), 435-38.

suggestion is that the text remained relatively stable until its printing. Of course, not all scholars have been convinced. Irving Ribner still feels that the text "suffered much alteration and degeneration between the times of its composition and its printing".[17] But on this point, Ribner is a lonely voice; for Richard Van Fossen notes: "in recent years, ... it has become more and more common to defend the 1633 text as very probably a faithful version of what Marlowe wrote".[18] This view of textual conservation, however, is directly related to the fact that recent critics have found the text fits their interpretations of the play. We no longer see the play, as did Eliot's generation, dividing sharply in the middle with a tragic Jew at the beginning and a comic Jew at the end. Again critical interpretation has governed our confidence in the text. Ultimately, the belief in the play's textual integrity is not founded on a new set of facts, but on a new faith.

In *Edward II*, we meet the ghost of a first edition which is no longer extant. In the Dyce Collection at the Victoria and Albert Museum, South Kensington, there is a copy of the 1598 edition in which a missing titlepage and the first seventy lines of text have been supplied in a seventeenth-century hand. The date written on the titlepage is 1593. Though it may be argued that "1593" is simply an error for "1598", the manuscript version has apparently been supplied from an earlier edition which is closer textually to the 1594 than the 1598 quarto. Both Tucker Brooke and Sir Walter Greg have argued for the existence of an earlier, now-lost edition, but unless a copy comes to light – not an impossible event as we know from the discovery of the first quarto of Shakespeare's *Titus Andronicus* in 1904 – we cannot be certain.[19] However, most

---

[17] Irving Ribner (ed.), *The Complete Plays of Christopher Marlowe* (New York: Odyssey, 1963), p. 420.

[18] Richard W. Van Fossen (ed.), *The Jew of Malta* (Lincoln: University of Nebraska Press, 1964), p. xiv.

[19] See C. F. Tucker Brooke, "On the Date of the First Edition of Marlowe's *Edward II*", *MLN*, 24 (1909), 71-73, who lists the variants between the MS. and the printing of 1594, and W. W. Greg (ed.), *Edward the Second* (Malone Society Rpts., 1925), pp. vii-viii. See also *Edward II*, ed. by H. B. Charlton and R. D. Waller, revised by F. N. Lees (London: Methuen, 1955), p. 212. Lees notes that the play was registered 6 July 1593 and that "publication usually followed quickly upon registration".

of the variants between the 1594 edition and the Dyce manuscript can be ascribed to errors in transmission or attempts at correcting the text. If there were a 1593 printing, it is quite possible that it was textually very similar to the 1594. But again this is conjecture.

One further suggestion about the 1594 text of the play must be recorded. In 1858, Dyce noted that the abbreviation "Matre." has been substituted for "Arundel" in the speech headings and also in the text. He thought that the "mistake ... was occasioned most probably by the parts of Arundel and Matrevis having been played by one and the same actor".[20] Greg, noticing this mistake along with an early entrance of "Bartley" at line 2097, theorized "that the piece was printed from a playhouse manuscript, and also apparently this had undergone some kind of revision for the stage".[21] It seems fairly clear that Dyce and Greg are right in their analyses of the mistakes, and what may appear on the surface to be a good text of *Edward II* has in all likelihood been through a reviser's hands. How much that reviser tampered with the text cannot be ascertained.

In surveying the Marlovian canon, we find almost every type of Renaissance textual problem, and these problems cannot be satisfactorily and conclusively solved by modern textual scholars. Our knowledge is too limited. Facing the textual situation objectively, the critic must admit that we proceed on literary faith, with the belief that through the extant texts we are able to see the essential Marlowe. The critic must approach his material with a due sense of humility and tentativeness. The further question of Marlowe's hand in other plays, such as *Arden of Feversham*, is interesting and perhaps important in assessing Marlowe's total theatrical commitment and influence, but in the present study we will be studying the seven now-undisputed plays in the canon.

The problem of establishing a chronology for these seven plays is as perplexing as the problem of text. In most cases, the external evidence is not very helpful. The publication dates range from

[20] Alexander Dyce (ed.), *The Works of Christopher Marlowe* (London, 1858), p. 203.
[21] Greg (ed.), *Edward the Second*, p. xii.

1590 for *Tamburlaine*, Parts I and II, to 1633 for *The Jew of Malta*. Although most critics have considered *Dido* an early effort and *Edward II* one of Marlowe's final plays, both were published in 1594, or if the Dyce copy is reliable evidence, the latter first appeared the previous year. *Faustus*, which some critics consider 'early' and others 'late', was first published in 1604. The undated first edition of *The Massacre at Paris* has been tentatively placed, on textual evidence, in 1592.[22] For most scholars, the chronology suggested by the publication record will not do.

The Tamburlaine plays have been dated as early as 1587 on the strength of Philip Gawdy's letter of 16 November of that year, in which he describes a theatrical shooting accident, and on the supporting evidence of Greene's *Perimedes the Blacke-Smith* (1588), which contains an allusion to Tamburlaine's tempting God from heaven.[23] Both references have been taken as pointing to incidents in *2 Tamburlaine*: the shooting of the Babylonian Governor and Tamburlaine's repudiation of Mahomet. Since, on the evidence of the Prologue of Part II (2317-19), the first part was written before the second, then it naturally follows that both were written before or during 1587. The logic is flawless, but the evidence is not. The Gawdy letter speaks of a character who is tied to a post and shot to death with "callyvers". In *2 Tamburlaine*, the action is not perfectly clear (V. i. 4259ff.), and modern editors usually add stage directions to indicate what happens on stage. In the text, however, Amyras points out how "the Captaine hangs" (4260), not how neatly he is tied to a post. Since Gawdy's letter does not specifically name *Tamburlaine*, he may well be recalling another, perhaps lost, play in which a similar execution was performed on stage. Greene's reference, on the other hand, may possibly be to a line in Part I: "His looks do menace heauen and dare the Gods" (I.ii.352), for Greene writes of "daring God out

22 Robert Ford Welsh, *The Printing of the Early Editions of Marlowe's Plays* (Ann Arbor, Michigan: University Microfilms, 1964), pp. 48-49.
23 Gawdy's letter is quoted by E. K. Chambers, *The Elizabethan Stage*, revised ed. (Oxford: Clarendon, 1951), II, 135, and *Perimedes* is in *The Life and Complete Works in Prose and Verse of Robert Greene*, ed. by Alexander B. Grosart (Huth Library, 1881-83), VII, 8.

of heauen with that Atheist *Tamburlan*". As Don Cameron Allen points out, in the Renaissance 'atheist' does not necessarily mean one who believes there is no God, but may mean one who acts as if there is none, that is, immorally or sacrilegiously.[24] Thus Greene may not be referring to the scene in Part II where Tamburlaine denies the existence of Mahomet, and the value of Greene's allusion for dating purposes is cut in half.

In fact, Greene may not have had either part of Marlowe's play in mind. Greene first mentions "*Tamburlaine*, the most bloody butcher in the world", in *Mamillia*, Part I, printed in 1583,[25] and few Marlovian scholars would care to push the date of the play back to the early eighties. Apparently Greene's knowledge of Tamburlaine antedates Marlowe's play, and as "the most bloody butcher in the world", Tamburlaine may be said to tempt God's vengeance. In *Perimedes*, then, Greene may simply be recalling Tamburlaine's monstrous actions already familiar to him in 1583. Moreover, in *Menaphon* (1589), Greene again writes of the Scythian conqueror: "I reade that mightie *Tamburlaine* after his wife *Zenocrate* (the worlds faire eye) past out of the Theater of this mortall life, he chose stigmaticall trulls to please his humorous fancie."[26] As far as we now know, only Marlowe calls Tamburlaine's wife Zenocrate; most tellers of the tale leave her nameless. But if Greene did "reade" this fact, it was apparently not in Marlowe's play which was printed the following year and which does not contain this incident. We are faced with a series of possibilities: (1) Greene is Marlowe's source for the name. (2) Greene read, in manuscript, a lost version of Marlowe's play which contained a suggestion that Tamburlaine consorted with prostitutes after Zenocrate's death. (3) Greene knew a non-Marlovian version of the story in which Tamburlaine's wife was called Zenocrate and from which Marlowe derived her name. (4) Greene's memory is confused, and he is incorrectly recalling

---

[24] Don Cameron Allen, *Doubt's Boundless Sea: Skepticism and Faith in the Renaissance* (Baltimore: John Hopkins Press, 1964), p. 4.
[25] Robert Greene, *Mamillia: A Mirrour or Looking-glasse for the Ladies of Englande* (London, 1583), sig. Gl^r (STC 12269). See Grosart, II, 81-2.
[26] Grosart, VI, 84.

an incident in Part II (4045ff.), which he had seen on stage, but had not read. Since Greene's evidence is susceptible to various interpretations, a cautious scholar will be forced to reject it as useless in dating Marlowe's plays. Greene is not a very reliable witness.

Marlowe's use of secondary sources may, at first glance, indicate a more conclusive dating. In Part II, Marlowe paraphrases a military description from Paul Iue's *Practise of Fortification*, and if we may assume that he used the printed text of 1589, we may date Part II between 1589 and the following year when the play was printed.[27] But Marlowe also quotes from Spenser's *Faerie Queene* in Part II (IV.ii.4098), and since Spenser's work was not printed until 1590, it has been generally assumed that Marlowe read the *Faerie Queene* in manuscript.[28] We know that manuscripts were circulated before, or even instead of, printing, and that in the Renaissance, 'publication' was not synonymous with 'printing'. Although well enough known to his contemporaries, Sidney's first version of *The Arcadia*, for a prime example, was not printed until this century. Quite possibly, then, Marlowe read Iue's treatise in manuscript. But this is not the only possibility. F. S. Boas suggests that Spenser's lines were added to the play when Marlowe put both parts through a complete revision before the printing in 1590,[29] and the passages based on Iue may have been inserted at the same time. Although J. D. Jump presents evidence that the first quarto was set up from Marlowe's foul papers rather than from a revised fair copy,[30] Boas's hypothesis cannot be completely disproven, and it forces us to hesitate before accepting a date based on the evidence of borrowing. We can never be sure when or where Marlowe read the material he used.

For *Dido* and *Edward II* firm dating evidence is wholly lacking. *Dido* is generally dated before *Tamburlaine* because it is based on

---

[27] See F.-C. Danchin, "Études critiques sur Christophe Marlowe", *Revue germanique*, 8 (1912), 32-33.

[28] See Roy Battenhouse, *Marlowe's Tamburlaine: A Study in Renaissance Moral Philosophy* (Nashville: Vanderbilt University Press, 1964), pp. 178-92.

[29] Boas, p. 73.

[30] John D. Jump (ed.), *Tamburlaine the Great, Parts I and II* (Lincoln: University of Nebraska Press, 1967), p. xxv.

the *Aeneid* and thus supposedly linked with Marlowe's studies. Perhaps the play was written for a group of travelling children actors, "the Children of her *Maiesties Chappell*", as the titlepage states, while Marlowe and Nashe were students at Cambridge. Militating against this supposition is the maturity of verse and dramatic technique which some scholars detect in the play.[31] Of course, this maturity may be the product of a later revision, but ultimately, place and date and revision are conjectural, and maturity is a matter of personal taste. *Edward II* is tentatively dated by Tucker Brooke in 1591 or early 1592.[32] Most editors and critics concur. The late dating is based on the 'obvious' maturity of the verse and construction, but Leo Kirschbaum argues that the rigidity he finds in the play is not the sign of a mature dramatist.[33] Esthetic criteria will apparently never yield a firm date for the writing of a play.

The *Jew of Malta* and *The Massacre at Paris* are generally linked by critics as the least popular of Marlowe's plays. *The Jew* may be dated after the death of the Duke of Guise (23 December 1588), referred to in the Prologue, and before 26 February 1592, when Henslowe records its performance.[34] This dating assumes that the Prologue was written by Marlowe and at the same time as the play – possibly a naive assumption, when we consider that prologues were in general not indispensable equipment and that two of the Prologues used for this play were apparently penned by Heywood. The *terminus a quo* cannot be firmly established. In dating *The Massacre*, we have two dates: the death of Henry III of France on 2 August 1589, which is dramatized in the play, and Henslowe's record of the play as "ne" [i.e., new] on 30 January

---

31 See T. M. Pearce, "Evidence for Dating Marlowe's *Tragedy of Dido*", *Studies in the English Renaissance Drama in Memory of Karl Julius Holzknecht*, ed. by J. W. Bennett *et al.* (New York: New York University Press, 1959), pp. 231-47, who dates the play in 1591.

32 Tucker Brooke (ed.), *Works*, p. 307.

33 Leo Kirschbaum (ed.), *The Plays of Christopher Marlowe* (Cleveland: World, 1968), p. 15.

34 See Philip Henslowe, *Henslowe's Diary*, ed. by R. A. Foakes and R. T. Rickert (Cambridge: Cambridge University Press, 1961), p. 16, assuming that the "Jewe of malltuse" is Marlowe's play.

1593, assuming that the play which Henslowe calls "the tragedey of the gvyes" is Marlowe's.[35] In a recent textual study, however, R. F. Welsh adduces evidence to suggest that *The Massacre* was already in print in 1592. If this date is correct, and if we still wish to accept Henslowe's "gvyes" as Marlowe's work, we are forced to interpret "ne" as 'new to his repertory', a meaning not unique for Henslowe. In any case, we can no longer use Henslowe's evidence with absolute confidence. If *The Massacre* were printed in 1592, it must have been written some time before.

The *Historia von D. Johann Fausten*, the basis for Marlowe's *Doctor Faustus*, was issued twice in 1587. Marlowe may well have read the history in that year and written a first draft of the play immediately. Since the play is linked in several ways with the morality tradition, it can be argued that *Faustus* is an early play revealing Marlowe's transition from religious drama, which he undoubtedly knew as a youth, to popular drama, which he practised as a playwright in London. Tucker Brooke argues from the historical allusions to the "fiery keele at *Antwarpes* bridge" and to the Duke of Parma, and from the fact that the company for which the play was written was probably silenced on 6 November 1589, that Marlowe completed the play during the winter of 1588-89.[36] His case is called in question by W. W. Greg, who argues for a date of 1592 or early 1593. According to Greg, Marlowe based his work on the English translation of the *Historia*, printed in 1592.[37] However, knowing Marlowe's probable penchant for manuscript reading, we cannot dismiss, with Greg, the possibility that Marlowe read the translation before it was printed. Even though we cannot accept Greg's arguments as conclusive, we must acknowledge that the weight of evidence and scholarly opinion has shifted. At present, it seems possible that *Faustus* is a late play.[38]

---

[35] Henslowe, p. 16. Later (p. 22), Henslowe records "the Gwies" and "the masacer" (19 June 1594, and 25 June 1594). They may be the same or separate plays. Henslowe was not only odd in his spelling, but inconsistent as well.

[36] Tucker Brooke (ed.), *Works*, p. 139.

[37] W. W. Greg (ed.), *Marlowe's Doctor Faustus*, pp. 1-14.

[38] The tides of opinion may be changing once again. See Curt Zimansky, "Marlowe's *Faustus*: The Date Again", *PQ*, 41 (1962), 181-87, who argues for an early date (circa 1588-89) on the basis of parallels from *A Knack to Know a Knave*.

However, in dealing with Marlowe, the terms 'late' and 'early' which we have been using mean relatively little. Marlowe came down from Corpus Christi, Cambridge, in 1587, and was murdered early in 1593. Even if we are willing to accept the baseless assumption that Marlowe wrote *Dido* and *1 Tamburlaine* at the University, which he entered in 1580, we have only a twelve-year span from the beginning of his career until his death. And the meager evidence points toward the late eighties and the early nineties as his most productive period. We are, then, in all likelihood, speaking of a dramatic career of five or six years. This is a very important fact to remember in criticizing the plays.

The present study proposes that the seven plays which Marlowe wrote during this brief period do not reveal a significant development in thought. The dramatic world of the plays is basically the same, and what we have is the first phase of a writing career, unfortunately cut short by an early death. In his drama, Marlowe is exploring the possibilities of a certain type of protagonist, the aspiring man, a character which Peele, Lodge, and Greene were also using; and he is building an essentially evil background before which his protagonist moves. In the Marlovian world, the aspiring man is simply a super-villain among knaves. Some few characters are conventionally virtuous; and although they may be functionally important, they do not guide the action of the play, and they are clearly in the minority.[39] By and large, the protagonist functions among other characters who are very like himself in attitude and action. If he distinguishes himself, it is because he is better at intrigue or warfare than they; his schemes run deeper; his armies are more vicious; he is more clearly allied to the devil, or more completely perverted. Throughout his plays, Marlowe uses similar characters in a dramatic world which remains, in general qualities, constant.

Although we may feel that Marlowe's dramatic techniques change from play to play, there are similarities which should not

---

[39] See Alfred Harbage, "The Safe Majority", *As They Liked It: A Study of Shakespeare's Moral Artistry* (New York: Harper, 1961), pp. 163-73, who suggests that 72% of all Shakespeare's characters are good. The contrast with Shakespeare is an index to the world Marlowe was creating.

be ignored. There is a recurrent use of declamation, long passages of description or narration, and monologues or soliloquies of aspiration. In a specialized form, the soliloquy becomes the protagonist's boast to have a peculiar control over his destiny. To reveal struggle, there is a continuing use of the confrontation, where one faction meets to bandy words with another. Tamburlaine confronts Bajazeth in much the way that Edward confronts his recalcitrant Barons or Barabas confronts his Christian adversary, Ferneze. There is a feeling that the characters are declaiming at full volume, not communicating with each other. In fact, all of these recurring techniques point to the 'loudness' of Marlowe's rhetoric, a loudness which distances the audience from the action, allowing them to remain always emotionally detached. This is a basic Marlovian technique.

Although there are constant factors in Marlowe's thought and technique, there are certain changes in his dramaturgy which divide the seven plays into two groups. In the first group, *Dido, Edward II*, and *The Massacre at Paris*, Marlowe seems most interested in the 'world' of the play. These plays are in the tradition of *Gorboduc* (1561), where the eponymous hero does not dominate the action of the play and where the authors, Sackville and Norton, emphasize the 'unnaturalness' of their dramatic world. It is a drama of unnatural conflicts, brother against brother, parent against child, and the interest lies not so much in the fortunes of a central character, as in the total effect of the action. In the second group, *1* and *2 Tamburlaine, Faustus*, and *The Jew of Malta*, Marlowe focuses attention on the central character. Our interest is now dominated by the aspiring protagonist and only secondarily are we interested in the dramatic world. If the first plays were in the *Gorboduc* tradition, the second group may be seen as the offspring of Thomas Preston's *Cambises* (1569). In *Cambises*, Preston emphasizes the dominance of his eponymous hero, and though the action may appear to be presented serially, Cambises is not a static character. Beginning as a just ruler, he degenerates to an inhumane dictator and finally dies on his own sword, destroyed by his own weapon. In our study of Marlowe's second group of plays, we will see how he develops and elaborates this basic degenerative pattern. We may call this type of play 'mono-drama' to distinguish it from the 'drama of unnatural conflict'.

In the following chapters it will be suggested that the chief thrust of Marlovian drama was away from the drama of unnatural conflict and toward monodrama, that Marlowe's genius lay in the creation of figures like Tamburlaine, Faustus, and Barabas, and that these figures, in turn, are the best embodiments of Marlowe's thought. Since the present dating of Marlowe's plays is, as we have abundantly seen, based on tenuous evidence, and since we are dealing with a dramatic career of only a few years, we may be justified in arranging the plays according to theme and idea, and in such a way as to see clearly the playwright's evolution of the aspiring hero. So arranged, the plays make up a closely inter-related group from *Dido* to *The Jew of Malta*. At the same time, it should be noticed that, according to our present lack of knowl-edge, Marlowe may well have written the plays in the order they will here be discussed.

The biographical question still remains. Was Marlowe a reli-gious skeptic, and if so, how did this skepticism affect his art? Once again we cannot answer our questions with any degree of certainty. After Marlowe's murder, Kyd and Baines both accused him of atheism and homosexuality; but the accusations are sus-pect, Kyd's because he was desperate to acquit himself of similar charges, and Baines's because he was obviously currying official favor by his gratuitous maligning of Marlowe.[40] Henry Oxinden's diary, which contains comments on Marlowe's atheism, is hearsay evidence.[41] Although these accusations are similar in certain details, the similarities may be explained in more than one way. Marlowe used both homosexuality and atheism as motifs in his plays, and it has always been the tendency among naive critics

---

[40] See, e.g., Boas, pp. 236-52. But cf. Arthur Freeman, *Thomas Kyd: Facts and Problems* (Oxford: Oxford University Press, 1967), pp. 31-32.

[41] Henry Oxinden's notebooks are now at the Folger Shakespeare Library and at the British Museum. I have examined those at the Folger (V.b. 100). The comments on Marlowe are transcribed by Mark Eccles, "Marlowe in Kentish Tradition", *N&Q*, 169 (1935), 20-23, 39-41, 58-61, 134-35.

to identify the creator with the created. We have all heard that Shakespeare put HIMSELF into Hamlet or Richard II. Quite possibly part of Marlowe's reputation comes from this kind of simplistic identification, which assumes that the playwright IS the atheist Tamburlaine or the homosexual Edward. Or, was Marlowe that familiar type of young theological student who revels in blasphemy? Blasphemous jokes, we are told, often begin in theological seminaries, not because seminarians are skeptics, but because their faith is strong enough to tolerate a good, robust joke. A man cannot be condemned for what he says, but for what he truly believes and does.

Marlowe may indeed have made the comments attributed to him, but since they are taken out of context, the tone is almost impossible to determine. If, for example, we catch a glimmer of Marlovian irony in the statement that "all they that loue not Tobacco & Boies were fooles",[42] it becomes not an indication of personal preference, but a piece of social commentary. Marlowe may well have felt that smoking and homosexuality were too prevalent in sixteenth-century London, and his comment ironically underscores the fact. But without a full context we can hardly make a final decision. Marlowe may simply have been a Renaissance manifestation of the young artist who thoroughly enjoys shocking his contemporaries with his outrageous opinions on life and letters. In our own day and on a different level, we have only to think of the youthful essays of T. S. Eliot, wherein he tells us that both Milton and *Hamlet* are failures. Must we conclude that Eliot had no literary taste? Or, to return to Marlowe, must we conclude that a young dramatist's shocking statements – if he made them – are an index to his character?

Further, it may be noticed that the moralists, Thomas Beard and William Vaughan, who criticize Marlowe's character shortly after his death, do not feel it is necessary to condemn his plays as blasphemous. Beard notes that Marlowe was "by profession a

---

[42] The Baines note is quoted by Paul Kocher, *Christopher Marlowe: A Study of His Thought, Learning, and Character* (Chapel Hill: University of North Carolina Press, 1946), pp. 34-36.

scholler, ... but by practise a play-maker",[43] calls his poetry
scurrilous, and passes over his plays in silence. Vaughan recalls
that "it is reported, about 14. yeres a goe" that Marlowe "wrote
a Booke against the Trinitie".[44] Since Vaughan's preface is dated
1599, Marlowe composed it about 1585, or just about the time he
was leaving Cambridge. One wonders if the essay were not an
advanced student paper on the Trinitarian controversy. It was
also "credibly reported", writes Beard, that Marlowe affirmed
"our Sauiour to be but a deceiuer, and *Moses* to be a coniurer and
seducer of the people, and the holy Bible to be but vaine and idle
stories, and all religion but a deuice of pollicie".[45] The accusations
sound suspiciously like the Kyd-Baines reports. But the essential
point is that, although they are fully aware of Marlowe's reputed
faults, Vaughan and Beard do not take this opportunity to attack
his 'atheistic' plays. Assuming that they both knew Marlowe's
drama, we might expect them to attack its supposedly pernicious
effect. That they did not may suggest that these two critics saw
nothing particularly reprehensible in Marlowe's work – in spite
of what they saw as his extremely sinful nature.

We may be more certain, however, that R. H. (possibly Robert
Henderson) in his *Arraignement of the VVhole Creatvre* (1631), felt
that Marlowe's Tamburlaine plays, at any rate, were completely
orthodox. In a chapter on the uncertainty of riches, honor, and
pleasure, R. H. cites *2 Tamburlaine* as an illustrative example.[46]
Thus, Marlowe makes a grand step, within three decades, from
a horrible example of atheistic Epicurianism, to an author quoted
for his moral insight into human impermanence. From the evidence
we have, it seems possible that Renaissance audiences never saw
Marlovian drama as unorthodox.

Nevertheless, the picture of Marlowe which emerges from the
anecdotes, the bits of evidence, and the accusations is that of a

---

[43] Thomas Beard, *The Theatre of Gods Iudgements* (London, 1597), p. 147 (STC 1659).
[44] William Vaughan, *The Golden-groue, Moralized in Three Bookes* (London, 1608), sig. C4ᵛ (STC 24611). A first edition appeared in 1600.
[45] Beard, p. 147.
[46] *The Arraignement of the VVhole Creatvre* (London, 1631), p. 240, sig. Hh4ᵛ (STC 13069).

mentally active, skeptical young man, one not given to accepting unexamined values, a questioner reluctant to participate in faddish enthusiasms. So far, we have the conventional picture of the 'subversive' Marlowe popular with the Romantic critics. But the Romantic critics tend to see Marlowe as selectively skeptical. While questioning certain religious and moral assumptions, he was, for them, quite able to accept and endorse, with a good deal of youthful fervor, the Renaissance passion for aspiration. With a kind of ingenuousness, Marlowe was supposed to have kept skepticism in abeyance and to have thoughtlessly glorified the materialistic ambition for earthly power and riches. But given Marlowe's skeptical nature, such naive acceptance seems improbable, if not impossible. More accurately, we may believe that Marlowe was keenly aware of the limitations of his aspiring protagonists and of the evil world which they inhabit. If we wish to see the plays as socially relevant, they do not sing the praises of the Renaissance conquistadors and their bloody battles, but detail their weaknesses and failings. Marlowe and his generation had witnessed, at a distance to be sure, and were fully alive to the horrors of Spanish aggression. "There was neuer Captayne", Gomara writes of Cortez in Central America, "that did with like army ouercome so infinite a people, & bring both thē and their coūtrey vnder subiectiō."[47] And every Englishman knew that The Netherlands and then England herself were targets for Spanish ambitions. This is to say nothing of the competitive striving of England's own nobility, of Raleigh, Essex, and Leicester. Surely Marlowe's disillusioned eye did not mistake this greedy struggle for the stuff of romance.

That Marlowe's drama has social implications, that he viewed Renaissance European society with disinterested critical eyes is not an hypothesis generally held. Northrop Frye, for example, suggests that "Marlowe ... presents his heroes more or less as demigods moving in a kind of social ether."[48] Frye's critical

---

[47] Francisco Lopez de Gomara, *The Pleasant Historie of the Conquest of the VVeast India* (London, 1578), p. 23, sig. D4ʳ (STC 16807).
[48] Northrop Frye, *Anatomy of Criticism: Four Essays* (New York: Atheneum, 1968), p. 284.

authority notwithstanding, if Marlowe did not see the essential social evils of sixteenth-century Europe, he certainly was not a very perceptive young artist. Critics of the contemporary scene, men with far less insight than Marlowe, perceived the problem of the "*aspiring mind to be above others*".[49] Sir Richard Barckley complains that the "pride, ambition, and vaine glorie and corruption of these latter dayes hath engendered a confusion of all things".[50] Matthieu Coignet argues that "with very great reason may a man impute, all sects, heresies, & diuisions, foolish enterprises, combats, and vnnecessarie warres, to the ambition of vnquiet & mouing spirits, which neuer content theselues in their vocation".[51] William Vaughan, who, as we have seen, uses Marlowe himself as an illustration in his chapter on Atheism, discusses the "fiue mischiefes" of "ambition":

> The first is, that causeth a man neyther to abide a superior or an equal. The second, an ambitious man by attributing honour vnto himselfe, goeth about to defraud God of his due. The 3. plague in ambition is, that it considereth not what chaunced to such, as exercised it.

As an example of the "patterne of ambition", Vaughan cites Cardinal Wolsey, "who beyng preferred by King Henry the eight of famous memorie, would notwithstanding haue exalted himselfe aboue the King, for which his intolerable ambition, his goods were cofiscated, and himselfe apprehended". All ambition ends by overreaching itself.

> The fourth mischiefe in ambition is, that hee hunteth after false and deceitful glory … . The fift, an ambitious man waigheth not his owne fraylety and weaknesse.[52]

---

[49] Jean de L'Espine, *A Very Excellent and Learned Discovrse, Touching the Tranquilitie and Contention of the Minde* (Cambridge, 1592), p. 134ᵛ, sig. T1ᵛ (STC 15516).

[50] Sir Richard Barckley, p. 499, sig. Kk1ʳ.

[51] Matthieu Coignet, *Politiqve Discovrses Vpon Trveth and Lying* (London, 1586), p. 179, sig. M4ʳ (STC 5486). On p. 175, sig. M2ʳ, he comments: "presumption is the mother of all vices."

[52] Vaughan, sigs. H1ʳ-H1ᵛ. Cf. George Cavendish's "Life and Death of Thomas Wolsey", in *The Renaissance in England*, ed. by Hyder Rollins and Herschel Baker (Boston: Heath, 1954), p. 58.

In the metaphysical realm, ungovernable ambition leads to the practise of black arts:

This ambition and vaineglory the diuell knoweth to be so offensiue to God, & enemy to the felicitie of men, that he leaueth nothing vnpractised to stirre vp mens mindes to the desires thereof, him selfe being always ready at hand, where he findeth a disposition meete for this purpose, to assist them to worke straunge feates, and counterfeit miracles, not to the destructiõ of them only that are entred into his societie, but to vse them as instruments to seduce many others, from whom onely commeth mans felicitie, to seeke helpe of his hands.[53]

But the aspiring mind does not merely desire to attain the ultimate of power. There are other, no less destructive aspects of this acquisitive desire:

what greater calamity hath hapned to man than such as hath beene procured by inordinate and vnsatiable loue. Was not *Paris*, soone to *Priamus* king of Troy, the very cause by his inord inat loue, that brought to passe such cruell wars betwixt the Greekes and Troyans, wherein both his aged father and brethren were slaine, his country spoyled, and the citie of Troy mightely defaced with fire, & throwen flat to the ground, with the slaughter of many thousand of his coũtreymẽ.[54]

"Thus", concludes Fenne, "it remaineth euident & extant at this day."[55] The aspiration for an absolute physical love is unnatural and destructive. All in all, Renaissance critics saw discontent with human limitations as the prime factor in social disruption. And these moral generalizations of the critics may easily be documented from the lives and loves of the Tudor nobles and courtiers.[56] Marlowe, as well as the critics, was confronted by this recklessly ambitious society.

Marlowe's vision of this brave new world has much in common with Young Goodman Brown's experience of the diabolical

---

[53] Barckley, pp. 206-07.
[54] Thomas Fenne, *Fennes Frutes* (London, 1590), p. 50ᵛ (STC 10763).
[55] Fenne, p. 53ʳ.
[56] See Anthony Esler, *The Aspiring Mind of the Elizabethan Younger Generation* (Durham, N. C.: Duke University Press, 1966), pp. 24-50. Cf. Thomas Wyatt's "If thou wilt mighty be", an adaptation from Boethius, but which suggests the problems of ambition Marlowe later deals with. Kenneth Muir (ed.), *Collected Poems of Sir Thomas Wyatt* (London: Routledge, 1949), pp. 180-81.

society in the forest. In Marlowe's plays, all those apparently religious pillars of the state have joined the dance of ruthless aspiration. Respectable queens lust after spotless warriors; sedate scholars yearn to control the powers of darkness. Marlowe's drama represents an inverted world, where evil has become dominant and, in many cases, has been accepted in the place of good.

Without pushing the concept of the inverted world too far, we may suggest that Marlowe's dramatic world is, in a sense, 'upside down'.[57] His heroes are not heroic in the way Shakespeare's Hamlet and Lear are. They are parts of a far-different dramatic milieu. Perhaps one of the problems with Marlovian interpretation has been that the critics have concentrated on the central characters while excluding a thorough investigation of the surrounding dramatic world. Only by examining the character in his world can we see the point of Marlowe's drama. His world is not creative in its response to the challenges it receives. In *Dido*, the heroine ends her life on a funeral pyre, with her sister and her unrequited lover joining her in a joint suicide. The scene may readily stand as a central symbol of the Marlovian world. In place of a Christian savior, Marlowe creates Tamburlaine, the scourge and destroyer. Instead of Shakespeare's gallant Italian merchants, Marlowe presents the greedy and murderous Barabas. The perverted saints of this world are the Guise and Faustus, both willing to use religion in order to gain earthly power. The inept rulers, Dido and Edward, destroy kingdoms in search of impossible sexual gratifications. Here passions always control reason. Marlowe's world is the anti-utopia, the contra-ideal. Most of the principles upon which civilized life is based are forgotten or dismissed as irrelevant. It is a world where evil grows from the ambition to attain impossible ends. But, given the finite nature of man, aspiration for ultimates becomes ludicrous, even comic. We tend to laugh at hyperbolic posturing and frenetic declamation. Nevertheless, this is not a totally comic world; it is one where aspiring evil ultimately destroys

---

[57] Ernst Robert Curtius, *European Literature and the Latin Middle Ages*, trans. by Willard Trask (New York: Harper, 1963), pp. 94-98, provides the medieval background for this 'topos'.

itself, hoist with its own petard. Marlovian drama is a warning against the quest for infinity.

Marlowe was hardly the propagandist for Renaissance materialism, however romantic, colorful, and exciting that materialism may seem today. He appears most clearly as the incisive critic, with a full understanding of the vanity of human ambition. His vision is radical in its criticism, conservative in its nature. He is never a preacher, but always a seer, and his moral vision of the insanely aggressive world is turned into art. Along with this vision of evil is an increasing awareness in the playwright that his artistic strength is in 'monodrama' where the concentration is on the individual aspirer. Marlowe came to see that, in the drama dominated by the central character, he could say most clearly what he had to say about human evil. The following chapters are arranged to reveal Marlowe's movement toward Faustus and Barabas, the ultimate aspirers and the ultimate cosmic clowns. The first plays we will examine, *Dido* and *Edward II*, are predominantly concerned with the destructive power of an impossible love. In them, the eponymous protagonists are caught in highly emotional situations; they are the centers of conflict, more acted upon than acting.

II

DIDO, QUEEN OF CARTHAGE

Dido, Queen of Carthage is a play about destructive love.[1] Since Aeneas is fated by the gods for Lavinia and consequently for an Italian empire, Dido's attempt to hold him in an illicit love affair is doomed from the beginning. Her sexual desires are not consonant with the impersonal historical movements of her world. By struggling against the inevitable, by her great desire for Aeneas, she destroys herself and her dependents, and throws her country into turmoil. Her uncreative, irrational love becomes a kind of perversion, and the normal process of love and procreation is denied. This theme of perverted love is announced in the first scene.

However, before turning to the play's first scene, we should notice some of the major additions Marlowe made to the story that Virgil tells in the first four books of the *Aeneid*. The additions should point toward the emphasis Marlowe was trying to attain in the play and help to give us an initial focus. An extremely minor character in Virgil, Iarbas becomes, as the jealous but unrequited lover of Dido, an important foil to Aeneas. Ironically, it is he who first helps the Trojans find safe harbor in Carthage,

---

[1] The few valuable studies of the play are John P. Cutts, "Dido, Queen of Carthage", *N&Q*, 5 (1958), 371-74; David M. Rogers, "Love and Honor in Marlowe's *Dido, Queen of Carthage*", *Greyfriar*, 6 (1963), 3-7; Don Cameron Allen, "Marlowe's *Dido* and the Tradition", *Essays on Shakespeare and Elizabethan Drama in Honor of Hardin Craig*, ed. by Richard Hosley (Columbia: University of Missouri Press, 1962), pp. 55-68; Brian Gibbons, "Unstable Proteus: Marlowe's *The Tragedy of Dido Queen of Carthage*", *Christopher Marlowe*, ed. by Brian Morris (New York: Hill and Wang, 1969), pp. 27-46; and G. S. Rousseau, "Marlowe's *Dido* and a Rhetoric of Love", *EM*, 19 (1968), 25-49. There is an interesting chapter in Douglas Cole, *Suffering and Evil in the Plays of Christopher Marlowe* (Princeton: Princeton University Press, 1962), pp. 75-85.

and, later, after reversing his position because of jealousy, provides them with the sailing equipment they need to leave for Italy. Unlike Virgil's Dido, Marlowe's heroine, in a fit of extreme jealousy, dismantles the Trojan ships and confiscates the sails and oars after Aeneas's first, unsuccessful attempt to escape her power. The idea of this initial attempt is also a Marlovian addition; for, when Virgil's Aeneas resolves to go, he goes. The comic love scenes, including the dialogue between the Old Nurse and Cupid, are not found in Virgil, and it may be suggested that the Virgilian love scenes which are adapted for the play are sexually heightened. Cupid plays a much more important, albeit comic role here, and the suggestiveness of Virgil's objective description of the cave and the storm is made much more explicit. Dido here burns with undeniable passion. From this brief sketch of the dramatist's use of the *Aeneid*, it is fully apparent that Marlowe adds new material and emphasizes the old for the major purpose of enlarging and underscoring the theme of love.

The action begins rather shockingly with the discovery of "Iupiter *dandling* Ganimed *vpon his knee*" (Stage Directions, I.i.1); this also is a Marlovian innovation.[2] At least one critic sees the opening scene, with its emphasis on homosexuality, as an indica-

---

[2] The relevance of the scene is suggested by Henry Peacham (*Minerva Britanna, 1612*, ed. by John Horden [Menston, Yorkshire: Scolar Press, 1969], p. 48), who uses Ganymede as an emblem:

> Vpon a Cock, heere *Ganimede* doth sit,
> Who erst rode mounted on IOVES Eagles back,
> One hand holdes *Circes* wand, and ioind with it,
> A cup top-fil'd with poison, deadly black:
>   The other Meddals, of base mettals wrought,
>   With sundry moneyes, counterfeit and nought.
>
> These be those crimes, abhorr'd of God and man,
> Which Iustice should correct, with lawes severe,
> In *Ganimed*, the foule Sodomitan:
> Within the Cock, vile incest doth appeare:
>   Witchcraft, and murder, by that cup and wand,
>   And by the rest, false coine you vnderstand.

Although this particular emblem appeared too late for Marlowe's use, it indicates something about the figure of Ganymede in the Renaissance.

tion of Marlowe's own emotional orientation rather than as an integral part of the play's action.[3] More probably, the innovation is calculated to shock the audience into a re-evaluation of the traditional story of Dido and Aeneas. The homosexual love here evinced forces the playgoer, assuming that he is normally oriented toward the opposite sex, to stand aloof from the action, to evaluate critically the words of the old god and the young boy. The viewer can hardly sympathize with what he sees and hears. As Don Cameron Allen remarks, the "affair of Jupiter with Ganymede is an example of *amor illegitimus et praeternaturalis*",[4] and we must stress the meaning of 'unnatural' in *praeternaturalis*. Marlowe's initial presentation invites, or even demands, this emphasis, and it is from this tainted framework that we are introduced to the love story of Dido and Aeneas.

Jove's opening lines – the words of an old homosexual pleading for the love of his young paramour – set the tone of the first part of the scene:

> Come gentle *Ganimed* and play with me,
> I loue thee well, say *Iuno* what she will.   (I.i.1-2)

The lines indicate the extreme infatuation of the old man as well as revealing that he has deserted his natural orientation toward his wife, Juno, in order to pursue a child. Ganymede's reply:

> I am much better for your worthles loue,
> That will not shield me from her shrewish blowes: (3-4)

is, of course, openly ironic, but suggests, with the phrase "worthles loue", more than he intends. Outraged that his wife should strike his boy, Jupiter vows to "hang her meteor like twixt heauen and earth, / And bind her hand and foote with golden cordes" (13-14). Should Jupiter accomplish his vow, Ganymede promises to spend his time in Jupiter's arms, and the old god answers that all things are at Ganymede's command: "Controule proud Fate, and cut the thred of time" (29):

---

[3] Leonora Leet Brodwin, "*Edward II*: Marlowe's Culminating Treatment of Love", *ELH*, 31 (1964), 148: "*Dido* begins with an irrelevant scene which portrays the love of Jupiter for Ganymede."

[4] D. C. Allen, "Marlowe's *Dido*", p. 68.

> *Hermes* no more shall shew the world his wings,
> If that thy fancie in his feathers dwell,
> But as this one Ile teare them all from him.   (38-40)

Since Hermes is Jupiter's messenger to the earth, he becomes, in
the abstract, a symbol of divine control of earthly affairs. Thus,
Jupiter, by offering to incapacitate Hermes at Ganymede's whim,
offers to abrogate his divine responsibility. His complete degradation is suggested when he places Juno's wedding jewels, stolen
from her, upon the neck, arms, and shoulders of his "owne sweet
heart", Ganymede (44). Although overtly comic, the scene is
serious in content.

Had the playgoer missed the point of the initial colloquy,
Venus underlines it when she enters:

> I, this is it, you can sit toying there,
> And playing with that female wanton boy,
> Whiles my *AEneas* wanders on the Seas,
> And rests a pray to euery billowes pride.   (I.i.50-53)

In reality, the Father of Gods and Men has already given over
his duties and responsibilities as providential caretaker for the
sake of an illegitimate and rather jealous young lover. His easy
words to Venus:

> thy *AEneas* wandring fate is firme,
> Whose wearie lims shall shortly make repose
> In those faire walles I promist him of yore: (83-85)

in extenuation of his laxity do not completely exonerate him. We
have caught him in the act, and we can hardly blame Juno, when
she later enters, for being frustrated and irascible. Traditionally
the symbol of unity and creativity, love is presented in these
opening lines as unnatural, disruptive, and potentially destructive.
The traditional expectations are forcibly denied. Moreover, the
first scene may be viewed as a thematic microcosm of the play's
total action. Like Jupiter, Aeneas will succumb to an illegitimate
love which will keep him from his duty, the founding of an Italian
empire; and as Jupiter is brought back to a consciousness of his
dereliction by Venus, so Aeneas will be reminded of his destiny by

Hermes. Although one would not like to push these similarities too far, they do indicate that the first scene is a meaningful part of the action, not a dramatic miscalculation.

If the introductory scene suggests that illegitimate love is universal in space, present even among the gods of Marlowe's world, then the "woeful tale" of Troy which Dido bids Aeneas to recount indicates that it is universal in time. Although the main parts of the story are taken from Virgil, the incidents selected for Aeneas's heroic narrative are suggestive of events that will later take place in Carthage. Hecuba, the "frantic queen" of Troy, looks forward to Dido, the frantic queen of Carthage; both have lost the men they love. The blood-thirsty Pyrrhus who leaves Troy in flames (II.i.508) foreshadows the adamant Aeneas who leaves Dido burning on her funeral pyre. If the playgoer should refuse to recognize these parallels, the description of the "franticke Queene" (II.i.539-43), Marlowe's addition to Virgil's account, is, at least, an emotional analogue to Dido's tragic death. Furthermore, it is noteworthy that Marlowe has Aeneas desert three women in order to escape the carnage at Troy. First, he loses his wife, Creusa, much more perfunctorily in the play than in the *Aeneid*: "O there I lost my wife" (565), he exclaims, and she is forgotten. Second, he finds Cassandra in the streets, carries her in his arms for a short time, but is "forst to let her lye" (574) when he is attacked by a troop of Greeks; she either has been or is later to be raped by Ajax at the shrine of Diana. Although Marlowe leaves the time sequence unclear, it seems that she is raped after Aeneas deserts her. Probably taking details from Ovid and Lydgate,[5] Marlowe elaborates this incident from the *Aeneid* where Cassan-

---

[5] Ovid's allusion is translated by Marlowe: "So, chaste Minerva, did Cassandra fall, / Deflower'd except, within thy temple wall" (*Poems: Christopher Marlowe*, ed. by Millar MacLure [London: Methuen, 1968], p. 120). John Lydgate (*The Avncient Historie and Onely Trewe and Syncere Cronicle of the Warres Betwixte the Grecians and the Troyans* [London, 1555], sig. Aa2ᵛ [STC 5580]), writes that Ajax took Cassandra as his ward "Out of the temple longing to Mynerue", thus linking the two characters. Fenne, *Fennes Frutes*, sigs. Ee2ᵛ-Ee3ʳ, describes Cassandra's rape from Hecuba's viewpoint: "To Pallas temple she was drawn, in *Troy* a sacred place, / And there my daughter was abusde before her mothers face." That Cassandra was raped seems to have been an accepted fact; that it was done by Ajax in the temple of Diana seems to be a Marlovian addition.

dra's loss is obscured by Virgil's rhetoric. Third, Polyxena calls to Aeneas while he is sailing away: "*AEneas*, stay, / The Greekes pursue me, stay and take me in" (576-77). Aeneas begins to swim back for her, but as he swims, he sees her "by the cruell Mirmidons surprizd" (582), and he returns to the ship without more ado. Afterward Polyxena is sacrificed by Pyrrhus on his father's tomb. Possibly from Ovid, this incident is Marlowe's addition to Virgil.[6]

The repetition of Aeneas's desertion of a Trojan woman serves as an ironic comment on Dido's growing belief that she can hold Aeneas in Carthage. Polyxena's cry, "*AEneas* stay", reechoes through the play. Preparing to leave Carthage for the first time, Aeneas says of Dido: "Her siluer armes will coll me round about, / And teares of pearle, crye stay, *AEneas*, stay" (IV.iii.1201-02). When he finally leaves, Anna calls after him: "*AEneas*, false *AEneas* stay" (V.i.1636). We are asked to recall the deserted Polyxena sacrificed at Troy. What happened there will again happen, on a more limited scale, in Carthage; the details may be different, but the motivation for the destruction will be much the same. Dido unconsciously points to the continuity when she asks, "But how scapt *Helen*, she that causde this warre?" (II.i.587), and then exclaims, "O had that ticing strumpet nere been borne!" (595). As Dido realizes, Troy has been destroyed by the illegitimate love of Helen and Paris. Later, when Aeneas is initially preparing to leave Carthage, Achates, echoing Dido's words, forbids him to speak of the Queen: "Banish that ticing dame from forth your mouth" (IV.iii.1181). Ironically, Dido herself has now become the temptress, the woman whose love destroys rather than creates. In the last scene, she notices: "all the world calles me a second *Helen*" (V.i.1552). Aeneas's story of Troy's fall forms an analogue to the immediate action of the play.

It should be remembered, however, for an Elizabethan audience the details of Aeneas's narrative were questionable. In the Dictys account, with which the Renaissance was familiar, Aeneas is not the hero, but the villain who helped to plot the Fall of Troy. Lydgate uses the story, and Fenne, following Lydgate, points

---

[6] *Metamorphoses*, XIII.448ff. See also Lydgate, sigs. Aa3ʳ-Aa4ʳ and Fenne, sig. Y3ʳ.

out that "*Troy* was tracherously yelded vp by *AEneas* and his traiterous crew".[7] Attempting to explain Aeneas's behavior in Carthage, Fenne comments: "being a *Troian* he could not digresse from his vnfaithful progenitors".[8] The Trojans are a "wicked race, who alwayes were the chiefe cause of their own destruction, and procurers of their fatall destinie by their periurie, vnfaithfull dealing, churlish conditions, and vnsatiable lecherie".[9] The playgoer who came to a performance with this attitude toward Aeneas and the Trojans would see the story Dido hears as a tissue of lies, the first step in her deception by a Trojan adventurer.

Significantly, Aeneas's "ruthfull tale" is followed at once by the substitution of Cupid for Ascanius. Putting her mortal grandson asleep, Venus commands:

> Now *Cupid* turne thee to *Ascanius* shape,
> And goe to *Dido*, who in stead of him
> Will set thee on her lap and play with thee:
> Then touch her white breast with this arrow head,
> That she may dote vpon *AEneas* loue: (II.i.618-22)

And Cupid assents: "I will faire mother, and so play my part, / As euery touch shall wound Queene *Didos* heart" (III.i.627-28). Consequently the end of Aeneas's story of an epic love tragedy (whether the playgoer accept this story as true or not) is punctuated by the beginning of another. Marlowe takes pains to make the connection between the two fully apparent, and in so doing, he out-Virgils Virgil. Ironically neither Aeneas who vigorously tells his story, nor Dido who attentively listens, seems to understand its significance for his or her own actions.

Further, Marlowe is careful to link the fruitless love of Dido and Aeneas with the unnatural love of Jupiter for Ganymede and the resulting disruption in heaven. Explaining to Venus why she dislikes Aeneas, Juno makes it clear that part of her hatred stems from "Troian *Ganimed*" as well as her grudge against Paris for not awarding her the golden apple (III.ii.852). The confrontation of Juno and Venus, which ends by giving the love

---

[7] Fenne, sig. Bb1ʳ.
[8] Fenne, sig. Bb1ᵛ.
[9] Fenne, sig. Bb3ʳ.

affair between Dido and Aeneas some kind of divine approval, must be read with Virgilian stage directions. Ostensibly the scene commemorates the new-made amity of Venus and Juno; but when Juno suggests that she and Venus join in confirming the union of Dido and Aeneas, her plan, according to Virgil, is spoken "with fainid mind / That *Rome* she might reiect, and *Carthage* kingdome empier make" (IV.105-06). When Venus answers, "Well could I like this reconcilements meanes" (891), she has already penetrated Juno's deception, and "she gan to smile, so glad she was she coulde perceyue the gile" (IV.128).[10] As Juno has before tried to destroy Aeneas with a storm, she will try again:

> Ile make the Clowdes dissolue their watrie workes,
> And drench *Siluanus* dwellings with their shewers.
> Then in one Caue the Queene and he shall meete,
> And interchangeably discourse their thoughts.   (III.ii.900-03)

This time the attempt will be more subtle; the storm itself will not be destructive, but the human situation into which it forces Dido and Aeneas will be potentially so. Love, which has caused almighty Jupiter to neglect his duty, will certainly, thinks Juno, turn Aeneas aside from his fated destiny.

Juno's scene mirrors that of her husband. Like Jupiter, the goddess begins by expressing her emotions for a child, Ascanius. "Here lyes my hate, *AEneas* cursed brat" (III.ii.811). And her emotions are as perverted as his. We do not expect this kind of hatred for a comparatively innocent, sleeping child especially in the Queen of the Gods. Her purpose is to murder him. Nevertheless, as in the opening scene, Venus arrives to change the course of action. Before she had rescued her son; now she rescues her grandson.

The storm scene, which Juno and Venus have planned, is also symbolically joined to the Jupiter-Ganymede scene. In that scene, Jupiter tells Ganymede:

> these linked gems,
> My *Iuno* ware vpon her marriage day,
> Put thou about thy necke my owne sweet heart,
> And tricke thy armes and shoulders with my theft.   (I.i.42-45)

---

[10] Thomas Phaer, *The Whole. xii. Bookes of the AEneidos of Virgill* (London, 1573), sigs. L3ʳ-L3ᵛ (STC 24801).

In the storm scene, Dido performs the same kind of ritualistic action with Aeneas as recipient:

> Hold, take these Iewels at thy Louers hand,
> These golden bracelets, and this wedding ring,
> Wherewith my husband woo'd me yet a maide,
> And be thou king of *Libia*, by my guift.   (III.iv.1056-59)

At this point, they licentiously "*Exeunt to the Caue*". In both cases, Jupiter's and Dido's, the giving of the jewels is a renunciation of a former love: Jupiter's for Juno; Dido's for her dead husband, Sichaeus. And, in both cases, the new loves are illegitimate. That Dido has given herself wrongly is underlined by Iarbas as he rants of "these adulterors surfetted with sinne" when Dido and Aeneas are discovered coming from their love making "in this darksome Caue" (IV.i.1079, 1083). If the giving of the jewels, which connects the two scenes, suggests *amor illegitimus*, it may also suggest *amor praeternaturalis*. The unnatural quality is indicated by the reversal of roles: in the first scene, Jupiter gives the jewels of his wife to a male lover; in the second, Dido uses her wedding jewels to woo a man, thus assuming the traditionally masculine role. It follows that the love relationship she establishes with Aeneas is as unnatural, in its way, as that between Jupiter and Ganymede. Obviously this love is not, nor it cannot come to, good.

The idea that Aeneas's new found passion will be an impediment to his public duty, the founding of a new Troy, is immediately underscored. Dido complains that Aeneas loves fame, not her, but that she "dyes for him" (III.iv.1035). He rapidly succumbs to her complaints and vows:

> Neuer to leaue these newe vpreared walles,
> Whiles *Dido* liues and rules in *Iunos* towne,
> Neuer to like or loue any but her.   (III.iv.1044-46)

The fair walls of Rome which Jupiter has promised of yore have been forgotten. Dido commands Aeneas to make her "armes" his "*Italy*"; now, "*Sicheus*, not *AEneas* be thou calde: / The King of *Carthage*, not *Anchises* sonne" (1052, 1054-55). If this liaison robs him of his mission, it also attempts to rob him of his identity;

Dido tries to change him into another Sichaeus. If one were searching for symbolic confirmation of this strange rebirth, one might see Aeneas's entry into the cave with Dido as a symbol, not so much of sexual union, as of reabsorption into the maternal womb. In her fashion, Dido desires to be the spiritual mother of a new Aeneas with a new destiny.

The beginnings of this attempt to make a permanent change in Aeneas are found in his first scene with Dido. Although she proclaims,

> AEneas is AEneas, were he clad
> In weedes as bad as euer Irus ware.   (II.i.379-80)

seeming to insist that his identity is unchangeable, she sends for the "garment which Sicheus ware:" and has Aeneas clothed in it (375). For Aeneas, these are borrowed robes, and with them Dido tries to force upon him a borrowed personality. After his first attempt to leave Carthage, she recalls him and "to make amends" commands him to "Weare the emperiall Crowne of Libia" and to hold "the Punike Scepter" as her vicegerent (IV.iv.1239-41). Aeneas argues that these are not his proper clothes:

> How vaine am I to weare this Diadem,
> And beare this golden Scepter in my hand?
> A Burgonet of steele, and not a Crowne,
> A Sword, and not a Scepter fits AEneas.   (IV.iv.1246-49)

But Dido insists:

> O keepe them still, and let me gaze my fill:
> Now lookes AEneas like immortall Ioue,
> O where is Ganimed to hold his cup,
> And Mercury to flye for what he calles?   (1250-53)

She ironically tries to make Aeneas into another Jove, the unnatural and unfaithful husband who opens the play; and, though she now appears to believe that "Not all the world can take" him from her arms (1267), Aeneas soon leaves Libyan shores at Jupiter's command delivered by Mercury. As he goes, he casts off his borrowed robes along with his alien identity, and Dido is left with the "garment" which she "cloath'd him in, / When first he came on shoare" (V.i.1706-07), the empty shell of a misguided and unsuccessful attempt at transformation.

Dido's attempt to change Aeneas is linked, at least in part, with the Renaissance allegorization of the mythic love affair between Mars and Venus.[11] According to his attitude toward war and physical violence, a Renaissance man might see Venus's domination of Mars either as a symbol of peace, or as a sign of emasculation and degeneration. As the playgoer may expect, the Trojans adhere to the latter interpretation. Achates claims that "daliance doth consume a Souldiers strength, / And wanton motions of alluring eyes / Effeminate our mindes inur'd to warre" (IV.iii.1184-86). And Aeneas finally decides: "I may not dure this female drudgerie" (1205), implicitly comparing himself to Hercules at the spindle of Omphale, the symbol of effeminate man.[12] That Dido has become a surrogate for the seductive Venus is subtly suggested in the hunting scene (III.iii), where Dido has put aside her "princely robes" for "*Dianas* shrowdes" (III.iii.913-14). Superficially, of course, it may seem that Dido is being identified with the goddess of the hunt and chastity, but when Achates notes that the hunt takes place in the same forest in which he and Aeneas "met faire *Venus* virgine like, / Bearing her bowe and quiuer at her backe" (III.iii.964-65), another association is suggested. Although one editor believes that the "identification of this wood with the earlier one ... is desirable for staging with the fixed set", the reason for Achates' words seems ultimately more artistic than practical.[13] I would like to hypothesize that, when the play was originally performed, Dido wore the same costume in the sixth scene that Venus wore as the Diana-like huntress of scene one. The costume is equally ironic for both goddess and queen. Achates' identification of the place is, then, a way of forcing the viewer to sense that the interchange of costume

[11] The Venus and Mars myth is discussed by Edgar Wind, *Pagan Mysteries in the Renaissance*, revised ed. (London: Faber, 1968), pp. 86-96, 270-71. See also Raymond Waddington, "*Antony and Cleopatra*: 'What Venus did with Mars'", *Shakespeare Studies*, 2 (1966), 210-27.

[12] Cf. Spenser, *Faerie Queene*, V.v.23-25, in J. C. Smith (ed.), *Poetical Works*, (Oxford: Oxford University Press, 1909).

[13] Oliver, p. 52, note on lines 50-53.

is not a product of inadvertence or economy. At this point in the action, Dido is assuming the role of the love-goddess. In the next scene, when she asks Aeneas how he found the cave, he replies with the completely un-Virgilian line: "By chance sweete Queene, as *Mars* and *Venus* met" (III.iv.999). Although Aeneas's assurance that the meeting is governed by chance is ironic, his simile points to the fact that he and Dido are recapitulating the Mars-Venus affair, and like Mars and Venus, their adultery will become a matter of public knowledge. Marlowe does not dwell on the possibly incestuous implications of the identification, though maternal aspects of Dido are evident; his prime purpose is to suggest that Dido-Venus attempts to emasculate or pacify her Aeneas-Mars, to force him into the ways of love, not martial conquest. It is interesting to note that this struggle between Dido and Aeneas foreshadows the similar struggle between Tamburlaine and Zenocrate. Although the situations and emphases are quite different, Dido and Zenocrate equally fail to change their respective partners. Aeneas and Tamburlaine remain agents of destruction.

The destructive nature of the central love affair in the present play is mirrored in the loves of Iarbas for Dido, and Anna for Iarbas, both of which are destined to failure. The frustration of Iarbas's love begins with the work of Cupid-Ascanius in a scene which is only partially serious (III.i). Wavering back and forth, Dido bids Iarbas stay one minute and go the next: "thou art no loue of mine" (673). To which Iarbas replies: "*Iarbus* dye, seeing she abandons thee" (674). Dido hesitates:

> No, liue *Iarbus*, what hast thou deseru'd,
> That I should say thou art no loue of mine?
> Something thou hast deseru'd. Away I say,
> Depart from *Carthage*, come not in my sight. (675-78)

There are no stage directions, but the wavering is undoubtedly punctuated by comic stage business, Cupid hitting Dido's breast with his golden arrow to incline her toward Aeneas. The comedy, however, has tragic overtones, and Iarbas says, "I goe to feed the humour of my Loue, / Yet not from *Carthage* for a thousand worlds" (684-85). Like Dryden's Antony, he is willing to give all for love. Nevertheless, as Iarbas reminds Dido, he is "King of rich *Getulia*" (679), and his decision, like that of Aeneas, involves not only his private pleasure but also his public trust.

On the other hand, Anna's problems, though she also knows "too well the sower of loue" (III.i.695), are different. Unrequited in her passion for Iarbas, she tacitly decides to influence Dido to pursue her love for Aeneas, thus leaving Iarbas free for her. In Virgil, of course, her similar actions are otherwise motivated. When asked if Aeneas is "faire and beautifull", she answers, "Yes, and *Iarbas* foule and fauourles" (697-98):

> O sister, were you Empresse of the world,
> *AEneas* well deserues to be your loue,
> So louely is he that where ere he goes,
> The people swarme to gaze him in the face.   (703-06)

Having succeeded in the first part of her plan, she must now convince Iarbas to change his love: "Be rul'd by me, and seeke some other loue" (IV.ii.1129), she tells him. Iarbas, however, refuses to be persuaded: "Mine eye is fixt where fancie cannot start, / O leaue me, leaue me to my silent thoughts" (1131-32). But Anna in her turn also refuses:

> I will not leaue *Iarbas* whom I loue,
> In this delight of dying pensiuenes:
> Away with *Dido*, *Anna* be thy song,
> *Anna* that doth admire thee more then heauen.   (1137-40)

Impervious, Iarbas answers: "I may nor will list to such loathsome chaunge, / That intercepts the course of my desire" (1141-42), and he flees from Anna's "alluring eyes" (1144). Iarbas who has the chance to love a woman who will return his affection refuses to do so, and the scene ends with Anna frustrated and alone. In contrast to her sister's successful seduction of Aeneas, Anna's sexual aggressiveness bears no fruit at all.

When Dido's old nurse is commanded to care for Cupid-Ascanius, even she is struck by the arrow of love:

> That I might liue to see this boy a man!
> How pretilie he laughs, goe ye wagge,

Youle be a twigger when you come to age.
Say *Dido* what she will I am not old,
Ile be no more a widowe, I am young.
Ile haue a husband, or els a louer. (IV.iv.1389-94)

The scene is darkly comic with the old crone desiring the young
child, and D. C. Allen remarks: "the awakened old woman is a
fine sample of *amor illegitimus et naturalis*".[14] However, in this case,
Allen's *naturalis* seems to give the wrong emphasis, for, in the light
of Renaissance ideas of natural hierarchy, the nurse has conceived
an 'unnatural' passion. Cupid's quip, "A husband and no teeth!"
(1395), points in that direction. The nurse is old enough to have
gained some control over her sexual impulses. Although her
comment, "Say *Dido* what she will I am not old", is ambiguous,
it probably does NOT mean that "Dido has told me that I am too
old", but rather, "Dido may have said that she herself is too old
(and thus abjured marriage – until Aeneas arrived); on the contrary, I am not." The comment suggests that her case is analogous
to Dido's, for both women are following the same pattern: "Ile
be no more a widowe."

Although the lines of cause and effect are not tightly drawn, after
falling into this unnatural passion, the nurse ends rather sadly.
Having lost Cupid-Ascanius, who was indeed beyond her ability
to hold and control, she is berated by Dido:

O cursed hagge and false dissembling wretch!
That slayest me with thy harsh and hellish tale,
Thou for some pettie guift hast let him goe,
And I am thus deluded of my boy:
Away with her to prison presently,
Traytoresse too keend and cursed Sorceresse.[15] (V.i.1624-29)

To the charge of traitoress, the nurse replies: "I am as true as any
one of yours" (1631), and the retort may be taken as unintentional-
ly ironic. Although the nurse has indeed been unnatural in her

---

[14] Allen, "Marlowe's *Dido*", p. 68.
[15] "Traytoresse to keend" may mean either 'traitoress to kind, i.e., to nature',
or 'traitoress too keen, i.e., sharp'. The first gloss, used by most modern editors,
is based on a conjecture by Collier and fits in with the present interpretation of
the passage.

lust for a young boy, so has everyone else been less than natural (in the Renaissance sense) in their passions – even Dido herself. Nevertheless, the aged nurse is taken to prison; her chance at a last fling is thwarted. Cupid, as a symbol of sexual love, is truly lost. All in all, the nurse provides a tragi-comic analogue to Dido, and her story suggests the kind of outcome illegitimate and unnatural love can expect.

The destructive power of love is reinforced by the imagery of flames. With one of the first allusions to fire, Jupiter predicts:

> poore *Troy* so long supprest,
> From forth her ashes shall aduance her head,
> And flourish once againe that erst was dead: (I.i.93-95)

The submerged image is that of the phoenix, which finds the fire both destructive and revitalizing, the new phoenix arising from the ashes of the old; and in the first scene, the emphasis is on rebirth after destruction, on the founding of a new Troy. Throughout the *Aeneid*, Virgil had managed to exploit the ambiguity of the fire imagery, suggesting both the death of the old and the growth of the new.[16] The major emphasis of fire in Marlowe's play, on the contrary, is destructive; and this adaptation of Virgil's imagery suggests the difference between the epic and the drama. Though Marlowe's Aeneas leaves Carthage in flames, he never reaches Italy. The promise of a resurrected Troy is not realized; no goal is attained to justify the suffering and destruction.

Moreover, we may see the flames as symbolic as well as real. The dual aspect of the imagery is suggested in Jupiter's love-speech to Ganymede:

> I exhal'd with thy fire darting beames,
> Haue oft driuen backe the horses of the night,
> When as they would haue hal'd thee from my sight. (I.i.25-27)

---

[16] See Bernard M. W. Knox, "The Serpent and the Flame: The Imagery of the Second Book of the *Aeneid*", *AJP*, 71 (1950), 379-400. Marlowe does not employ the Virgilian serpent imagery, an omission which suggests that he was aware of Virgil's artistic use of the fire imagery and that he consciously brought this imagery over into the play for calculated poetic effect. Had the serpent imagery also appeared, one might have seen both image patterns as part of an unselective or unconscious mimicking of Virgil.

Even though Jove is apparently being rather playful with his partial pun on "exhal'd" and "hal'd", his descriptive phrase, "exhal'd with thy fire darting beames", may be taken as relatively serious. On a strictly pedestrian level, Jove's words may be paraphrased (although the meaning is in some dispute): "consumed with burning passion", "set on fire".[17] The fire is induced by the lover's eyes. The convention that connects love with the eyes is an old one, and the play uses it effectively; but Marlowe here underlines the aspect of destruction.[18] The lover is the destructive agent in this metaphoric conflagration.

In Aeneas's story of Troy's destruction, metaphor merges with reality, for the fire of illegitimate passion in Paris and Helen leads to the burning of the city. Aeneas emphasizes the flames:

> a thousand Grecians more,
> In whose sterne faces shin'd the quenchles fire,
> That after burnt the pride of *Asia*.   (II.i.480-82)

> *Troy* is afire, the Grecians haue the towne.   (503)

> With balles of wilde fire in their murdering pawes,
> Which made the funerall flame that burnt faire *Troy:*   (512-13)

And Pyrrhus, the symbolically named son of Achilles, stands watching "the fire wherewith rich *Ilion* burnt" (559). The flames from this inferno glitter throughout the play.

One of the first things that Aeneas does after his arrival in Libya is to start a fire:

> Gentle *Achates*, reach the Tinder boxe,
> That we may make a fire to warme vs with,
> And rost our new found victuals on this shoare.   (I.i.166-68)

He commands one of his men: "Hold, take this candle and goe light a fire" (171). Though the incident is taken from the *Aeneid*,

---

[17] See Oliver's edition (p. 6), note on I.i.25, and Ribner, *Complete Plays of Christopher Marlowe*, p. 4. There is some possibility, though I think a slim one, that the phrase means 'drawn out of oneself' or 'exalted'. Cf. *1 Tamburlaine*, IV. ii.1487.

[18] See Robert K. Root's edition of Chaucer's *Troilus and Criseyde* (Princeton: Princeton University Press, 1926), pp. 416-17, note on I. 306-07.

it loses none of its suggestiveness in the play. Metaphorically, Aeneas starts a larger fire in Libya than he is initially aware of. Later, answering Aeneas's question about whom she loves, Dido answers:

> The man that I doe eye where ere I am,
> Whose amorous face like *Pean* sparkles fire,
> When as he buts his beames on *Floras* bed.
> *Prometheus* hath put on *Cupids* shape,
> And I must perish in his burning armes:
> *AEneas*, O *AEneas*, quench these flames.   (III.iv.1013-18)

Like father Jupiter, Dido is consumed with a burning passion enkindled by the fire-darting eyes of a lover, and her appeal to Aeneas to quench the flames is ironic: he can only make them burn more fiercely.

As we have abundantly seen, Marlowe makes certain that the parallels between the background story of Troy and the present action are not obscured in adapting Virgil's story to the stage. As Dido comes to see in herself another Helen, she tells Aeneas:

> So thou wouldst proue as true as *Paris* did,
> Would, as faire *Troy* was, *Carthage* might be sackt.   (V.i.1554-55)

In spite of Dido's reckless lack of concern for her city, Aeneas will not prove faithful to her, and she must be consumed by both the quenchless flames of passion and the fire of her suicidal funeral pyre: "Goe *Anna*, bid my seruants bring me fire" (V.i.1686). And Dido builds "a fire, / That shall consume all that this stranger left" (1692-93). Before her suicide, however, she prays to the gods:

> from mine ashes let a Conquerour rise,
> That may reuenge this treason to a Queene,
> By plowing vp his Countries with the Sword:
> Betwixt this land and that be neuer league.   (1714-17)

Dido then throws herself, followed closely by Iarbas and Anna, into the flames. Frustrated love has led to their destruction, and the phoenix-image which Dido evokes, balancing Jove's in the first scene, emphasizes not rebirth but the continuity of discord and separation.

The symbol that apparently points in the opposite direction is "walls". The word is used so often in the play that T. M. Pearce felt it must have something to do with the staging.[19] However, the image is taken from the *Aeneid*, and "walls" seem to be more a part of the play's poetic meaning than its production technique. The image is introduced as a metaphor in the first scene, where Ganymede speaks of being "walde in with Egles wings" (I.i.20). In the background story, Troy falls because Priam "Inforst a wide breach in that rampierd wall" in order to draw in the Grecian horse (II.i.469). After Troy falls, Jove promises that Aeneas will gain "faire walles" in Italy as a substitute for those destroyed (I.i.85). When he arrives in Libya, Aeneas is fascinated by the Troy story which he finds pictured (painted or carved in bas-relief) on "Carthage walles" (II.i.296). Having fallen in love with Dido, Aeneas promises:

> *Carthage* shall vaunt her pettie walles no more,
> For I will grace them with a fairer frame,
> And clad her in a Chrystall liuerie,
> Wherein the day may euermore delight.   (V.i.1412-15)

But Hermes interrupts his dream of African grandeur, telling him that he is to build his walls in Italy. Because of the repeated emphasis, "wall" becomes a significant image, conveying its traditional suggestions of safety, integrity, and unity. While Troy's walls stand, the city and its people are safe; the exposed position is untenable. "Walls" then are actually an affirmation of the power of "fire". Where destructive passions, represented by fire, are rampant, one seeks safety in isolation, encapsulation; one hides behind protective walls. Unfortunately for Dido, her storied walls, rather than repelling the Trojans, draw them on; and the Trojans in their way are as deceitful and destructive as the Greeks were at Troy. Love forces entrance through the walls, and the fire of passion follows.

The play is also very much concerned with the idea of fate. Perhaps Dido has no choice but to love Aeneas. In the first scene,

---

[19] See T. M. Pearce, "Evidence for Dating Marlowe's *Tragedy of Dido*", *Studies in the English Renaissance Drama in Memory of Karl Julius Holzknecht*, ed. by Josephine W. Bennett *et al.* (New York: New York University Press, 1959), 236-37.

Jupiter insists that "*AEneas* wandring fate is firme" (I.i.83). Apparently Aeneas is slated to be the founder of a second Troy whether he desires this distinction or not. The concept of fate working in history is derived from Virgil, but the idea is part of the Marlovian ideology as well. In *Hero and Leander*, Marlowe writes:

> It lies not in our power to loue, or hate,
> For will in vs is ouer-rul'd by fate.   (I.167-68)

As in the *Aeneid*, one may feel in Marlowe's plays a contrast between the human agents who are used and then tragically destroyed and the inexorable powers of superhuman fate which move to their preordained ends. There is the suggestion that we should see the characters as caught in predestined roles, controlled from without, and victims of an inescapably destructive world. But Marlowe at the same time leaves the question of determinism open. Dido seems to fall in love with Aeneas before the advent of Cupid, and their love seems to be growing without the help of Juno's rain storm. Possibly we should see the supernatural characters simply as personifications of human passion.[20] We can never be sure how far individual will is overruled by external fate, but the question of freedom of action is of recurring importance in Marlowe's drama. Ultimately, one may feel that Marlowe emphasizes personal responsibility. Although in some sense driven by outside forces, Marlowe's heroes are finally responsible for the world they inhabit.

Dido emphasizes the uncreative, disruptive aspects of love – the homosexual, the unnatural, the adulterous – those kinds of love which are socially unacceptable and which become personally as well as socially destructive. From high to low, from Jupiter to the Nurse, the social duties are neglected, and even perverted, because of passion. The world of the play has nothing to do with normally oriented love, with the fruitful passion of a man for a woman and the contentment of marriage. As Dido complains, she

[20] E.g., in the tradition of the psychomachia, where the gods are personifications of vices and virtues. See Erwin Panofsky, *Studies in Iconology* (1939; rpt. New York: Harper, 1962), p. 149, and fig. 107.

has had no children with Aeneas. In Dido's world, to remain safe from love's frustration, despair, and destruction, one must either forego all passion or "transgresse against all lawes of loue" (IV. iii.1198). Though Aeneas may claim that beauty calls him back to Dido, he is finally able to break away from her and sail for Italy. His decision, even if it is beyond his power of free choice, can hardly be regarded with admiration. Behind him, he leaves three lives destroyed, and Dido's curse will lead, in the historical world beyond the play, to the Punic Wars in which Rome itself will be threatened. The action of the play is not resolved in a vision of unity. There is no tragic resolution, but a sense of continuing destruction and alienation.

But if *Dido* underlines the personal aspects of tragic love, it is not without political overtones. As we have noted, the love of Dido and Aeneas initially stands in the way of the founding of Rome, while its unfortunate outcome leads to problems between their countries in the imagined future. The tragedy of love points to the tragedy of empire. Sidney's "Discourse ... to the Queenes Majesty Touching Hir Mariage with Monsieur" may help us see the love tragedy of Dido in an Elizabethan perspective, for Sidney details the "evilles & dangers"[21] which were attendant upon Elizabeth's possible match with the adventurous French prince, the duc d'Alençon. Such a union, among other things, would lead to the disaffection of a great number of her subjects, and might result in social and political disorders. Certainly there is an analogy here between the two queens, an analogy which gains even more cogency when we find an Elizabethan reminding us that Dido was "otherwise called *Elisa*".[22] In the twentieth century, with different attitudes toward love and marriage, we may possibly miss the point both Sidney and Marlowe are making. For them, romantic love is not an ultimate value to be pursued at all costs. Throughout his plays, Marlowe suggests that personal actions have social and political reverberations which are of primary concern. The individual should, to preserve the respect

---

[21] Albert Feuillerat (ed.), *The Prose Works of Sir Philip Sidney* (Cambridge: Cambridge University Press, 1962), III, 55.
[22] Fenne, sig. Bbl^r.

of the playgoer, consider the common good in his quest for personal satisfaction. In *Dido*, the world of political action forms a vivid background for the central love tragedy; in the next play we shall consider, *Edward II*, love and politics are more intricately united.

III

EDWARD II

The unnatural situation presented in the first scene of *Dido* is reflected in the basic situation of *Edward II*. Queen Isabel herself draws the parallel:

> Like franticke *Iuno* will I fill the earth,
> With gastlie murmure of my sighes and cries,
> For neuer doted *Ioue* on *Ganimed*
> So much as he [i.e., Edward, her husband] on cursed
> *Gaueston*.   (474-77)

Like Jupiter, Edward has forsaken both his wife and his political duties in order to devote himself to a homosexual love; but in *Dido*, the perverse triangle forms the background, not the center of the play. Looked at as a personal tragedy, *Edward II* is based on a series of interlocking and unnatural love affairs, and the first in point of dramatic time is that of King Edward for Piers Gaveston.

Although it has been suggested that the king and Gaveston, by Renaissance standards, do not have an abnormal relationship,[1] this position can hardly weather Gaveston's opening soliloquies. Gaveston enters reading a letter from the king:

> My father is deceast, come *Gaueston*,
> And share the kingdom with thy deerest friend.
> Ah words that make me surfet with delight: (1-3)

Although Gaveston's chief delight may come from his friend's desire

---

[1] L. J. Mills, "The Meaning of *Edward II*", *MP*, 32 (1934-35), 11-31: "the dramatic effectiveness of *Edward II* ... may be explained by the dramatist's use ... of the Elizabethan friendship ideas" (p. 31).

to share the kingdom with him, his words suggest that he is also
delighted with the death of Edward's father. The playgoer immediately suspects such morbid happiness. Perhaps the juxtaposition of death and delight is a species of Elizabethan dark
humor, and though the shock of the disjunction may force a chuckle
from the audience, we must doubt the mental balance of the
character who has made us laugh. Gaveston goes on:

> What greater blisse can hap to *Gaueston*,
> Then liue and be the fauorit of a king?   (4-5)

The incongruous juxtaposition of bliss with royal favor forces
us to wonder at the perversity of the question. The favorites of
kings were traditionally disliked and even hated, and during
times of unrest, not infrequently murdered. Furthermore, the
instability of royal favor was widely noted by moralists and critics.
Most sane Elizabethans could have listed many more blissful
positions than royal favorite. If Gaveston's greatest bliss results
from filling this despised station, such an admission points to his
distorted vision.

But Gaveston's abnormality becomes even more apparent in
the lines following:

> Sweete prince I come, these these thy amorous lines,
> Might haue enforst me to haue swum from France,
> And like *Leander* gaspt vpon the sande,
> So thou wouldst smile and take me in thy armes.
>
> ...
>
> [London] harbors him I hold so deare,
> The king, vpon whose bosome let me die.   (6-9, 13-14)

The phrase "Sweete prince" is conventional enough, as we know
from *Hamlet*, but Edward's "amorous lines" to his male friend suggest
a relationship less than asexual. Moreover, Gaveston compares
himself to Leander, the masculine lover of the priestess Hero,
and imagines, in this context, that the king will embrace him. The
phrase, "vpon whose bosome let me die", carries a possible double
meaning. The first is conventional and alludes to Leander's
swimming the Hellespont for his lover just as Gaveston has crossed
the Narrow Seas for his. The allusion is, of course, a piece of

dramatic irony, since Gaveston, like Leander, will die for his love. But that Gaveston is so pessimistic may be questioned. He is probably punning on the Elizabethan meaning of "die" as sexual consummation, implying that the king will become his homosexual partner. In this exalted position, Gaveston resolves neither to bow to the lords, nor to help the commons. The following interview with the three poor men reveals his overweening egoism and his lack of social responsibility. He thinks of employing only the lying traveller, not the active men who merit some reward for their service to England. These men see Gaveston as, essentially, he is, and the old soldier's curse, "perish by a souldiers hand" (37), looks forward to his death.

In his second and more well-known soliloquy of scene one (perhaps better-known because part of it has been used by Aldous Huxley as an epigraph for *Antic Hay*), Gaveston becomes even more fanciful and sensuous, as he dreams of drawing "the pliant king which way" he pleases by means of his "showes" (53, 56). In his perverse imagination, his pages will be dressed like "*Syluan Nimphes*" and his men "like Satyres" (58, 59). As a variation, he will have a "louelie boye" dress like the goddess Diana, and "in his sportfull hands an Oliue tree, / To hide those parts which men delight to see" (61, 64-65). In the likeness of Actaeon, another boy will be transformed into a hart and thus run to earth by his hounds "and seeme to die" (70). This is the kind of verbal description which captures the imagination of the playgoer, even though it has been painstakingly constructed by the playwright. The passage is a complex tissue of suggestion and allusion. The transvestism may be conventional, but when added to the growing evidence of Gaveston's unnatural desires, even the conventional tends to confirm our suspicions. The "parts which men delight to see" is ambiguous; obviously in the case of Gaveston's lovely boy they are male rather than female organs, and we may wonder if he is projecting his own predilections on all men. The olive branch as a protective covering dictated by modesty is as old as *The Odyssey*, where, in Book Six, Odysseus, after his final shipwreck, holds one before him while addressing Nausikaa. The comparison with Odysseus reveals that the olive branch in the sportful hands of the boy is not at all modest: it is tempting and prurient. The boy's act is related to the modern fan dance.

Bestialism also forms a part of Gaveston's daydream, for his men are not only changed into women but transformed into animals. The descent of man into animal is again an ancient idea, and again it can be traced back to Homer, where Circe changes Odysseus's men into swine. The transformation was soon allegorized into a fable of the bestialization of man through the uncontrolled dominance of his passions. Spenser uses the idea in the second book of *The Faerie Queene*, where the Circe-like Acrasia turns her passionate lovers into beasts. This concept of man's degradation through sensuality became attached to the Actaeon myth. Beneath an emblem showing the transformed Actaeon being torn by several hounds, Geffrey Whitney comments:

> ACTAEON heare, vnhappie man behoulde,
> When in the well, hee sawe Diana brighte,
> With greedie lookes, hee waxed ouer boulde,
> That to a stagge hee was transformed righte,
>   Whereat amasde, hee thought to runne awaie,
>   But straighte his howndes did rente hym, for their praie.
>
> By which is ment, That those whoe doe pursue
> Theire fancies fonde, and thinges vnlawfull craue,
> Like brutishe beastes appeare vnto the viewe,
> And shall at lengthe, Actaeons guerdon haue:
>   And as his houndes, soe theire affections base,
>   Shall them deuowre, and all their deedes deface.[2]

---

[2] See Geffrey Whitney, *A Choice of Emblemes*, p. 15; and R. H., *The Arraignement of the VVhole Creatvre*, p. 246, sig. Ii3ᵛ. Cf. John M. Steadman, "Falstaff as Actaeon: A Dramatic Emblem", *SQ*, 14 (1963), 231-44. In contrast, Giordano Bruno, *The Heroic Frenzies*, trans. by Paul Eugene Memmo (Chapel Hill: University of North Carolina Press, 1964), in the "Fourth Dialogue", explains Actaeon as a positive seeker after divine knowledge, who finds that knowledge within himself. For the conflicting interpretations, see DeWitt T. Starnes and Ernest W. Talbert, *Classical Myth and Legend in Renaissance Dictionaries* (Chapel Hill: University of North Carolina Press, 1955), pp. 204-09. See also Philippe de Mornay, *A Woorke Concerning the Trewnesse of the Christian Religion* (London, 1587), p. 278, sig. U3ᵛ (STC 18149): "man doth couertly carie in his breast all maner of Beasts, ẽ which it behoveth him to kil in himselfe, according to this saying of the *Platonists*. That the readiest way to return vnto God, and consequently to a mans first nature, is to kill his owne affections." Cf. L'Espine, p. 100ʳ, sig. 07ʳ, and p. 101ʳ, sig. 08ʳ.

The Actaeon myth is more relevant to his own situation than Gaveston is aware. Like Actaeon, he is brutalized and finally destroyed because of those "thinges vnlawfull" which are so much a part of Gaveston as a dramatic character.

Further, it is important to note that Gaveston's description ends with death – or in this case, apparent death – "and seeme to die". His entrance, as we have seen, is introduced with the announcement that Edward's father is dead, and some fourteen lines later, he imagines himself dying on the king's breast. One may hypothesize that the recurrence of death in his two soliloquies indicates something about Gaveston's character, a kind of morbid sexual preoccupation with dying. But even the old soldier connects Gaveston and death, and there is a broader suggestion that Gaveston's function in the play will be destructive. He is the agent who precipitates the personal and political catastrophes of the play.

Introduced in the first seventy lines, the themes of passion, degradation, bestiality, ambition, and death, Gaveston's homosexuality, his sensuality, his unthinking selfishness, and his presumptuous determination not to accept his rank in the social hierarchy, all are important in the dramatic situation. Gaveston's two speeches form an overture to the play. Later, as Edward is being drawn to his final outrage, he cries, "O *Gaueston*, it is for thee that I am wrongd" (2306); and in the sense that Gaveston is a prime embodiment of the play's evils, Edward is perfectly right.

Edward's other lover, his wife Isabel, functions initially as a contrast to the selfish Gaveston. She appears as the long-suffering wife who desires only to please her husband, and nothing more. When Edward demands that she persuade the Barons to recall Gaveston, Isabel feels that she must "be a meanes to call home *Gaueston*", even while she understands that Edward will "euer dote" on his minion and she will thus be "euer miserable" (480-82). But Isabel's action is not completely selfless. Edward has threatened her: "till my *Gaueston* be repeald, / Assure thy selfe thou comst not in my sight" (464-65).[3] In a way, Isabel's exile

[3] A pattern of exile and estrangement runs through the play. It is linked with a recurring denial of the sight of loved ones. E.g., Edward is denied his last sight of Gaveston; Prince Edward is denied sight of his father.

from Edward is commensurate with Gaveston's exile from England.
Later, when Warwick accuses her of being Gaveston's advocate,
she replies: "Tis for my selfe I speake, and not for him" (516).
Although the queen is not as selfless as she first appears, she
suffers with a kind of grace, and her single desire seems to be the
gaining of Edward's love.

Having achieved Gaveston's recall, Isabel receives Edward's
promise to "hang a golden tongue about" her neck because she
has "pleaded with so good successe" (625-26). She gently answers:

> No other iewels hang about my neck
> Then these my lord, nor let me haue more wealth,
> Then I may fetch from this ritch treasurie:
> O how a kisse reuiues poore *Isabell*.   (627-30)

The stage business at this point must be interpolated, but it
seems that "these" of line 628 refer to Edward's arms which are
now around Isabel's shoulders: his arms, she insists, are jewels
enough for her, and the wealth which she gathers from the rich
treasury of his lips sufficient. Considered in relation to Gaveston's
concern with manipulating the king for material gain and selfish
pleasure, this metaphor suggests a startlingly different attitude.
If Gaveston sees his relation to the king as a means to an end,
Isabel feels that her relationship with her husband has intrinsic
worth. Perhaps the main trait in the queen's character is that she
desires a mate with whom she can exchange a true and entire love.

Earlier critics were concerned to explain how she changes from
the dutiful wife of Edward to the passionate mistress of Mortimer.[4]
In some ways her change of heart may seem abrupt, but it can be
shown that from the beginning, she favors the young man. She
selects him for private audience and asks him to be her advocate
for Gaveston's recall. After he succeeds, she tells him: "when this
fauour *Isabell* forgets, / Then let her liue abandond and forlorne"
(594-95). Given her desire for a perfect love relationship, the playgoer may feel that she has already decided, perhaps unconsciously,

---

4 See, e.g., Osborne W. Tancock (ed.), *Marlowe: Edward the Second* (Oxford:
Oxford University Press, 1879), pp. xi-xiii.

to turn her quest toward Mortimer if Edward proves unfit for a heterosexual union. When Gaveston charges that the queen has fallen in love with Mortimer, his allegation may not be completely without foundation.

Moreover, the queen's apparent triumph over the Barons in attaining Gaveston's pardon is deceptive. According to Mortimer's argument, Gaveston is recalled so that he may be carefully watched and then assassinated. The playgoer is left to wonder if the queen concurred in, or even suggested this plan. The reconciliation with the king, which follows, is fraudulent and shortlived, since the Barons are merely seeking an occasion to rid themselves of Gaveston. The "second marriage", which Edward promises his queen because she has won over the lords, is founded on false grounds of hope. The king honestly believes that she has recovered his homosexual companion for him; but Isabel knows that he is deceived. Near the end of the play, after Isabel has made a particularly deceitful speech, Mortimer says: "Finely dissembled, do so still [i.e., always] sweet Queene" (2218). His advice seems superfluous. In evaluating the queen's development, we must realize that she is not, even at the beginning of the play, innocent of political intrigue. The queen's emotions and actions are never completely pure, and her moral step from wife to mistress may not be as far as we sometimes think.

If we see Isabel as a character whose main function in the play is to desire a stable and mutually loving relationship with a man, NO MATTER WHO, NO MATTER HOW – then her actions become fully explicable, and she herself becomes a more pathetic figure. Even after winning her deceptive victory over the Barons, she remains the abused wife. Edward quickly forgets his vows of second marriage and accuses her of loving Mortimer, while she protests: "Heauens can witnesse, I loue none but you" (1112). Whatever we think of her assertion, she plays the traditional role of the rejected but dutiful wife. Having been pushed physically away, she laments:

> O that mine armes could close this Ile about,
> That I might pull him to me where I would,
> Or that these teares that drissell from mine eyes,

> Had power to mollifie his stonie hart,
> That when I had him we might neuer part.   (1114-18)

But these are impossibilities. As Edward's wife, Isabel has been a usable tool, "a meanes", but the signs of any shared love between them are indeed few. Edward seems incapable of establishing a close relationship with a woman, and Isabel needs exactly what he cannot, because of his homosexual nature, give.

For Isabel, the turning point is marked by her soliloquy:

> So well hast thou deseru'de sweete *Mortimer*,
> As *Isabell* could liue with thee for euer.
> In vaine I looke for loue at *Edwards* hand,
> Whose eyes are fixt on none but *Gaueston:*
> Yet once more ile importune him with praiers.
> If he be straunge and not regarde my wordes,
> My sonne and I will ouer into France,
> And to the king my brother there complaine,
> How *Gaueston* hath robd me of his loue:
> But yet I hope my sorrowes will haue end,
> And *Gaueston* this blessed day be slaine.   (1157-67)

Although Gaveston is killed, the queen still leaves England. There is an ambiguity, derived from the historical sources, in her journey to France. On the one hand, Edward sends her to negotiate with her brother, the French king; on the other, she departs voluntarily in order to plot a retaliatory invasion.[5] In any case, her departure is a kind of exile, and there is no one to plead for her recall.

In France, she becomes Mortimer's mistress, but her quest for an absolute union of love is not accomplished. Again, she is a political tool rather than a beloved woman. The kind of relationship Mortimer and she establish is suggested by his recurrent impatience with her speeches. Twice within a hundred lines (1761, 1854), he peremptorily stops her. After she and the prince are made figureheads for the rebellion which places power in Mortimer's hands, he tells her: "Be rulde by me, and we will rule the realme" (2147). She is governed, not loved. As Leicester quips, "What cannot gallant *Mortimer* with the Queene?" (1917). What not indeed?

[5] See Raphael Holinshed, *The Laste Volume of the Chronicles of England, Scotlande, and Ireland* (London, 1577), II, 875-77 (STC 13568b).

In the second half of the play, Mortimer's political ambitions become fully evident. His earlier actions now appear to have been motivated by his desire to rule, not by any altruistic thought of England's welfare. In the manner of Tamburlaine, he claims to control fortune (2197), and boasts:

> I stand as *Ioues* huge tree,
> And others are but shrubs compard to me,
> All tremble at my name, and I feare none.   (2579-81)

And with the usual Marlovian irony, his boast is followed immediately by his fall from power. But Mortimer is given some limited insight into his condition:

> Base fortune, now I see, that in thy wheele
> There is a point, to which when men aspire,
> They tumble hedlong downe: that point I touchte,
> And seeing there was no place to mount vp higher,
> Why should I greeue at my declining fall?
> Farewell faire Queene, weepe not for *Mortimer*,
> That scornes the world, and as a traueller,
> Goes to discouer countries yet vnknowne.   (2627-34)

Although his nonchalance sounds forced, Mortimer now understands one of the most pertinent facts about the dramatic world he inhabits: there is a limitation on human accomplishment; not all desires are attainable. Mortimer may be able to control the queen, but neither he nor she can attain those absolutes of power and love to which they aspire.

The relationship of Isabel to Mortimer parallels Edward's to Gaveston. In the broadest sense, the relationships are immoral, adulterous, and unnatural. Both the king and the queen are used by their lovers as the means to power. Ultimately, Gaveston and Mortimer are unsuccessful in their attempts to hold power, and both are beheaded by their political enemies. The tools of their ambitions, Isabel and Edward, are powerless to help them, and are themselves destroyed. But, where Edward seems blind to Gaveston's motives, Isabel apparently sees the monster she has created in giving her love and power to Mortimer. When Mortimer broaches the question of murdering the imprisoned king, she replies:

so the prince my sonne be safe,
Whome I esteeme as deare as these mine eyes,
Conclude against his father what thou wilt,
And I my selfe will willinglie subscribe. (2159-62)

She sacrifices the father to save her son. For as her relationship with Mortimer deteriorates, Isabel becomes more and more concerned with the prince, who must fill the vacuum of love left by her loss of both Edward and Mortimer.

In the final scene, her last love proves as worthless to her as the others. When Edward III condemns Mortimer to death as a traitor, the queen pleads: "As thou receiuedst thy life from me, / Spill not the bloud of gentle *Mortimer*" (2636-37). But Edward turns on the queen, questioning her own involvement in the king's death, and he commits her to the tower, pending further investigation. "Nay", she answers, "to my death" (2651). The queen has been unable to establish, on any level, that lasting relationship she so strongly desires. Even her son, for whom she has given so much, betrays her love. As Edmund comments on her affair with Mortimer, "Fie on that loue that hatcheth death and hate" (1801). But all the love affairs in this play seem to be exactly of that nature: destructive.

At the center of these personal entanglements is the king, who forms a contrasting parallel to the queen. If she seeks the ultimate male-female relationship, the king seeks his happiness in the impossible fruition of homosexuality, first with Gaveston, and then with the Spencers and Baldock. He further mirrors the queen in his conviction that a love relationship is beyond material value. Both believe in the intrinsic merit of love, which far surpasses material wealth. Mourning Gaveston's exile, the king says:

Did neuer sorrow go so neere my heart,
As dooth the want of my sweete *Gaueston*?
And could my crownes reuenew bring him back,
I would freelie giue it to his enemies,
And thinke I gaind, hauing bought so deare a friend. (603-07)

In isolation the king's attitude is certainly admirable, but Edward has royal responsibilities and duties, and these have been completely forgotten in his attempt to perfect a homosexual union with his minions.

From one point of view, the unnatural relationship with Gaveston has led directly to the anarchy which England experiences under Edward. By devoting his wealth to lascivious ends, the king has weakened his political power. Mortimer, who espouses this point of view, tells him:

> The idle triumphes, maskes, lasciuious showes
> And prodigall gifts bestowed on *Gaueston,*
> Haue drawne thy treasure drie, and made thee weake,
> The murmuring commons ouerstretched hath.   (959-62)

Lancaster adds: "Looke for rebellion, looke to be deposde" (963). In his desire to satisfy his perverse appetites, the king undermines the social and political stability of his realm. Shakespeare's Hal indicates the proper solution to the monarch's problem: the disruptive character (Falstaff, or in this case, Gaveston) must be banished from Court. In the king, the personal merges with the public, and the king's private desires must be accommodated to the "loue" the subjects "beare" their "soueraigne" (832). When the king allows his personal proclivities to stand in the way of his general relationship with his subjects, political upheaval, as Lancaster warns, is sure to follow.

Looked at from a political standpoint, however, Edward's homosexuality merely reflects the 'unnatural' state of the realm. It becomes a symbol of a more total inversion. The disintegration of the body politic is a complex affair, and though the Barons may wish to place the full blame on the king, his fecklessness is symptomatic rather than precipitative of the civil strife England undergoes.

The Barons themselves must share the blame for the national upheaval, for their pride has caused them to overstep the bounds of their traditional function in government. Kent comments on what has happened:

> Barons & Earls, your pride hath made me mute,
> But now ile speake, and to the proofe I hope:
> I do remember in my fathers dayes,

> Lord *Percie* of the North being highly mou'd,
> Brau'd *Mowberie* in presence of the king,
> For which, had not his highnes lou'd him well,
> He should haue lost his head, but with his looke,
> The vndaunted spirit of *Percie* was appeasd,
> And *Mowberie* and he were reconcild:
> Yet dare you braue the king vnto his face.   (107-16)

Kent uses the past to illustrate the 'natural' subordination of lord to king, while the present situation is an inversion of the traditional order. If the king oversteps the bounds of nature in his private life, the nobles have assumed political powers which have not been theirs in the orderly past.

The conversation between the two Mortimers, before the elder leaves for Scotland, is instructive. First, it seems quite clear that the Barons are not worried about the morality of Edward's homosexual attachment to Gaveston:

> seeing his minde so dotes on *Gaueston*,
> Let him without controulement haue his will.
> The mightiest kings haue had their minions,
> ...
> And not kings onelie, but the wisest men.   (686-88, 692)

Mortimer Senior goes on to list a compelling number of classical examples and concludes that Edward should be allowed to "Freely enioy that vaine light-headed earle" (697). Second, Mortimer Junior makes it clear that Gaveston is not hated because of his homosexuality, but because of his low birth and his present wealth:

> this I scorne, that one so baselie borne
> Should by his soueraignes fauour grow so pert,
> And riote it with the treasure of the realme.   (700-02)

The opposition of the Barons grows then from a combination of class pride and downright greed, and the derogatory references to Gaveston's use of the nation's wealth, frequently made in the first part of the play, suggest that greed overshadows pride. Unlike the king and the queen who seem willing to give all for love, the lords (like Gaveston himself) are preoccupied with the preservation and implementation of their material possessions.

They, however, are not unopposed in their struggle for wealth and political power. The discussion of Gaveston by the two Mortimers is juxtaposed to a discussion of him by Spencer and Baldock. The latter respects him as a "liberall earle" and a favorite of the king (730). Through Gaveston's example, Spencer instructs Baldock in the ways of political aspiration:

> learne this of me, a factious lord
> Shall hardly do himselfe good, much lesse vs,
> But he that hath the fauour of a king,
> May with one word aduaunce vs while we liue:
> ...
> You must be proud, bold, pleasant, resolute,
> And now and then, stab as occasion serues.   (726-29, 762-63)

As self-seeking and conscienceless as the Mortimers, Spencer and Baldock represent the 'new men' who serve the king, taking the place of the alienated Barons.

Gaveston, the object of both discussions, epitomizes the 'new men' like Spencer and Baldock who have become the king's favorites not because of their place in the stable social hierarchy, but because of their intrinsic worth to the crown.[6] The Barons find the king's men "base and obscure" (101), and the class conflict, influenced, as we have noted, by economic considerations, breaks into fire when the king and Gaveston confront the factious lords. Watching Gaveston enter with the king, Mortimer Senior asks: "What man of noble birth can brooke this sight?" (307). And Mortimer Junior reminds Gaveston that he is hardly "a gentleman by birth" (324). Later in a parallel scene, Pembroke lashes out at Spencer Senior: "Away base vpstart, brau'st thou nobles thus?" (1513). The Barons insist that persons of the lower and middle classes have no business in the service of the king. In opposition, the king asserts that he himself, rather than the accident of birth, will decide on social priority: "Were he [Gaveston] a

---

[6] The Tudors were troubled by the antagonism between the established aristocracy and the 'new men' like Wolsey and Thomas Cromwell who gained political power through their personal abilities and royal favor. See, e.g., A. L. Rowse, *The England of Elizabeth: The Structure of Society* (London: Macmillan, 1950), pp. 244-52.

peasant, being my minion, / Ile make the prowdest of you stoope to him" (325-26). Of course, the irony of the situation is that, by breaking the rules of hereditary right, Edward opens the gates to social disintegration. If the Barons are no longer certain of their traditional ranking in the political and social hierarchy, then the king's position as leader of the system is likewise called into question. If a peasant may take precedence over a noble, a noble may in consequence replace a king. The recurring confrontations between the king's men and the nobles implicitly ask whether England will be built on a system of 'worth' or a system of 'birth'.[7] Thus Edward's bland assertion that his birthright allows him to determine questions of human worth is paradoxical. As Lancaster informs him, "you may not thus disparage vs" (327). Once the stable hierarchy is eliminated, any member of the society with ability and ambition may aspire to a position of power and control. The static order of traditional society disappears, and in its place is the turmoil of individual aspiration and class struggle.

Neither side in the struggle receives the endorsement of the playwright. Both Barons and king's men seek their own selfish ends, and their methods are strikingly similar. When Isabel tries to gain the support of her brother, the King of France, Spencer Filius sends Levune to undermine her diplomatic endeavors:

> be gon in hast, and with aduice
> Bestowe that treasure on the lords of Fraunce,
> That therewith all enchaunted like the guarde,
> That suffered *Ioue* to passe in showers of golde
> To *Danae*, all aide may be denied
> To *Isabell* the Queene. (1573-78)

Levune asks Spencer and Baldock to have no doubts, for he will "clap so close / Among the lords of France with Englands golde, / That *Isabell* shall make her plaints in vaine" (1586-88). Two

---

[7] The debate over the relative merits of birth and worth was of considerable interest to the Renaissance. E.g., Henry Medwall's play, *Fulgens and Lucrece* (1497), is built on the debate, and decides in favor of worth. The issue is part of a greater Renaissance tension between art and nature. See Edward William Tayler, *Nature and Art in Renaissance Literature* (New York: Columbia University Press, 1964), pp. 13-14.

points should be noted in Levune's commissioning. First, Levune is apparently sent to France without King Edward's immediate knowledge. The king leaves the stage before Spencer gives Levune his instructions. Second, Levune is certain that the bribery will work, even though the King of France is Isabel's brother. This is a question of finances not morality.

In an analogous situation, Mortimer, without the queen's knowledge, commissions Lightborn. Just as the queen was a threat to the security of the king's men, the imprisoned Edward is a potential threat to Mortimer, and he must be assassinated. In the confident manner of Levune, Lightborn sees no moral objections to the murder. When Mortimer suggests that he will be filled with human compunctions, Lightborn answers ironically: "I vse much to relent" (2359). He is a willing tool:

> You shall not need to giue instructions,
> Tis not the first time I haue killed a man,
> I learnde in Naples how to poison flowers,
> To strangle with a lawne thrust through the throte.[8]   (2361-64)

For Lightborn, the assassination is merely a financial transaction. The analogy between Levune and Lightborn not only suggests that the Barons and the king's men are playing the same political game with similar equipment and ruthlessness, it highlights a major characteristic of the play, the intrigue. From Gaveston's manipulation of the king to Kent's secret talks with the young Prince Edward, the action has a quality of cloak-and-dagger. Deception, secrecy, rumor are all elements of this heavy atmosphere of intrigue which pervades the action.[9]

The intriguers of both parties hide behind the façade of patriotism. Publicly, all claim to be motivated by their "countries cause" (1190),[10] and the phrase and its variants echo through the

---

[8] Cf. *Jew of Malta*, II.946ff.; IV.1962-63.

[9] See, e.g., 420ff., 677, 737, 1026, 2175, 2227, 2641ff.

[10] Cf. *Massacre at Paris*, 651-52, and Balliol's speech in Peele's *Edward I*: "Tis not ambitious thoughts of private rule, / Hath forst your king to take on him these Armes, / Tis countreis cause, it is the common good, / Of us and of our brave posterity" (2029-32). *Edward I*, ed. by Frank Hook, *The Dramatic Works of George Peele* (New Haven: Yale University Press, 1961), II, 145-46. Balliol is in the act of rebelling against his sworn allegiance to Edward. There are indications that Peele was borrowing consciously from Marlowe.

play. In betraying his vow and murdering Gaveston, Warwick claims: "it is my countries cause I follow" (1297). Escaping from England with the rebellious Mortimer, Edmund calls on Nature to give them fair winds: "yeeld to my countries cause in this" (1594). In open rebellion against the king, Mortimer says it is "for our countries cause" (1766) that the rebels swear allegiance to Prince Edward, who is, of course, in Mortimer's control. In each case where love of country is evoked as a guiding principle, self-interest – the "commodity" of Shakespeare's *King John* – is actually at work. Each group is struggling to maintain its political power; there is no genuinely disinterested concern for the nation. Although Johnson's definition of patriotism as the last refuge of a scoundrel was apparently not uttered after a reading of this play, the definition does suggest something of the political hypocrisy rampant here. Marlowe's characters realize as surely as Shakespeare's Angelo that good words will disguise bad deeds to the satisfaction of most people.

The violence which results from the pervasive self-interest mirrors the moral and political disintegration of the society. From promise to fulfilment, beheading is a prominent pattern in the play. Edmund announces it when he suggests that Edward "let these their [i.e., the Barons'] heads, / Preach vpon poles for trespasse of their tongues" (117-18).[11] The blustering Lancaster replies by threatening to throw the "glozing head" of Gaveston at the king (133). Later, both Edmund and Lancaster are beheaded, along with most of the Barons, Gaveston, and the king's men. Mortimer is completely dismembered (2621), and the play ends with Edward III holding his severed head and placing it on the dead king's coffin: "accursed head, / Could I haue rulde thee then, as I do now, / Thou hadst not hatcht this monstrous treacherie" (2663-65). Although Marlowe derives the pattern from the histories, he converts beheading into a dramatic symbol for unnatural dismemberment of the state.[12] In an age when the state was

---

[11] Edmund is probably playing on a partial pun on "perch" and "preach".
[12] See Holinshed, pp. 868, 893, 894. Cf. Christopher Ricks, "*Sejanus* and Dismemberment", *MLN*, 76 (1961), 301-08, who points out a similar image pattern in Jonson's play.

imaged as a "body politic", the equation between the human body and the state was easily made. One need only remember the graphic titlepage of Hobbes' *Leviathan*, where the healthy state is symbolized by the king who literally incorporates his subjects. In the play, the opposite is true: the chaotic state finds an external correlative in the dismembered and headless bodies of the king's subjects who are alienated from him.

The minor violence done to Edward's person was probably taken from Stow's account. Matrevis and Gurney, Edward's guards, decide "to disfigure him that hee mighte not be knowen":

> they determined to shaue as well the heare off hys heade as also off his bearde, wherefore comming by a little Water which ranne in a ditche, they commaunded him to alighte from his horsse to be shauen: to whome being set on a Molehill, a Barbour came with a Bason of colde Water taken out of the ditch, to whō *Edwarde* sayd, shall I haue no warme water? the Barber answered, this wyll serue ... .[13]

Marlowe follows this departure from Holinshed's basic account for symbolic purpose. The forcible removal of Edward's hair points to the loss of his royal identity, which is only a part of the disintegration of social identity – the world turned upside down.

For Edward's murder, Marlowe found sufficient material in Holinshed, but again he uses the material with dramatic significance. Marlowe's stage directions for Edward's murder are missing, but Lightborn requires several tools: a red hot spit, a table, and a featherbed. Until recently, editors and commentators, laboring under a sense of false propriety, have obscured what the playwright wished to have presented. Holinshed describes the scene:

> they came sodenly one night into the chamber where he lay in bed fast asleepe, and with heauie feather beddes, (or a table as some write) being cast vpon him, they kept him downe, and withall put into his fundament an horne, and through the same they thrust vp into his bodie a hote spitte ... the which passing vp into his intrayles, and being rolled to and

---

[13] John Stow, *The Chronicles of England* (London, 1580), p. 356, sig. Z2ᵛ (STC 23333). The story also appears in Stow's *Annales of England* (London, 1592) and subsequent editions.

fro, burnt the same, but so as no appearāce of any wounde or hurt out-
wardly might bee once perceyued.[14]

This is the kind of action Marlowe must have had in mind. Edward's death results from a deadly re-enactment of the homosexual
act. If death by beheading mirrors the dismemberment of the
body politic and Edward's disfiguration its loss of social identity,
then his death symbolizes the moral perversion which accompanies
the political upheaval.

Viewing the play as a chronicle of moral and political instability,
we can perhaps more accurately describe the function of Edmund,
Earl of Kent. Traditionally, Kent has been seen as the weathervane of audience sympathy, supporting first Edward, then the
Barons, and finally Edward again.[15] He apparently joins each
party in its time of greatest appeal to the playgoer. But the playgoer can surely make up his mind without the aid of a vacillating
earl. The function of the role is not well-defined by the weathervane
theory, and possibly Edmund is better seen as a political whirligig,
a creature of constant change, who unlike the queen, never uses
his power to seek a reconciliation between the struggling factions.
No matter how much we may sympathize with Kent, his incon-
stancy is of negative value in the play. Of course, it may be argued
that Kent brings about the resolution of the action. His secret
conversations with the young King Edward III are feared by the
queen and Mortimer: "If he haue such accesse vnto the prince, /
Our plots and stratagems will soone be dasht" (2221-22). But
ironically it is not Kent's words but his death that motivates the
young king to act against Mortimer. As Kent is being taken away
to execution, young Edward asks: "What safetie may I looke for
at his [Mortimer's] hands, / If that my Vnckle shall be murthered
thus?" (2441-42). The question suggests an interpretation of the
end of the play. Although the young king may be genuinely moved
by his father's assassination, his impatience to see Mortimer's head

---

[14] Holinshed, p. 883. Cf. John Rastell, *The Pastime of People* [1529] (London,
1811), pp. 213-14. See also William Empson, "Two Proper Crimes", *Nation*,
163 (1946), 444-45.
[15] Cf. F. P. Wilson, *Marlowe and the Early Shakespeare* (Oxford: Oxford University
Press, 1953), p. 94.

stems from motives of self-interest. Mortimer may decide that the royal figurehead is dispensable. The play ends with no promises of political or personal renewal, for Edward III is as ruthless and uncompromising as Mortimer.

Kent, in his irresponsibility and his lack of success, only reflects his brother the king, who again and again expresses his willingness to sell, give away, or divide his country so that he may enjoy his private pleasures. In seeking perverse gratification, Edward assists the collapse of political stability, a stability which he, as a king, should be dedicated to preserving and building. We may see Edward as a male Dido, willing to give all for his love, but finding that the love he has chosen to pursue is denied by the very nature of his universe. His homosexual desires are destructive, and form a center of unnaturalness in the play. His search for an ultimate consummation outside the bounds of human possibility, combined with the ambitions both personal and political of his subjects, leads to his confusion and the disruption of his realm.

In *Edward II*, Marlowe, like Sophocles in *Oedipus Rex*, successfully blends unnatural love with unnatural disturbances in the body politic. Although many critics seem to agree with Harry Levin that Marlowe is concerned "not with the state, but, as always, with the individual",[16] their position ignores a great deal of what Marlowe has to say. In one of its major aspects, the play is about "that commonweale, where lords / Keepe courts, and kings are lockt in prison" (2328-29), an inverted world of political confusion. The play is not an endorsement of Renaissance aspiration, but a critique of a society which allows selfishness and ambition to destroy itself utterly.

In the following plays, *The Massacre at Paris*, *1* and *2 Tamburlaine*, and *Doctor Faustus*, the love relationships become subordinate to political aspirations. The Guise's affair with the Queen Mother is a political convenience, and even Tamburlaine's vaunted love

[16] Harry Levin, *The Overreacher: A Study of Christopher Marlowe* (Cambridge, Mass.: Harvard University Press, 1952), p. 88, and *Edward II*, ed. by H. B. Charlton and R. D. Waller, revised by F. N. Lees (London: Methuen, 1955), p. 222.

for the divine Zenocrate is secondary to his ambition for earthly conquest. With *Faustus*, we step into the world of Renaissance science fiction, and like many heroes of science fiction, Faustus is not greatly interested in love. His immortal Helen is a spirit, no woman of flesh and blood. Perhaps Faustus's one true passion is for himself.

These four plays form an interesting progression, for in them Marlowe examines the desire for sovereignty. The plays are here arranged in ascending order of aspiration. *The Massacre* deals with the struggle for France; *Tamburlaine*, with the struggle for world dominion; and *Faustus*, with the struggle for universal power. We begin with the conquest of France.

IV

THE MASSACRE AT PARIS

The Massacre at Paris was called, apparently, *The Guise* by Henslowe and his men, and the play, beyond losing its original name, has come to us in a more mutilated form than any other of Marlowe's plays. The textual problem is very important in a critical evaluation of the play, and we must discuss it more fully than we have done in Chapter I before we turn to the possible interpretations of the action. Both the reason for and the degree of textual mutilation are in doubt. The play is possibly a memorial reconstruction, the chief actor involved in the reconstruction being the Guise, for his lines are, it seems, fullest.[1] This explanation is most widely accepted at the present and explains the number of parallels with other plays: they were inserted by the reconstructing actor who remembered them from the plays in which he had acted. But there is also the possibility that *The Massacre* underwent a cutting process such as has been theorized for *Macbeth*.[2] In order to accommodate the play to a special performance, someone (probably not the author) cut and revised the text. In articulating what remained of the scenes, the unknown reviser added the rather crude exit lines: "Come then, lets away" (339), "Then come my Lords, lets goe" (486).[3] However, both of these solutions for the

---

[1] H. J. Oliver (ed.), *Dido Queen of Carthage and The Massacre at Paris*, p. lix, argues that there may have been as many as three actors involved: the actors of the Guise and Anjou-Henry III, and the actor who doubled such roles as the Cardinal and the Soldier.

[2] See Kenneth Muir (ed.), *Macbeth* (Cambridge: Harvard University Press, 1962), p. xii.

[3] The exit lines quoted, however, are not atypical of Marlowe's usual technique. Cf., e.g., *Edward II*, ll. 286, 438, 721, 1493, 2312; *Jew of Malta*, l. 1508. This fact severely qualifies their cogency as evidence for revision.

textual problem are conjectural; and it is quite possible that the play as we have it was not finished by Marlowe, and that what we have, in this third hypothesis, is the bare trunk of a play, somewhat like Shakespeare's *Timon of Athens*. It is an intermediate draft – perhaps a rough draft – replete with unturned phrases and lines remembered from plays Marlowe had seen or read.

Against this third hypothesis stands what is now called the 'Collier leaf'. Discovered by a London bookseller, the leaf was purchased and its discovery announced by John Payne Collier. Since Collier's scholarly reputation has been stained by his carelessness and his penchant for forging, the leaf was long under suspicion, but it has now been rehabilitated by several scholars.[4] The leaf gives an expanded version of the beginning of scene xix, indicating that Marlowe indeed wrote more (at least of this scene) than we have in the printed version. Further, it has been suggested that the Collier leaf is from Marlowe's 'foul papers' of the play, that the leaf reveals signs of hurried composition, especially in matters of speech-heads, punctuation, and character names (or lack of them). However, these signs of hurried composition are not self-evident, and there is no conclusive proof that the leaf is holograph of the 'foul paper' variety. It seems more likely that it is part of an advanced draft. There is little or no indication of blotting and rewriting, the kind of stumbling one expects in a first attempt. The manuscript is quite clean. Nevertheless, the possibility still remains that the printed version was set up from a surviving rough draft, written before the draft from which the Collier leaf is extant.

The Collier leaf contains a rather full speech for the soldier who is about to shoot and kill Mugeroun, and this speech compares closely with the printed text. However, the Guise's following speech, only four lines in the printed version, is sixteen in the manuscript. If the actor who played the Guise were one of the actors compiling

---

[4] Although Tucker Brooke was suspicious, Joseph Q. Adams ("The *Massacre at Paris* Leaf", *Library*, 14 [1934], 447-69) believes it to be authentic. J. M. Nosworthy ("The Marlowe Manuscript", *Library*, 26 [1945], 158-71), argues that the leaf is from "an original first draft". His reasons are given below in the main text.

he reconstruction, we might expect to have a full version of his
peech in the printed text; and, of course, we do not. The omission
casts some doubt upon the hypothesis that the play is a memorial
reconstruction.

At this point, it may be best to ascertain exactly what is missing
rom the Guise's printed speech in order to see if another explana-
ion is possible. The manuscript version[5] reads:

> Hold thee tale soldier take the this and flye   Exit
> thus fall Imperfett exhalatione
> wch our great sonn of fraunce cold not effecte
> a fyery meteor in the fermament
> lye there the kinges delyght and guises scorne
> revenge it henry yf thow liste or darst
> I did it onely in dispyght of thee
> fondlie hast thow incenste the guises sowle
> y^t of it self was hote enoughe to worke
> thy lust degestione wth extreamest shame
> the armye I have gathered now shall ayme
> more at thie end then exterpatione
> and when thow thinkst I have foregotten this
> and y^t thow most reposest one my faythe
> then will I wake thee from thie folishe dreame
> and lett thee see thie self my prysoner   Exeunt

The printed text reads:

> Holde thee tall Souldier, take thee this and flye.
> Lye there the Kings delight, and *Guises* scorne.
> Reuenge it *Henry* as thou list or dare,
> I did it only in despite of thee.   (824-27)

The printed text gives only the bare essentials of the speech: the
magery is gone. However, the comparison does not allow us at
present to determine the precise relationship of printed version
o manuscript. It is, for example, at least a remote possibility that
Marlowe himself excised the twelve lines from the speech. He may
have felt that they were not artistically apt.[6] Perhaps more plausi-

---

Oliver, pp. 165-66, transcribes the manuscript. I have compared it with the
original at the Folger Shakespeare Library. The transcript in Ribner's edition
p. 267) is often incorrect.
The phrase "with speed" (reinforced by "speedily" and "speedy") echoes

bly, Marlowe may have written the four lines in a first draft of the play, intending to expand them later; and the Collier leaf contains that expansion.

But the printed text DOES seem to suggest a cut. The four lines are the essential, non-imagistic portion of the speech. The soldier is paid, and the idea of revenge is introduced. Henry's revenge will lead to the Guise's fall. A reviser who wished to shorten the play might well cut the other lines for economy. This observation does not completely eliminate the theory of memorial reconstruction, for such a reconstruction could have come from actors who knew only a cut version. The Guise-actor may never have known the other lines of the speech.

This purposefully inconclusive discussion of the text points to the basic question of *The Massacre*: in the extant, verbally truncated play, how much do we have of Marlowe's to examine critically? Because of our inability to reach an undisputed conclusion about the nature of the text, the answers to the question have been various. Boas, taking one position, writes: "If the [Collier] leaf is genuine I look upon it as a support to my view ... that in the octavo text of *The Massacre at Paris* we have, though in a cut version, the essential features of Marlowe's play."[7] For the kind of criticism that Boas offers us, the play as it stands is sufficient. J. B. Steane, on the other hand, feels that Boas may be wrong:

If its *action* [i.e., Boas's "essential features"] remains more or less unaffected, then we must ask what made the 1263 extant lines up into a play of normal length. It may have been fooleries, as in *Faustus* but with the massacre as their excuse. Or it may have been passages of sustained writing; and 'the pith of the matter' may then be precisely what is lost to us.

And, using the Collier leaf as evidence, Steane concludes "that the places where attitudes might have been shaped and thought

---

through the play. If Marlowe were emphasizing speed, he might be expected to keep long speeches to a minimum.

[7] Boas, *Christopher Marlowe*, p. 171.

[8] J. B. Steane, *Marlowe: A Critical Study* (Cambridge: Cambridge University Press, 1964), pp. 237-38. We may deprecate Steane's description of the relevant comic scenes of *Faustus* as "fooleries".

developed have been exactly the places cut".[9] Since Steane's criticism is generally linked to a close reading of the text, he finds the attenuated play insufficient for more than a suggested reading of the action.

I find myself in a position similar to Steane's. Since we are so very uncertain about the grounds for interpretation, we can venture only hesitant suggestions about the unity of action and language. Indeed, the ambiguities are such – and we cannot be sure that they are unintentional – that one interpretation of the play cannot be offered as conclusive. We shall try here to explore two possibilities and to suggest that the second more nearly conforms to the Marlovian dramatic world as we have seen it and will see it in later chapters.

Before turning to the interpretive possibilities, however, we should notice some general features of the structure. The play is divided into twenty-four scenes.[10] The first twelve deal with the initial unity of France, symbolized by the rite of marriage, and its dissolution in the Massacre. In this sequence, the Guise is all-powerful, and his chief enemies (excluding Navarre) are put to death: in the third scene, the Queen Mother of Navarre is poisoned, and in the fifth, the Lord High Admiral is assassinated. In scene thirteen, the beginning of the second group of scenes, King Charles dies (apparently poisoned by his mother),[11] and the throne is assumed by his brother, King Henry. This sequence begins with the rites of death and coronation. Henry appears to be a more powerful king than Charles, and his minion, Mugeroun, wins the Duchess of Guise as his lover. Vowing revenge, the Guise has Mugeroun shot (in a way parallel to his having the Admiral

[9] Steane, p. 238.

[10] This is my count of absolute scenes, i.e., scenes which begin and end with a clear stage.

[11] Catherine says: "As I doe liue, so surely shall he dye" (526). When Charles dies unexpectedly, the playgoer may surmise that she has poisoned him. See *Martine Mar-Sixtus* (London, 1592), sig. E4ʳ (STC 24913a), and Henri Estienne, *A Mervaylous Discourse vpon the Life, Deedes, and Behauiours of Katherine de Medicis* (?Heydelberge, 1575), p. 138, sig. I5ᵛ (STC 10550), for contemporary conjectures of poisoning. See also Jean de Serres, *The Fourth Parte of Cōmentaries of the Ciuill Warres in France* (London, 1576), p. 125 (STC 22243).

shot earlier in the play). Mugeroun's murder is the immediate motivation for King Henry's bloody action against the Guise and his party, and the Massacre in the first sequence of scenes is balanced by the purge of the Guisian party in the second.[12] The death of the Queen Mother of Navarre is paralleled by the promised death of Catherine, Queen Mother of France: "Since the *Guise* is dead, I will not liue", she says; and the death of King Charles, which marks the turning point of the action, is parallel to the death of his brother, King Henry, which ends the play. The union of Navarre and France announced in the first scene is again announced in the last, when the King of Navarre joins Henry at the siege of Paris. As this brief outline of the play's construction indicates, *The Massacre* is a well-balanced play, and Marlowe has carefully selected and molded the material he gathered from the histories of contemporary France.[13] Boas was, in fact, correct in his assertion that the essentials of an integrated action are preserved in the printed text.

But still the essential critical question is how to interpret this action. First, the play may be seen as a conflict between the Guise, representing the Catholics, and Navarre, representing the Protestants. The Machiavellian Guise is attempting to capture the French throne:

> For this, I wake, when others think I sleepe,
> For this, I waite, that scornes attendance else:
> For this, my quenchles thirst whereon I builde
> Hath often pleaded kindred to the King.   (105-08)

The Catholicism that he espouses is merely a façade behind which he operates and which allows him to gain foreign support from the Papacy and from Spain:

> My policye hath framde religion.
> Religion: *O Diabole.*
> Fye, I am ashamde, how euer that I seeme,

---

[12] Cf. Antony Colynet, *The True History of the Ciuill VVares of France* (London, 1591), p. 263 (STC 5590), who notes the parallel in historical incidents.
[13] See Paul Kocher, "François Hotman and Marlowe's *The Massacre at Paris*", *PMLA*, 56 (1941), 349-68, and "Contemporary Pamphlet Backgrounds for Marlowe's *The Massacre at Paris*", *MLQ*, 8 (1947), 151-73, 309-18.

> To think a word of such a simple sound
> Of so great matter should be made the ground. (122-26)

Like Caesar, to whom he recurrently compares himself, the Guise is enamoured of a crown.[14] He will seek the kingship with "flames" and "bloud" (92, 93), and he stresses his "resolution" to do so (96, 166). In this first soliloquy, in which he sets forth his aims, he realizes the enormity of his desires, his "aspiring winges" (103), and sees that striving to attain the heights of ambition may place him in the "deepest hell" (104). There is an undertone of the diabolic in the Guise's attitude.

Opposing the aspirations of the Guise is the Protestant Henry of Navarre, who, we may feel, is a genuinely religious man. In the midst of a hardheaded discussion of the Guise's political ambitions, Navarre interjects:

> he that sits and rules aboue the clowdes,
> Doth heare and see the praiers of the iust:
> And will reuenge the bloud of innocents,
> That *Guise* hath slaine by treason of his heart,
> And brought by murder to their timeles ends. (42-46)

Such scrupulous piety, the audience may be sure, will obtain its earthly reward. Just before the Guise is murdered by hired assassins, Navarre again looks to heaven for aid:

> That wicked *Guise* I feare me much will be
> The ruine of that famous Realme of France:
> For his aspiring thoughts aime at the crowne,
>
> ...
>
> But if that God doe prosper mine attempts,
> And send vs safely to arriue in France:
> Wee'l beat him back, and driue him to his death,
> That basely seekes the ruine of his Realme.
> (928-30, 934-37)[15]

---

14 Cf. Michel Hurault, *A Discourse vpon the Present Estate of France*, trans. by E. Aggas (London, 1588), pp. 36, 52 (STC 14004); Barckley, *A Discovrse of the Felicitie of Man*, p. 236; and Hurault, *An Excellent Discovrse vpon the Now Present Estate of France* (London, 1592), sigs. A2ᵛ, A3ᵛ (STC 14005). William Blissett, "Lucan's Caesar and the Elizabethan Villain", *SP*, 53 (1956), 562-66, suggests that Lucan is the source for the references in Marlowe.

15 Oxberry's edition of Marlowe (London, 1818) was the first to turn this speech into a soliloquy. He is followed by H. S. Bennett (ed.), *The Jew of Malta and The*

Navarre projects himself as an agent of divine providence working for patriotic ends, and "God" is much in his mouth. His extreme piety is overt.

The playgoer may decide, then, that there is a dominant contrast in the play between Navarre and the Guise, a contrast based on attitudes toward religion. The Guise admits that his religion is used to cover his diabolical machinations and to solidify his party against the Protestant opposition. If the Guise is Machiavellian, Navarre is conventionally pious in his political statements. Religion for him is not a tool; he submits himself wholeheartedly to the divine will. The play concludes in triumph for religious and political morality; Navarre, with his truth, honesty, and genuine piety, attains the kingship.

This interpretation of the action is supported historically by the parallels between the play and the pamphlet literature which abounded during the French Civil Wars. Beyond a doubt, the Protestant pamphleteers saw the Guise as a devil incarnate and Navarre as a divinely inspired hero (until his defection from the Protestant cause in 1593, at any rate). Paul Kocher has demonstrated conclusively that Marlowe must have drawn his material from these sources, for there are remarkable similarities in plot between the play and such pamphlets as François Hotman's *True and Plaine Report* (1573). The suggestion is that Marlowe uncritically accepted the attitudes of the pamphleteers along with their material.[16]

This point of view has led to some astounding conclusions about the play and the playwright. Wilbur Sanders calls the play a "nasty piece of journalistic bombast", and Marlowe a "brutal, chauvinistic propagandist" pandering "to the lowest appetites

---

Massacre at Paris (London, 1931), Ribner, and J. B. Steane (ed.), *Chistopher Marlowe: The Complete Plays* (Baltimore: Penguin, 1969). Oliver (note on xx.19) argues against this emendation, using the authority of the first edition. I accept Oliver's argument which indicates that this is a public statement and that the piety here evinced is not necessarily a matter of personal belief.

[16] Cf. Kocher, *Christopher Marlowe*, p. 208: "Marlowe could do nothing else but take the attitudes made mandatory by English sympathies. This meant glorifying the Huguenots, headed by Navarre, and vilifying the Catholic League, led by Guise."

of his audience".[17] In his use of the aspiring Guise, Marlowe pursues a "campaign of vilification", as he "invents and adapts incidents" to heighten the Guise's villainy.[18] Sanders does not temper his adverse criticism of either the play or the dramatist, and Marlowe is for him little more than a very dangerous psychotic, as willing to use religion for his private ends as is his character, the Guise.

However, that Marlowe does present a villainous Guise in sharp contrast to a Navarre who is a "sublime ... example of protestant virtue" is not completely certain.[19] Here we must examine an alternative interpretation of the evidence, an interpretation that does not whitewash Marlowe's Guise, but which does place him in a context from which he stands out much less sharply. Marlowe may have used the anti-Guisian pamphlets for historical information, but this does not mean that he saw the French Civil Wars as a struggle between saintly Protestants and diabolical Catholics. The lines were not that clear-cut, and given Marlowe's skeptical nature, we may strongly doubt that he was so blindly idealistic about the King of Navarre. It is quite possible that Marlowe was here working along the same lines as he worked in *Edward II*, where Mortimer is not alone in his quest for material gain and power. As we have seen, the play is a multilateral power struggle for the English throne with the participants hiding their greed and ambition behind the façade of patriotism. Perhaps the present play resembles the dramatic milieu of *Edward II* more than has, in the past, been suspected.

To begin, King Charles holds the throne, though he appears to be a weak and easily guided monarch. On the marriage of Navarre to his sister Margaret in the first scene, he comments:

> I wishe this vnion and religious league,
> Knit in these hands, thus ioyn'd in nuptiall rites,
> May not desolue, till death desolue our liues,　　　　(3-5)

underlining the importance of the marriage as a union of Catholic

---

[17] Sanders, *The Dramatist and the Received Idea*, pp. 20, 22.

[18] Sanders, pp. 26-27.

[19] Sanders, p. 28.

and Protestant interests.[20] Ironically, this union which the king apparently desires is threatened a few lines later in his mother's aside: "Which Ile desolue with bloud and crueltie" (26). The king, it seems, will be overruled. Three scenes later, as Charles, his mother, the Guise, Anjou, and Dumaine plot the St. Bartholomew Massacre, the king quietly objects to the plan, his primary reason being that

> it wilbe noted through the world,
> An action bloudy and tirannicall:
> Cheefely since vnder safetie of our word,
> They iustly challenge their protection: (211-14)

"Besides", he continues, his "heart relentes" that so many people must be killed for their corrupt religious views (215-18). For him, religion is not a greatly significant issue, and his main objection to the plan is that it will besmirch his public image. He is encouraged to go on with the Massacre by his brother and the Guise, and his mother warns him that he must "haue some care for feare of enemies" (228), ironic words on the lips of the woman who will later murder him. At this point, Charles steps into the background: "What you determine, I will ratifie" (231). For the man whose chief objection to the plot is political expedience, this move out of the limelight is perfectly timed. The Guise and his companions will take the blame for the Massacre, while Charles will reap the benefit of the eliminated Protestant faction. Navarre will no longer be a threat to his security. At the same time, Charles will be able to remain friends with both sides, solidifying his position in the realm.

Charles, of course, is guided in his initial decisions by his powerful mother. As the plotters finish planning the Massacre, a messenger arrives to announce that the Admiral, one of Navarre's intimates, has been wounded by a musket shot and wishes to see

---

[20] Marlowe had authority for beginning the play here. Jean de Serres, p. 7, writes that King Charles "woulde for the more certaine continuing of the same [peace], gyue his sister Margaret in marriage to Prince Henrie, sonne to the Queene of Nauar. But this was the beginning of the lamentable tragedie of Bartholmewtide."

King Charles. To the messenger Charles replies: "tell him I will see him straite" (251), and turns to his mother for advice: "What shall we doe now with the Admirall?" (252). Catherine instructs him to visit the Admiral and "make a shew as if all were well" (254), and the Guise adds that he "will goe take order" for the Admiral's death (256).

In the wounded man's bedroom, Charles's dissembling is masterful as he tells the Admiral:

> I vow and sweare as I am King of France,
> To finde and to repay the man with death:
> With death delay'd and torments neuer vsde,
> That durst presume for hope of any gaine,
> To hurt the noble man their soueraign loues. (259-63)

Since the speech is aimed only at the noblemen whom Charles loves, it misses the Admiral, who seems totally oblivious to Charles's equivocation. The king's vow of assurance is another façade behind which he hides, for this scene between him and the Admiral is the prelude to the murders which begin in the following scene. We may be sure that the death of the Admiral's assassin will be "delay'd" and that the "torments" will "neuer" be used. A king who is able to equivocate so perfectly is not entirely weak, in the Machiavellian sense of weakness, even if his mother is an acknowledged virago; and the playgoer will certainly feel that Charles will hold his own in the developing struggle for power. There is an underlying toughness in his character.[21]

Although he implicitly sanctions the Massacre, Charles remains aloof from the general slaughter, and his non-participation allows him to ally with Navarre against the Guise after the Massacre has ended. Lorraine, the Cardinal, informs the Queen Mother that he has heard Charles "solemnly vow, / With the rebellious King of *Nauarre*, / For to reuenge their deaths vpon vs all" (521-23). Even if we are not prepared to trust this brother of the Guise,

---

[21] Cf. Jean de Serres, *The Lyfe of the Most Godly ... Iasper Colignie Shatilion*, trans. by Arthur Golding (London, 1576), sigs. F6ʳ-F7ʳ (STC 22248), and Ernest Varamvnd (i.e., François Hotman), *A True and Plaine Report of the Furious Outrages of Fraunce* (?Striveling, Scotland, 1573), sig. I1ᵛ (STC 13847): Charles is told, "He that can not skill to dissemble, can not skill to be a king."

the Queen Mother seems to believe him: "I, but my Lord let me alone for that, / For *Katherine* must haue her will in France: / As I doe liue, so surely shall he dye" (524-26). When Charles enters in scene thirteen complaining of a "griping paine" (542), supported by Navarre and Epernoun (soon to be a minion of King Henry), we suspect that the Queen Mother has been at work with a draft of poison and that Lorraine has been correct in his report. Symbolically, the entrance suggests that Charles has repudiated his Guisian alliance and has formed a coalition on the one hand with the Protestant Navarre and on the other with the anti-Guisian faction which will support the future King Henry.

Only superficially weak, Charles has not, in effect, reacted foolishly to the political situation. (Marlowe's foolish king is Mycetes in *1 Tamburlaine*.) Finding political unity impossible, Charles sanctions a Catholic purge of the Protestants. Then, having weakened one of the warring factions, he unites with it in order to contain the aspiring Guise.[22] His actions seem perfectly consonant with the harsh rules of Renaissance power politics, and we may conclude that his weakness is more apparent than real. He is not the effeminate mother's boy he at first appears to be, and when Catherine sees his potential as a Machiavellian prince, she murders him.

Catherine herself, as we realize by now, is also one of the contenders for royal power, though she can have no expectation of actually wearing the crown. After confiding to Lorraine that she will murder Charles, she continues:

> *Henry* then shall weare the diadem.
> And if he grudge or crosse his Mothers will,
> Ile disinherite him and all the rest:
> For Ile rule France, but they [her sons] shall
>   weare the crowne:
> And if they storme, I then may pull them downe.   (527-31)

---

[22] Cf. Hurault, p. 3, sig. A2ʳ, who defines three factions: Guisians, royalists, Navarrists. For a modern analysis of the political scene, see Henri Noguères, *The Massacre of Saint Bartholomew*, trans. by Claire Eliane Engel (New York: Macmillan, 1962).

In a parallel scene (xiv), after Henry's coronation, Catherine and
Lorraine again discuss the political situation *vis-à-vis* the new king.
Lorraine tells her that the Guise has gathered an army supposedly
to exterminate Protestants, but actually to oppose "the house of
Burbon" (649), the royal house of Navarre:

> Now Madam must you insinuate with the King,
> And tell him that tis for his Countries good,
> And common profit of Religion. (650-52)

The Queen Mother replies in familiar tones:

>   let me alone with him,
> To work the way to bring this thing to passe:
> And if he does deny what I doe say,
> Ile dispatch him with his brother presently,
> And then shall *Mounser* weare the diadem,
> Tush, all shall dye vnles I haue my will,
> For while she liues *Katherine* will be Queene. (653-59)

The parallels in these two speeches are possibly to be blamed upon
memorial reconstruction. Oliver, who suggests this possibility,
argues that "Marlowe can hardly have been" so uninventive;
and thus "one is forced to adopt the hypothesis that two scenes,
similar in function in the original script, have been somehow
confused".[23] The artistic use of parallels, however, is not a sign of
uninventiveness, but a way of imposing form and meaning on
material. In the theater, these scenes would not clash on the playgoer's sensibility, for the parallel merely highlights Catherine's
continuing aspiration for royal power and, at the same time, her
inability to handle or destroy Henry as she has handled and
destroyed the recalcitrant Charles. Henry does not use her as his
chief counselor, and from this point, Catherine has no control over
the political action.

Emotionally as well as politically Catherine is closely allied to
the Guise. Although there seems little to indicate a sexual union,[24]
theirs is certainly a union of like minds. When Henry tells his

[23] Oliver, p. liv.
[24] Lines 133-34 are suggestive: "The Mother Queene workes wonders for my
sake", the Guise says, "And in my loue entombes the hope of Fraunce."

mother that he has slain the Guise, her spirit is broken, and she asks to be alone to meditate on her defeat:

> Sweet *Guise*, would he [Henry] had died so thou
>   wert heere:
> To whom shall I bewray my secrets now,
> Or who will helpe to builde Religion?
> The Protestants will glory and insulte,
> Wicked *Nauarre* will get the crowne of France,
> And Popedome cannot stand, all goes to wrack,
> And all for thee my *Guise*: what may I doe?
> But sorrow seaze vpon my toyling soule,
> For since the *Guise* is dead, I will not liue.   (1094-1102)

At first glance, this soliloquy appears implicitly to deny her professions to Lorraine – that she desires to rule at all costs. Here she emphasizes, with a good deal of self-sorrow, her fondness for the dead leader and laments that Catholicism will not, in her opinion, be dominant in France. The playgoer readily sees that her lament for the Guise and Catholicism is in actuality a lament for her own lost power in France. No longer is she the king-maker, placing successive and obedient monarchs on the throne. Allied with the Guise, Catherine was a source of political and religious power. With the Guise gone and Catholicism apparently going, she sees the end of her career. Speaking with Lorraine, she emphasized her living strength; now she resolves to die. Another contender for political supremacy is destroyed.

Her son Henry, from the opening scenes when he is simply the Duke of Anjou, reveals himself as a shrewd and unscrupulous political manipulator. To encourage his brother Charles to massacre the Protestants, he admits (with Chaucer) that pity is natural in "gentle mindes",

> Yet will the wisest note their proper greefes:
> And rather seeke to scourge their enemies,
> Then be themselues base subiects to the whip.   (219-22)

Set forth in this scene as a general political maxim, the policy becomes Henry's operating rule as a king. He is guided fully by a kind of brutal and unenlightened self-interest.

As the Duke of Anjou, he is very conscious of his place in the line of succession to the crown, and though he is willing, and indeed eager, to participate in the Massacre, he wishes to make sure that his reputation remains unsullied:

> I am disguisde and none knows who I am,
> And therfore meane to murder all I meet.   (282-83)

On the one hand, his brutal nature cannot resist joining in the bloodbath, but on the other, he knows that it will not be politic for a possible future king of France to be murdering prospective subjects in the streets. Incognito, he participates fully in the slaughter, killing Ramus with his own hand and ordering the murder of the Protestant schoolmasters of Navarre and Condé. These are Marlovian additions to history, and they suggest Henry's violent rejection of civilized logic and learning.[25]

Immediately after these bloody scenes, Anjou negotiates with two lords of Poland about his assuming the Polish throne. The Electors have chosen him as heir, and Anjou is elated to be asked to rule such a "martiall people" (460), who war with the Muscovite on one side and the Turk on the other. This elation confirms that Henry's bloodthirsty behavior is an essential part of his character; he is basically aggressive and violent. His unconcern whether the Poles fight with Christian Muscovites or Moslem Turks argues his lack of any religious attachment; he values the violence itself, not the principles. In context, his deep enthusiasm for the "greatest warres within our Christian bounds" (465) is ironic. Anjou has just returned from murdering defenseless teachers in cold blood, and this is not the type of man the playgoer expects to extol heroic action. Ironically, the Poles have selected a murderer for their king.[26]

Nevertheless, when he attains the throne of France a few scenes later (scene xiv), Henry has full knowledge of the state's political divisons and of the Guise's machinations. He himself has been party to them in the past. Catherine's welcome to the returning

[25] Cf. Hotman, sigs. H2ʳ and K1ᵛ.

[26] Cf. Jean de Serres, p. 86: "A great scruple and doubt was obiected about the murders of Paris, the causes whereof by open rumors were layde vpon the Duke of *Anjou*."

Henry commands attention because it is so obviously a tissue of lies. "Heere", she tells her son,

> hast thou a country voide of feares,
> A warlike people to maintaine thy right,
> A watchfull Senate for ordaining lawes,
> A louing mother to preserue thy state,
> And all things that a King may wish besides:
> All this and more hath *Henry* with his crowne.   (596-601)

France, as we have seen, is a disordered nation, divided against itself, and its warlike people fight not for Henry's right, but for their own benefit or protection. We see no sign of a vigilant senate or of any law but that of survival of the fittest. In reality, Henry inherits a hollow crown. The pleasant picture presented by Catherine is undoubtedly meant to give him a false sense of well-being, to lull him into unpreparedness.

Henry's reply suggests that he is not taken in by her inflated speech. He has a purpose of his own:

> The guider of all crownes
> Graunt that our deeds may wel deserue your loues:
> And so they shall, if fortune speed my will,
> And yeeld your thoughts to height of my desertes.
> What saies our Minions, think they *Henries* heart
> Will not both harbour loue and Maiestie?
> Put of that feare, they are already ioynde,
> No person, place, or time, or circumstance,
> Shall slacke my loues affection from his bent.
> As now you are, so shall you still persist,
> Remooueless from the fauours of your King.   (604-14)

Although beginning with a bit of conventional piety – camouflage for the political manipulator – the speech is a bid for active support, a bid answered by Mugeroun and Epernoun. The cutpurse incident, which follows immediately, comments dramatically on the new political situation. Mugeroun cuts off the thief's ear, offering to exchange it for the buttons which the thief has removed from his coat. When the Guise intervenes to send the thief to prison, Henry stops the Guise's man: "Hands of good fellow, I will be his baile / For this offence: goe sirra, worke no more, / Till this our Coronation day be past" (627-29). The incident is darkly humorous, but it makes an important point. The Guise is pushed into the background, publicly snubbed, and King Henry and his minions are now at the center of power.

The shift is more cogently underlined in the following scene (xv), where the Guise finds his wife writing a love letter to Mugeroun. The scene suggests an intertwining of the political and the personal. Speaking of her lover *in absentia*, the Duchess soliloquizes: "Sweet *Mugeroune*, tis he that hath my heart, / And *Guise* vsurpes it, cause I am his wife" (665-66). The word "vsurpes" links the affair of the heart with the affairs of state, and the scene is complexly related to the main action. The Guise's ultimate goal entails wresting the throne from the reigning house – political usurpation, while at home, he is accounted an amatory usurper by his wife. However, the usurping male is not the Guise, as his Duchess suggests, but Mugeroun; and like Henry on the public level, the Guise takes murderous steps to safeguard his possession. At the same time, we may see Mugeroun, Henry's favorite, as an extension of the royal power. Henry is fully aware of, and apparently sanctions, the affair with the Guise's wife. In this way, Henry makes a further inroad on the Guise's security. First, Henry publicly embarrasses him; then, he allows his minion to disrupt the Duke's private life.

The Guise's reaction to his wife's infidelity deserves consideration. He is naturally furious:

> Is *Guises* glory but a clowdy mist,
> In sight and iudgement of thy lustfull eye?
> *Mor d*[ie]*u*, were not the fruit within thy wombe,
> Of whose encrease I set some longing hope:
> This wrathfull hand should strike thee to the hart.   (692-96)

Although the reference to the clouding of the Guise's glory is premonitory, what is more interesting is the Guise's inability to kill his wife because she is pregnant. He desires progeny – obviously to inherit the kingdom he intends to obtain. Like Tamburlaine, he wishes to pass his conquered world on to his children. But the Guise is blinded by his desire to found a dynasty, as blinded as he always believes others to be; for if his Duchess is unfaithful, there is no assurance that the fruit of her womb will not be more legitimately Mugeroun's heir. Though he calls her "strumpet", he seems never to sense the implications of the epithet. This is the first time that the Guise has shown such blindness to reality, and it is this blindness which allows him finally to be lured into Henry's trap.[27]

When the Duchess leaves the stage, the Guise moralizes upon the affair:

> O wicked sexe, periured and vniust,
> Now doe I see that from the very first,
> Her eyes and lookes sow'd seeds of periury,
> But villaine he to whom these lines should goe,
> Shall buy her loue euen with his dearest bloud.   (699-703)

The first three lines are comic when we realize that they apply as easily to the Guise as to his Duchess. The Guise's own sexual faithfulness is not above question, and, of course, the Guise is infamous for his perjury. But the next two lines are serious, for they not only pronounce the death of Mugeroun, they settle the Guise's fate. Mugeroun's death leads directly to the Guise's own assassination.

After Mugeroun's death, the Guise is confronted by an angry Henry who is ready for a showdown: "I cannot brook thy hauty insolence, / Dismisse thy campe or else by our Edict / Be thou proclaimde a traitor throughout France" (869-71). Although the Guise stalls for time, Henry sees through his verbal façade. He realizes that Paris has rallied behind the house of Lorraine, and he dismisses his council, taking emergency power into his own hand. Though "I seeme milde and calme", says Henry, "Thinke not but I am tragicall within" (900-01). Deteriorating in his ability as a political manipulator, the Guise has met his match. Within two scenes, the king lures the Guise into an ambush and has him murdered. Ironically, Henry tells him before he is stabbed to

---

[27] The motif of trap or ambush runs throughout the play. Navarre says that the Guise "beates his braines to catch vs in his trap, / Which he hath pitcht within his deadly toyle" (53-54). The Guise has both the Admiral and Mugeroun ambushed. Of the Massacre the Guise says: "Now haue we the fatall stragling deere / Within the compasse of a deadly toyle" (208-09). In the Guise's death, the trapper is trapped.

death that he will not be suspected of disloyalty, and the Guise is apparently satisfied by this equivocation. The playgoer remembers Charles's similar assurances given to the Admiral immediately before his death, and we are ready for a similar train of events.

One of the first acts of what Henry sees as his new liberty after the assassination is to call the Guise's son to witness his murdered father – possibly a piece of gratuitous sadism, but probably with calculated effect.[28] When the son draws his dagger to avenge his slain father, Henry speeds him to prison, with the promise: "Ile clippe his winges / Or ere he passe my handes" (1064-65). Henry then turns his attention to the Guise's brothers, Dumaine and the Cardinal, giving orders for their murder. In the following scene, the Cardinal is strangled by the two assassins who have already killed the Guise. Henry initiates, in the Guisian manner, another Massacre. With a kind of moral causality, the Guisians are hoist by their own petard.

Unfortunately for Henry, Dumaine prevents the plot against his life and mounts a counterplot against the king. Apostrophizing the dead Guise, Dumaine proclaims:

> I am thy brother, and ile reuenge thy death,
> And roote *Valoys* his line from forth of France,
> And beate proud *Burbon* to his natiue home,
> That basely seekes to ioyne with such a King,
> Whose murderous thoughts will be his ouerthrow. (1124-28)

To extirpate the Valois, Dumaine sends a friar, who will murder the king for "conscience sake" (1143), to stab Henry with a poisoned knife. Like the Guise, Henry reaps the reward of his own violence. His attempt to massacre the family of Guise is no more successful than the Guise's pogrom against the Protestants. Their immoral aspirations for absolute rule lead inevitably to destruction.

So far we have plotted the power struggle among the members

---

[28] Cf. Thomas Preston's *Cambises*, in *Chief Pre-Shakespearean Dramas*, ed. by Joseph Q. Adams (Boston: Houghton Mifflin, 1924), lines 466ff., where the son is taught a moral lesson from his father's death: "If thou beest proud, as he hath beene, even thereto shalt thou come" (468). See also Coignet, *Politique Discovrses Vpon Trveth and Lying*, sig. O1ʳ. In contrast, Henry probably wishes to force the Guise's son into a foolish attempt at revenge so that he may be confined. The attempted stabbing here foreshadows Henry's assassination by the friar.

of the French royal house and the family of Lorraine, but we have not examined critically the role of Sanders's "sublime ... example of protestant virtue", Henry of Navarre. As we have noticed in our preliminary glance at Navarre, he uses the conventional platitudes of piety. While Charles is dying, Navarre grandly tells him: "God will sure restore you to your health" (547). Eight lines later, Charles is dead, and Navarre has all the appearances of a pious ass. But these are only appearances, for as Charles is carried from the stage, Navarre communes with himself about the political situation:

> And now *Nauarre* whilste that these broiles doe last,
> My opportunity may serue me fit,
> To steale from France, and hye me to my home.
> For heers no saftie in the Realme for me,
> And now that *Henry* is cal'd from Polland,
> It is my due by iust succession:
> And therefore as speedily as I can perfourme,
> Ile muster vp an army secretly,
> For feare that *Guise* ioyn'd with the K[ing] of Spaine,
> Might seeke to crosse me in mine enterprise.   (570-79)[29]

He ends his soliloquy with a two-line conventionally pious tag, perhaps for the listening ears of Pleshé, but his speech nevertheless reveals a firm grasp of the political realities and an awareness as strong as Anjou's of his position in the degrees of agnation. His vocabulary – "opportunity", "steale", "speedily", "secretly" – hardly justifies the title pious ass. What is the mysterious "enterprise" in which he is engaged? May it be the usurpation of the French throne? With this question in mind, we must remember that Navarre, not King Henry, is the first to put an army in the field.[30] We have already noted how both the Guise and King Henry use the terms of piety and the ornaments of religion to

---

[29] Following Dyce's second edition (London, 1858), p. 235, Tucker Brooke emends line 750 to "now Pleshé". Oliver (note on xiii.30) explains the original line as indicative of self-communion. Thus, Dyce's emendation seems unnecessary.
[30] Protestant apologists had to defend Navarre. See *An Excellent Discovrse vpon the Now Present Estate of France*, sig. B4ᵛ: "who could iustlie in so sudden taking of armes, distinguish which of these parties first began?" But the author goes on to justify Navarre's action.

cover their personal aspirations to power, and it is likely that we should think of Navarre as their Protestant counterpart.

In any case, Navarre is not a completely admirable character.[31] While his mother dies, poisoned by the fumes from a pair of poisoned gloves given her by the Guise's druggist, Navarre irrationally berates her for lack of caution. That this outburst (181-83) is not to be seen as an example of filial solicitude is indicated by his wife's words: "Too late it is my Lord if that be true / To blame her highnes" (184-85). During the Massacre, Navarre plays no heroic part, allowing with a minimum of protest his schoolmaster to be carried to death, while he and Condé seek the protection of King Charles. Indeed, it must be apparent to every playgoer that the Protestant Navarre is ever ready to ally himself with a Catholic King of France, especially when such an alliance is conducive to his political ends or his personal safety. Marlowe does not make his Navarre into a citadel of Protestant virtue.

It is also true that Navarre does not engage as fully in the plots, the ambushes, the murders, as do the Guise and King Henry, but at the same time, he acts in ways which reveal his political opportunism. His first act of the play, his marriage to Margaret, is politically advantageous, but it is hardly a triumph for Protestant religion to have one of its princes marry a Catholic princess. The various purges which follow this initial action are political in nature; and when Navarre ends the play with a threat:

> I vow for to reuenge his [Henry's] death,
> As Rome and all those popish Prelates there,
> Shall curse the time that ere *Nauarre* was King,
> And rulde in France by *Henries* fatall death.   (1260-63)

it appears that yet another purge is about to begin, hidden behind the sacred name of religion. Navarre is prepared to follow the bloody instructions given him by the Guise and Henry.

The end of the play gains interest from the entrance of Queen

---

[31] Robert Knoll (*Christopher Marlowe* [*TEAS*, 74] [New York: Twayne, 1969], p. 108) remarks that Navarre "seems to act from one set of motives – ambition and revenge – while believing himself to be acting from another". For him, Navarre is an unconscious (rather than conscious) hypocrite.

Elizabeth's "English Agent", who says nothing, but listens to a lengthy diatribe by the dying Henry. The main tenor of the speech is hatred for Rome and love for England:

> These bloudy hands shall teare his [i.e., the Pope's]
>   triple Crowne,
> And fire accursed Rome about his eares.
> Ile fire his crased buildings and inforse
> The papall towers to kisse the holy earth.
> *Nauarre*, giue me thy hand, I heere do sweare
> ...
> ... eternall loue to thee,
> And to the Queene of England specially,
> Whom God hath blest for hating Papestry.   (1212-16, 1219-21)

His sudden anti-Catholicism, strange for one of the chief partisans in the Massacre, does not seem to stem from any religious conversion. His assassination has been carried out by a friar, and the change in religious alliance seems to be a mixture of political expedience and personal vengeance. His "bloudy hands" are stained because he has killed the friar with his own knife; but the image carries us back to the Massacre, when instead of killing priests, he had just killed Ramus, who gave Protestant Englishmen one of their chief tools, a new logic. Ironically, Navarre promises to revenge this most violent of monarchs, while he, in turn, blesses Queen Elizabeth for "hating Papestry". Even a playgoer who was used to having plays end with compliments to his queen would hopefully see the irony of the present situation. By her alliance with Navarre, Marlowe's queen is drawn into the pit of intrigue where religion is simply a political tool. The introduction of Elizabeth's envoy is not Marlowe's sop to patriotism; it is an attempt to suggest that what has been true for Catholic France may also become true for Protestant England. England itself might be torn apart by men seeking power under the guise of religion. In this, Marlowe was a prophet.

If *Edward II* is, in part, a study of political self-seeking under the guise of patriotism, then *The Massacre at Paris* is a similar study where religion becomes the dominant means of disguising political aspiration. Both plays are about the struggle for national power, about civil conflict, and about the disintegration of the family. Whatever it is, *The Massacre at Paris* is not a piece of Protestant propaganda, vilifying the Guise while glorifying the King of Navarre. Navarre clearly looks forward to Governor Ferneze in *The Jew of Malta*, a man who turns his religious conscience into a dishonest sum of gold.

It is easy to see *The Massacre* as a piece of socio-political criticism, but it is also a carefully articulated and balanced piece of art. Critics have been hard on *The Massacre*, possibly because they have suspected that the skeptical Marlowe was potboiling, producing a topical play for the sadistic delectation of the undiscriminating audience in the chauvinistic London of the early 1590's – and all the while laughing up his sleeve, or perhaps even worse, believing what he wrote. But if we see the play in context as another product of Marlowe's continuing exploration of the inverted world of man's destructive self-assertion, then the true nature of the play, as we have tried to define it in this chapter, becomes readily apparent.

V

1 TAMBURLAINE

With the Tamburlaine plays, Marlowe moves from the MEN who wish to seize a kingdom to the MAN who wishes to rule the world. The movement is not merely toward amplitude. In the three plays we have looked at so far, the emphasis is on the total situation, on personal relationships and on national problems. No one character dominates the stage. But in *1 Tamburlaine* the playgoer is confronted with what we have called 'monodrama'. There is a movement away from the complexities of political machinations toward a kind of purity of form. The character of Tamburlaine rules the action, and our other interests in the play are subordinate to our interest in his destiny. In the next four plays, we will find that one character – Tamburlaine, Faustus, Barabas – will claim our attention, and this one character will be the embodiment of aspiration.

The Tamburlaine plays are best approached as individual plays, separate artistic entities. Because of their length, they were most certainly not acted together on the Elizabethan stage: the two-hours' traffic on the stage would have turned into an all-day affair.[1] Besides the consideration of acting time, the Prologue to the Second Part plainly indicates that "*The generall welcomes Tamburlain receiu'd, | When he arriued last vpon our stage, | Hath made our Poet pen*

---

[1] The phrase 'two-hours' traffic' may have been traditional, rather than an indication of the approximate length of Renaissance dramatic performances. See the Sidney-Golding translation of Philippe de Mornay, *A Woorke Concerning the Trewnesse of the Christian Religion* (London, 1587), p. 173 (STC 18149): "a Tragedie is plaied afore thee ... in the two howers space", and cf. *Romeo and Juliet*, Prologue, line 12. Nevertheless, Elizabethan performances probably did not last longer than an average modern play.

his second part" (Prologue, 1-3). The second part is a sequel to the first. We should note, however, that the parts have the structural parallels that seem characteristic of the Elizabethan two-part play,[2] and that the parts were, in the early editions, printed together. Although the two parts should initially be studied separately, Marlowe undoubtedly saw them as two parts of a total picture.

The problem, of course, is how to interpret this total picture. We may feel that the printer Richard Jones, by cutting what he considered inappropriate comic scenes, has deprived us of a valuable clue to interpretation. How, for example, would one explain Shakespeare's *1 Henry IV* without the comic subplot? Perhaps one way to gain perspective on Marlowe's Tamburlaine is through a consideration of the sources and the background material. In the following pages, we will survey a small part of this extensive background, trying to see what Marlowe inherited from the historians, what choices he made in using his inheritance, and what he added from other sources to the received history of Tamburlaine. By studying this diverse and complex background, we may by indirections find directions out.

I. BACKGROUND

During the Renaissance, a semi-mythical account of Timur the Lame developed in Western Europe. Although there were several contemporary descriptions of the historical Timur available, the legend current in sixteenth-century England bears little resemblance to the Tamburlaine of twentieth-century historians. The legend grew by accretion and accumulation, drawing to itself various elements of the romance tradition.[3]

[2] See G. K. Hunter, "*Henry IV* and the Elizabethan Two-Part Play", *RES*, 5 (1954), 239-41.
[3] Hilda Hookham (*Tamburlaine the Conqueror* [London: Hodder and Stoughton, 1962]) provides a good synthesis of modern knowledge about the historical Timur-i-Lenk (Iron the Lame). Hookham (p. 59) reports that the signal for a general pillage after a battle was the raising of a black banner over Timur's personal tent. When Marlowe received the story, the black banner had turned into three different colored flags signifying three different moods. J. Douglas Bruce

The complete history of this growth has yet to be written,[4] but we can reconstruct, in basic outline, the story as Marlowe must have initially received it: springing from poor stock, Tamburlaine began his career as a shepherd or as a lowly warrior and fought his way to power through robbery. Against this thieving outlaw, an anonymous ruler of Persia sent an unnamed leader with a thousand horsemen. But this leader was won to Tamburlaine's side without battle. Thereafter Tamburlaine entered into the Persian civil war which was then raging and defeated each party in turn. With Persia in his power, he waged war against the Turks under Bajazeth and beat them. The defeated Bajazeth was treated like a dog, used as a footstool, and imprisoned in an iron cage. In the meanwhile, Tamburlaine marched on and defeated the Soldan of Egypt and the King of Arabia. There is some question in the accounts whether he takes the city of Damascus before or after his campaign against the Egyptians and Arabians, but the city is in the list of his conquests. The story of Tamburlaine's geographical movements is followed by several anecdotes, among them, his use of white, red, and black accoutrements to reveal his varying states of mercy and severity; his slaughter of the women and children of an unidentified city (an anonymous account published

---

("The Three Days' Tournament Motif in Marlowe's *Tamburlaine*", *MLN*, 24 [1909], 257-58) compares the different colored armor in a three-day medieval tournament. Although Bruce was unaware that the details were not invented by Marlowe, his suggestion indicates a possible way in which Timur's black banner developed by analogy into Tamburlaine's three colors. John P. Cutts ("The Ultimate Source of Tamburlaine's White, Red, Black and Death?", *N&Q*, 5 [1958], 146-47) notes the parallel with the white, red, and black horses in Revelation 6:2-8. Like Bruce, Robert T. Taylor ("Maximinus and Tamburlaine", *N&Q*, 4 [1957], 417-18) forgets that Marlowe inherited the story, but his note suggests that part of the legend grew from Roman history, especially from the career of Emperor C. Julius Maximinus (A.D. 235-38). Ethel Seaton ("Marlowe's Light Reading", *Elizabethan and Jacobean Studies Presented to Frank Percy Wilson* [Oxford: Oxford University Press, 1959], pp. 20-21) points to medieval accretions. The introduction of the human footstool from Classical and Romantic sources is traced by John O'Connor ("Another Human Footstool", *N&Q*, 2 [1955], 332).

[4] A beginning is made by Eric Voegelin ("Das Timurbild der Humanisten", *Zeitschrift für öffentliches Recht*, XVII:5), but he is interested in only one strain of the legend, the idealized portrait of the conqueror, which Marlowe does not use.

in 1664 calls it "Damas", Damascus);[5] his telling a Genoese
merchant that he, Tamburlaine, is the wrath of God. The account
ends with the notice of Tamburlaine's natural death and a brief
description of the dissolution of his empire shortly thereafter.
Marlowe may easily have found this basic story in Thomas
Fortescue's translation of Pedro Mexia, *The Foreste or Collection of
Historie* (London, 1571), or in George Whetstone's *The English
Myrror* (London, 1586). But it must be remembered that this same
story, or one of its variants, may be found in as many as one
hundred Renaissance sources, told from varying points of view,
and it is now impossible to know how many or how few of these
sources Marlowe read. What we do know is that he took this inherited fable of an Eastern conqueror and molded it into a unified
play.

Certain details of the play, however, may be traced to specific
sources. Not every variant of the fable, for example, includes the
shameful handling of Bajazeth's wife and his subsequent suicide.
These incidents are present in Pierre de la Primaudaye's *The
French Academie*, an English translation of which was printed in
1586. In general structure, La Primaudaye follows the common
story given above, but he adds:

Baiazet ... ended his dayes in an iron cage, wherein being prisoner, and
ouercome with griefe to see his wife shamefully handled, in waiting at
Tamburlanes table with hir gowne cut downe to hir Nauell, so that hir
secrete partes were seene, this vnfortunate Turke beate his head so often
agaynst the Cage, that he ended his lyfe.[6]

Since Marlowe's stage women were played by boys, he was forced
to change the kind of ill-treatment Bajazeth's wife undergoes at
Tamburlaine's table, but it is from this detail that Marlowe creates
the captivity of Bajazeth and Zabina. That Bajazeth was "made
to die miserably in an yron cage" is also mentioned by John
Byshop, who further asserts, as most of the sources do not, that

---

[5] *The Conduct and Character of Count Nicholas Serini ... with his Parallels Scanderbeg
& Tamberlain* (London, 1664), p. 165. Published anonymously, the book may
either point to a tradition known to Marlowe, or have been influenced by *1
Tamburlaine*.
[6] La Primaudaye, p. 475, sig. Hh6ʳ (STC 15233).

Tamburlaine associated "him selfe with two capteines called *Chardares* and *Myrxes*".[7] Marlowe changes the names of these two associates to Techelles and Usumcasane.

But both La Primaudaye and Byshop derive their accounts from other writers, their main source of information probably being Pietro Perondini. As Ellis-Fermor has suggested, Marlowe may have studied the pages of Perondini with great care, and among the first scholars to argue that he did, were C. H. Herford and A. Wagner.[8] To support their contention, Herford and Wagner suggest that some of the salient features of Marlowe's description of Tamburlaine (II.i.461-84) have been drawn from Perondini's *Magni Tamerlanis Scytharvm Imperatoris vita* (Florence, 1553). The authors do not point out, however, that Marlowe may have found imaginary portraits of Tamburlaine in one of the editions of Paolo Giovio's *Elogia Virorum bellica virtute illustrium* or in André Thevet's *Les Vrais Povrtraits et Vies des Hommes Illvstres* (Paris, 1584), and that these may have suggested the description. But even more fundamentally, the judicious source hunter must be skeptical of finding a unique source for Marlowe's conventional description of his Scythian warrior as tall, broad shouldered, and fiery eyed. Most tellers of the tale, for example, comment on Tamburlaine's eyes flaming like fire.[9] It seems most probable that Marlowe gathered his material from many sources.[10]

In naming his characters, Marlowe was certainly eclectic, drawing names from Renaissance histories of the Turk, from Greek history, and even from the Golden Legend. By examining the background of the names, we are often able to see the ironies of his choice, and this system of ironies tells us something about

[7] John Byshop, *Beavtifull Blossomes* (London, 1577), pp. 148ʳ, 147ʳ (STC 3091).
[8] C. H. Herford and A. Wagner, "The Sources of Marlowe's *Tamburlaine*", *Academy*, 24 (1883), 265-66.
[9] See, e.g., Andrea Cambini, *Tvvo Very Notable Commentaries*, trans. by John Shute (London, 1562), p. 5ʳ, sig. B1ʳ (STC 4470): "with eyes flaming like fyre", and Loys le Roy, *Of the Interchangeable Covrse, or Variety of Things*, trans. by R. A. (London, 1594), p. 108ᵛ (STC 15488): "sparkling eies".
[10] See, e.g., Nicholas Nicholay, *The Navigations, Peregrinations and Voyages, Made into Turkie*, trans. by T. Washington (London, 1585), p. 102ʳ (STC 18574) and cf. IV.ii.1446-51. A reading of Nicholay's account suggests how an Elizabethan may have seen the Mediterranean and Middle East.

Marlowe's method. "Vsancasan", the name of Tamburlaine's henchman, was the Persian king who ultimately uprooted the empire which Tamburlaine had founded.[11] Techelles probably gained his name from a religious leader who "inuaded the Turkes dominion" during the reign of the second Bajazeth.[12] As names for Tamburlaine's chief warriors, Usumcasane and Techelles are ironic. The foolish king of Persia, Mycetes, also bears an ironic name. Either he is named after "*Mesites Bassa*", a Viceroy of Asia known for his "great wisedom, experience, and valour", or he is named after another Mesites, who fought against Tamburlaine, but was pardoned because of his "inuincible courage, and contempt of death".[13] In contrast, Marlowe's Mycetes is known for his stupidity and cowardice, and is slain by Tamburlaine in battle.

It is probably too whimsical to see "Cosroe" as an attempt to suggest "Corcutus", a Turkish name.[14] Ultimately Mycetes' brother gains his name from the Golden Legend, where Cosroe or Cosroes, a Persian king, attempts to keep the True Cross from the Christians. He is defeated in battle and slain, while the Cross is returned to Jerusalem. The legend had some contemporary currency,[15] and Marlowe may have found a reference to it in Cambini's history of Scanderbeg, a possible source for Part II: "Scanderbeg was muche lyke to the Emperour Eracleo, which by the helpe of God dyd ouerthrowe the proude hethen prynce Cosdroe."[16] Marlowe uses the name to draw an ironic parallel

---

[11] See, e.g., George Whetstone, *The English Myrror* (London, 1586), p. 83 (STC 25336), and Richard Knolles, *The Generall Historie of the Turkes* (London, 1603), p. 228 (STC 15051). Hugh Dick ("*Tamburlaine* Sources Once More", *SP*, 46 [1949], 154-66), argues that Marlowe may have known Knolles when he was working on the Turkish history, giving Marlowe access to a good Eastern library. The importance of this possible connection will be discussed in the next chapter. In any case, Knolles' sources were available to Marlowe, and Knolles provides a convenient compendium.

[12] Knolles, p. 469.

[13] Knolles, pp. 267, 234.

[14] Knolles, p. 471.

[15] See William Caxton (trans.), *The Boke Intituled Eracles* (London, 1481), STC 13175. The historical Chosroes is treated by Procopius, *History of the Wars*, I.xi.5f. (London: Heinemann, 1914), I, 82ff. Chosroes had to struggle with an eldest brother for the throne.

[16] Cambini, pp. 41ᵛ-42ʳ, Ee3ᵛ-Ee4ʳ.

between the legendary Persian king and his character. For in the play, Cosroe stands between Tamburlaine and his substitute for the Cross – a secular crown. "Cosroe" connotes an evil character, but he is here defeated by a warrior more greatly evil than himself. Ironically the righteous Emperor Hercules is replaced by Tamburlaine.

Zenocrate's name is more complex. It may be translated 'Divine Power' and thus suggest the force of her beauty on Tamburlaine.[17] But her name may have been derived from Xenocrates of Chalcedon (396-314 B. C.), who is chiefly remembered for his emphasis on virtue as the source of happiness. Greene alludes to the philosopher familiarly in one of his pamphlets; Ariosto excuses Ruggiero by insisting that Angelica's beauty "was so rare as well it might, / Haue made *Zenocrates* an Epicure"; and Matthieu Coignet recounts that "Xenocrates ... did so pearce the heart of his auditors, that of dissolute persons they became temperate and modest."[18] For the Renaissance, Xenocrates was an emblem of the virtuous man, and we may assume that Marlowe named his Zenocrate after the philosopher who believed that the virtuous man was pure in thought as well as deed. The complicated ironies involved in the naming will become apparent as we trace what happens to the virtuous Zenocrate in the course of the action.

Most important in discussing Zenocrate's developing relationship with Tamburlaine are those elements which are not intrinsically connected to the basic story or its Eastern background. Although several of the histories mention Tamburlaine's wife, his romantic love for Zenocrate is not part of the tradition. It is essentially a Marlovian addition, and as such, demands that we investigate Marlowe's reasons for adding it. Undoubtedly the reasons, as well

---

[17] Mary Mellen Wehling, "Marlowe's Mnemonic Nominology with Especia Reference to Tamburlaine", *MLN*, 73 (1958), 246.

[18] Robert Greene, *The Life and Complete Works in Prose and Verse*, ed. by Alexander Grosart (Huth Library, 1881-83), III, 161; Matthieu Coignet, *Politiqve Discovrses Vpon Trveth and Lying* (London, 1586), sig. C8ᵛ and sig. P7ᵛ (STC 5486); and Ludovico Ariosto, *Orlando Furioso in English Heroical Verse*, trans. by John Harington (London, 1591), p. 82, sig. G6ᵛ, and see sig. Oo3ʳ for a story of "*Zenocrates* a Stoike" (STC 746). References to Ariosto in the text will be to this edition.

as the background, are various and complex. First, the capture of Zenocrate may have been suggested by an incident in *Orlando Furioso*, where Mandricardo, the Tartarian knight (XIV, 37), captures the beauteous Doralice, fiancée of Rodomont of Sarza, in a single-handed fight against her armed entourage. He keeps her as a captive, and she, like Zenocrate, falls in love with her captor:

> But after supper what did passe betweene,
> Dame *Doralyce* and *Agricanes* haire,
> Cannot be told, because it was not seene,
> But they may guesse that haue with Ladies faire,
> By night alone in place conuenient beene,
> Where to disturbe them no mane did repaire.
> I doubte he did not so his passion bridle,
> To let so faire a dame lye by him idle.   (XIV, 53)

Harington adds a pointed marginal comment: "*If she were not idle, you may imagin what she was.*" Doralice later has the chance to return to her original love, Rodomont, but she prefers her Tartar. Although Doralice is quite obviously of easy virtue, Marlowe's Zenocrate is initially true to her namesake, the moral philosopher. She does not fall quickly, and Marlowe heightens the tension by making her complete conquest by Tamburlaine occur only during the last minutes of the drama when she receives the Persian crown.

Behind the Mandricardo-Doralice and Tamburlaine-Zenocrate stories stands a story recorded by Raymond de Beccaria in a chapter on "How Souldiers ought to gouerne themselues":

Scipio although that he was yoong, & a gallant man, yet he restored a Gentlewoman of most excellent beautie, vnto hir father & husband, without raunsome: and as he quitted hir freely so he restored her vnto her freendes as intirely in hir honour, as shee was at the time of hir taking: which act did profit him more then all his force.[19]

John of Salisbury tells the same story, coupling it with a similar story about Alexander the Great:

---

[19] See Paul Iue, *Instructions for the Warres* (London, 1589), pp. 260-61, sigs.T2ᵛ-T3ʳ (STC 1708.5). Formerly attributed to Guillaume Du Bellay, this work is now known to be translated from Raymond de Beccaria. See Gladys Dickinson, *The Instructions sur le Faict de la Guerre of Raymond de Beccarie de Pavie* (University of London: Athlone Press, 1954), p. cxiii.

When news was brought to him [i.e., Alexander] that a virgin of surpassing beauty, who was betrothed to the prince of a neighboring nation, was among the captives, he preserved the highest degree of abstinence with regard to her, not even going to look at her; and shortly afterwards he sent her back to her betrothed, and by this act of kindness won for himself the good-will of that whole nation. Thus by his humanity he won to him the minds of his own subjects, and by his justice those of alien peoples. We read that Scipio Africanus pursued the same course in Spain, when a noble virgin was brought before him ... .[20]

Both Alexander and Scipio illustrate their kindness and generosity by returning the captured maiden unsullied, and further, in Scipio's case, by foregoing any claim to ransom. Through their actions, they are able to conquer nations without bloodshed. When placed in a similar situation, Tamburlaine retains the maiden he has captured along with her wealth, refuses to accept any ransom for her, and finally kills her betrothed and conquers her father after sacking one of his chief cities. The point of the comparison is that Tamburlaine is not the kind of heroic military leader whom De Beccaria and Salisbury laud in their descriptions. Like Ariosto's Tartar, Tamburlaine stands in the list of anti-heroes. He lacks the honor and humanity exhibited by Scipio and Alexander.

Moreover, the story of Tamburlaine and Zenocrate is also related to the iconographic union of Venus and Mars which we have seen operating in *Dido*. In the latter, the emasculating effects of the union were emphasized: Mars is incapacitated by his love for Venus. But this *discordia concors* of love and hate can be seen, as it often was in the Renaissance, as a symbol of harmony, balance, and pacification. Erwin Panofsky records the old tradition that the marriage of the two gods resulted in the birth of Harmony, their daughter.[21] And painters as diverse as Veronese and Rubens celebrate the beneficial effects of the union.

However we may wish to interpret what happens to Mars, the same fate does not overtake Tamburlaine, who becomes neither

[20] John of Salisbury, *The Statesman's Book of John of Salisbury: Being the Fourth, Fifth, and Sixth Books, and Selections from the Seventh and Eighth Books of the Policraticus*, trans. by John Dickinson (New York, 1927), pp. 96-97.

[21] Erwin Panofsky, *Studies in Iconology*, p. 163. See also Robert Kimbrough, "*1 Tamburlaine*: A Speaking Picture in a Tragic Glass", *RenD*, 7 (1964), 25-30.

effeminate nor pacified. Rather, Venus-Zenocrate is brought to an unusual state of bellicosity – one of the variant results of the marriage myth.[22] From a captured and demure maiden, she moves toward Tamburlaine's position. She defends him in an argument with Agydas, an argument which leads to Agydas's death, and later, in the conflict with Bajazeth and Zabina, she verbally mirrors Tamburlaine's aggression. After the Turkish defeat, she participates in the cruelty with which her lover treats the ruler and his wife. There seems to be no realization that the royal couple mirror her own earlier plight when she herself was a captive and unwilling follower of Tamburlaine. As with her, Tamburlaine refuses to accept ransom for their freedom. Only after their tragic suicides does Zenocrate understand the total import of what she and the Scythian war lord have done, and she asks divine forgiveness:

> Ah myghty *Ioue* and holy *Mahomet*,
> Pardon my Loue, oh pardon his contempt,
> Of earthly fortune, and respect of pitie,
> And let not conquest ruthlesly pursewde
> Be equally against his life incenst,
> In this great Turk and haplesse Emperesse.
> And pardon me that was not moou'd with ruthe,
> To see them liue so long in misery. (V.ii.2145-52)

But even before this realization of the ruthless and implacable creatures they have become, Zenocrate tries to dissuade Tamburlaine from his final military action against her father, the Soldan of Egypt, and against his city of Damascus:

> If any loue remaine in you my Lord,
> Or if my loue vnto your maiesty
> May merit fauour at your highnesse handes,
> Then raise your siege from faire *Damascus* walles,
> And with my father take a frindly truce. (IV.iv.1708-12)

Tamburlaine refuses, declaring that he would conquer Egypt if it were "*Ioues* owne land" (1713). Two scenes later, the Virgins of Damascus come to plead with "this man or rather God of war"

---

[22] See Edgar Wind, *Pagan Mysteries in the Renaissance*, pp. 89-96. See also L'Espine, *A Very Excellent and Learned Discovrse*, p. 101ʳ, sig. 08ʳ.

(V.i.1782), and reaffirming his decision, Tamburlaine has them
slaughtered by his horsemen:

> I will not spare these proud Egyptians,
> Nor change my Martiall obseruations,
> For all the wealth of Gehons golden waues,
> Or for the loue of *Venus*, would she leaue
> The angrie God of Armes, and lie with me.   (V.ii.1902-06)

The allusion to the Mars-Venus myth implicitly contrasts Tamburlaine with Mars, who does succumb to the power of love. Tamburlaine claims, in effect, that he is more implacable than the God of
War.

After hearing that the "slaughtered carcases" of the Virgins
have been "hoisted vp" on the walls of Damascus – a piece of
unnecessary cruelty – Tamburlaine in soliloquy examines the
relative merits of Beauty and War. In "diuine *Zenocrate*" he sees
the embodiment of beauty: "Faire is too foule an Epithite for thee"
(1917), and feels a struggle within himself between beauty, which
urges him toward peace and love, and his own concept of military
honor. Zenocrate's plea for peace, he feels, has done more to
thwart him than the Persian or Turkish armies, and this understanding of beauty's power leads him to the question: "What is
beauty saith my sufferings then?" (1941). But even the poets,

> If these had made one Poems period
> And all combin'd in Beauties worthinesse,
> Yet should ther houer in their restlesse heads,
> One thought, one grace, one woonder at the least,
> Which into words no vertue can digest.   (1950-54)

Himself no mean verbal artist, Tamburlaine attains another
realization: words are inadequate to express spiritual concepts
like the perception of beauty.

But, at this point, Tamburlaine reasserts his will:

> But how vnseemly is it for my Sex
> My discipline of armes and Chiualrie,
> My nature and the terrour of my name,
> To harbour thoughts effeminate and faint?   (1955-58)

Thoughts of beauty and poetry are incompatible, he thinks, with
his nature as a soldier and with the military profession in general.

Still, the soul of each man is "toucht" with a feeling for beauty; and every warrior who commits himself to the pursuit of "fame", "valour", and "victory", must have a sense of beauty (1959-63):

> I thus conceiuing and subduing both
> That which hath stopt the tempest of the Gods,
> Euen from the fiery spangled vaile of heauen,
> To feele the louely warmth of shepheards flames,
> And martch in cottages of strowed weeds,
> Shal giue the world to note for all my byrth,
> That Vertue solely is the sum of glorie,
> And fashions men with true nobility.   (1964-71)

The former shepherd decides that beauty, which has pacified the anger of the gods and brought them down to earth masquerading as lowly shepherds, will be unable to bring him back to pastoral contentment. Again he asserts that his will is stronger than the divine will. As a man who has symbolically cast off his shepherd's weeds for a suit of armor, he will make the world see that military *vertu* rather than pastoral beauty endows man with glory, nobility, and (he might have added) honor. He later insists that his honor "consists in sheading blood" (V.ii.2259):

> The God of war resignes his roume to me,
> Meaning to make me Generall of the world.   (2232-33)

In Tamburlaine's long and famous soliloquy, Venus struggles with Mars and loses. The traditional motif in which beauty overcomes or modifies the savagery of war is inverted, and Tamburlaine denies the fundamental influence of love and beauty on his actions. Or, ironically, if they do influence him, they only urge him on to greater acts of violence and aggression. Concurrently, Zenocrate reveals a growing brutality, and, although she repents her cruelty after the deaths of Bajazeth and Zabina, her acceptance of the Persian crown at the end of the play suggests that she ultimately accepts Tamburlaine's scheme of values.

It may be argued, of course, that Zenocrate's influence does indeed force Tamburlaine, after his Egyptian conquest, to hang his armor "on *Alcides* poste" and take "truce with al the world" (2310-11). There may be an exchange of values, but the evidence

for it is slim. Instead of gratifying his future wife by giving up
military conquest, Tamburlaine pronounces:

> To gratify the sweet *Zenocrate*,
> Egyptians, Moores and men of Asia,
> From *Barbary* vnto the Western *Indie*,
> Shall pay a yearly tribute to thy Syre.   (2298-2301)

His gift is, in effect, another show of his military strength. The
declaration of peace follows and is addressed to his "Lords and
louing followers" (2304), not to his beloved wife. Her first plea
for a truce was denied, and this final speech is merely a further
assertion of Tamburlaine's indomitable will – not a surrender to
love and beauty.

That Marlowe did invert the usual outcome of the Mars and
Venus myth does not necessarily indicate iconoclastic intentions
on his part. It seems rather that the inversion is an implied
comment on Tamburlaine. Earlier in the play, Meander wonders
if "powers diuine, or els infernall, mixt / Their angry seeds at
his conception" (II.vi.820-21). The question of Tamburlaine's
fundamental nature lurks in the verbal texture of the play: should
we accept Tamburlaine's glorious estimation of himself as divinely
inspired and heavenly bound, or the estimation of his enemies, who,
like Bajazeth, see him as diabolic? Since Tamburlaine fails to
respond creatively to the beauty of Zenocrate, we may feel that
Marlowe, by thus slanting the Venus-Mars motif, has helped us
toward an answer. Tamburlaine's inability to allow love and
beauty to assuage his martial fervor does not argue the divine
nature of his aspiration, for according to Tamburlaine's own interpretation, the gods are swayed by beauty. Man alone of rational
creatures seems capable of perverting its use.

The addition of Zenocrate's story to the mythical history of
Tamburlaine lends perspective to his public triumph; his conquest
of the East is paralleled by his private conquest of his future wife.
Zenocrate's capitulation suggests that beauty and love are essentially powerless in Tamburlaine's world, and, as the play ends,
Tamburlaine stands among the lifeless bodies of Bajazeth, Zabina,
and Alcidamus, Zenocrate's fiancé, with the slaughtered Virgins
of Damascus in the background of our memory, and proclaims

that he and his friends must first conduct a funeral and then a wedding. The playgoer can hardly remain blind to the ironic juxtapositions and their implicit meaning.

The scene of Tamburlaine's triumph over the armies of his future father-in-law suggests another influence on Marlowe's conception of the Scythian conqueror. Although there is a lack of definite evidence for comparative dating, we should not forget that the playwright had probably translated the first book of Lucan's *Pharsalia* before writing the Tamburlaine plays, and Marlowe's translation of the first book of the unfinished epic argues that he was familiar with the whole. Frederick Boas, in fact, has suggested that Lucan "may have supplied Marlowe with hints for the background" of the play,[23] and it is entirely possible that behind the Scythian Tamburlaine stands the Roman Caesar, who is unwilling to allow family ties to come between him and imperial power. In Lucan, it is Pompey, Caesar's older son-in-law, who tries to stem the conqueror's growing military power, and the *Pharsalia* is as much a glorification of his hopeless defense of Roman liberty as it is a vilification of Caesar. Like Tamburlaine, Caesar is larger than life:

> Shaming to striue but where he did subdue,
> When yre, or hope prouokt, heady, & bould,
> At al times charging home, & making hauock;
> Vrging his fortune, trusting in the gods,
> Destroying what withstood his proud desires,
> And glad when bloud, & ruine made him way:
> So thunder which the wind teares from the cloudes,
> With cracke of riuen ayre and hideous sound
> Filling the world, leapes out and throwes forth fire,
> Affrights poore fearefull men, and blasts their eyes
> With ouerthwarting flames, and raging shoots
> Alongst the ayre and not resisting it
> Falls, and returnes, and shiuers where it lights.
>
> (Marlowe's trans., 146-58)

---

[23] Boas, *Christopher Marlowe*, p. 43. See III.iii.1252: "Nor in *Parsalia* was there such hot war." William Blissett (*SP*, 53 [1956], 562-66) feels that Lucan is a pervasive influence in Marlowe's plays. See also his "Caesar and Satan", *JHI*, 18 (1957), 221-32, and Michel Poirier, *Christopher Marlowe* (London: Chatto and Windus, 1951), pp. 92, 116.

This passage describing Caesar's elemental violence may be compared with Tamburlaine's boast after capturing Bajazeth:

> My sword stroke fire from his coat of steele,
> Euen in *Bythinia*, when I took this Turke:
> As when a fiery exhalation
> Wrapt in the bowels of a freezing cloude,
> Fighting for passage, make[s] the Welkin cracke,
> And casts a flash of lightning to the earth.
> But ere I martch to wealthy *Persea*,
> Or leaue *Damascus* and th'Egyptian fields,
> As was the fame of *Clymenes* brain-sicke sonne,
> That almost brent the Axeltree of heauen,
> So shall our swords, our lances and our shot
> Fill all the aire with fiery meteors.
> Then when the Sky shal waxe as red as blood,
> It shall be said, I made it red my selfe,
> To make me think of nought but blood and war.   (IV.ii.1485-99)

A comparison of the two passages indicates the similarity between the Roman and the Scythian, who are both identified with the gigantic destructive powers of nature.

Both decide in the course of their careers that they are the favorites of the gods and Fortune (see *Pharsalia*, V, 580-83), and they are able, with the perverse aid of Fortune, to become the rulers of their respective worlds. We are not, I believe, wrong in seeing Lucan's anti-hero as a classical prototype for Marlowe's Tamburlaine, and, if this is indeed the case, we have established another point of reference from which to judge Tamburlaine's actions. Although Lucan envisions Caesar as larger than life, the *Pharsalia* is a devastating picture of personal aggrandisement and conquest. Like Tamburlaine, Caesar is willing to sacrifice the freedom of others for his own increased power. That he may be free, all others must be slaves. The largeness of Lucan's character is not an index to his spiritual greatness.

This survey of the background material and its relationship to the play suggests an approach to the figure of Marlowe's Tamburlaine. We must see him not as the embodiment of Renaissance magnanimity, but as a Renaissance anti-hero. It is incorrect to take Jean Bodin's comparison of Tamburlaine to "the great

Hercules, who traueling ouer a great part of the world with wonder-full prowes and valour destroyed many most horrible monsters, that is to say Tirants",[24] as the key to Marlowe's intention. In the Renaissance sense, Marlowe's Tamburlaine is not a Herculean hero. Golding's translation of *De beneficiis* gives us the proper context: "Hercules winning nothing too himself, traveled over the whole world, not conquering it, but setting it at libertie. For what could he win, that was an enemye too evill, a defender of the good, and a pacifyer bothe of sea and Land?"[25] This idealized portrait of Hercules can only be used as a contrast to Marlowe's creation. But this indeed is Marlowe's method, to indicate the correct point of view by throwing Tamburlaine into high relief against the truly heroic past. Tamburlaine is not Hercules, Alexander, Scipio, nor was he meant to be. Implacable, he presents the voracious and insatiable lust to consume the world, and his greater capacity for evil should not blind us to the fact that he is no better than the more petty Gaveston, Mortimer, or Guise.

II. THE PLAY

Much has been written on the special verbal quality of Marlowe's poetry, and one cannot deny the playwright's masterful use of language. But there is a peculiar emphasis on 'words' in the ideas of *1 Tamburlaine*, and the Prologue seems to suggest that this play will contain an extraordinary combination of words and actions:

> *From iygging vaines of riming mother wits,*
> *And such conceits as clownage keepes in pay,*
> *Weele lead you to the stately tent of War,*
> *Where you shall heare the Scythian* Tamburlaine

[24] Jean Bodin, *The Six Bookes of a Commonweale*, trans. by Richard Knolles (London, 1606), pp. 220-21 (STC 3193). Bodin's work appeared in French in 1576. See Hugh Dick, p. 154. Eugene Waith, *The Herculean Hero* (London: Chatto and Windus, 1962), pp. 60-87, sees Tamburlaine as Herculean.

[25] *The Work of that excellent Philosopher ... Seneca concerning Benefyting*, trans. by Arthur Golding (London, 1578), p. 9ᵛ (STC 22215). See T. K. Dunseath, *Spenser's Allegory of Justice in Book Five of The Faerie Queene* (Princeton: Princeton University Press, 1968), p. 234.

Threatning the world with high astounding tearms
And scourging kingdoms with his conquering sword.   (Prologue, 1-6)

Of course, most drama is concerned with language and action, but here, Marlowe promises, there is to be a difference.

Coupled with Tamburlaine's remarkable rhetorical skill is his personal appearance, which may be either compelling or terrifying as he pleases, but in either case, is unusual. All the characters are struck by Tamburlaine's 'looks'. Nevertheless, we must remember that 'words' and 'appearances' are often deceptive, especially in Renaissance drama where the discrepancy between illusion and reality is a central theme. To take examples from Shakespeare, Richard III glories in his ability to blind others by his verbal witcheries, and *The Comedy of Errors* is built on the supposition that its characters are completely deceived by external appearances. In *1 Tamburlaine* these ideas of verbal deception and human gullibility are used far otherwise, but the basic assumptions are the same. The way the playgoer must evaluate the words and the appearance of a dramatic character is by his actions and their fruits: by a character's deeds the play-goer may know him. Early in the play, Tamburlaine tells Zenocrate: "I am a Lord, for so my deeds shall prooue" (I.ii.230), and the playgoer is given, through the action, a chance to make up his mind about the validity of Tamburlaine's assertion – "*And then applaud his fortunes as you please*" (Prologue, 8).

The play opens with the spotlight on a character who acts as a foil to Tamburlaine: Mycetes, King of Persia. Mycetes' inability to use words properly reflects his inadequacy as a ruler:

> Brother *Cosroe*, I find my selfe agreeu'd,
> Yet insufficient to expresse the same:
> For it requires a great and thundring speech: (I.i.9-11)

And he goes on to make some of the most egregious comic blunders. Though Mycetes is a failure in his public office, he recognizes the powers of language and personal appearance: "thy words", he tells Theridamas, "are swords / And with thy lookes thou conquerest all thy foes" (I.i.82-83). His realization that Therida-mas has the necessary natural equipment serves as an implied

comment on himself and prepares us for the later confrontation
of Theridamas and Tamburlaine.

When Theridamas actually meets Tamburlaine, his public
assets prove to be less potent than his adversary's. Although
Techelles belligerently insists, "Our swordes shall play the Orators
for vs" (I.ii.328), Tamburlaine stays him and asks to speak with
Theridamas. Theridamas's comments mark his progressive seduction by Tamburlaine:

> His looks do menace heauen and dare the Gods,   (352)

> Not *Hermes* Prolocutor to the Gods
> Could vse perswasions more patheticall.   (405-06)

> Won with thy words, & conquered with thy looks,
> I yeeld my selfe, my men & horse to thee: (423-24)

By overcoming Theridamas with his lengthy oration (360-404),
Tamburlaine proves his mastery of both rhetoric and public
appearance. The scene is, in effect, a test case. If Tamburlaine
can turn Theridamas from his primary allegiance by verbal
suasion and physical appearance, then the way is clear for his
similar conquests throughout the play. Shakespeare, it may be
noted, uses much the same technique, when, at the beginning of
Richard III, he has Richard seduce Anne while she is mourning
over the body of Henry VI. In much the same way as Anne,
Theridamas comes as an enemy and remains as a friend.

At the same time, Tamburlaine is not reluctant to praise
Theridamas:

> Noble and milde this Persean seemes to be,
> If outward habit iudge the inward man.   (357-58)

> With what a maiesty he rears his looks: (360)

But there are at least two ways of interpreting these lines. We may
feel either that Tamburlaine is genuinely impressed with Theridamas, or, on the contrary, that this is simply an example of
Tamburlaine's verbal mastery. Immediately before Theridamas
enters, Tamburlaine plays the orator with Zenocrate; and when
Techelles questions his intentions, Tamburlaine replies: "women

must be flatered" (303). Theridamas may also be the victim of
Tamburlaine's flattery. Both interpretations are tempting. In the
first, Theridamas reflects part of Tamburlaine's overt appeal; he
also is a man who conquers with his looks, and Tamburlaine's
conquest of him raises the conqueror's ability in our estimation.
In the second, we catch a glimpse of Tamburlaine's overwhelming
verbal power. Possibly the interpretations are not mutually
exclusive.

When Cosroe arrives in Tamburlaine's camp, Theridamas, who
even by the most liberal standards is a traitor, excuses himself by
emphasizing Tamburlaine's oratorical ability:

> You see my Lord, what woorking woordes he hath.
> But when you see his actions top his speech,
> Your speech will stay, or so extol his worth,
> As I shall be commended and excusde
> For turning my poore charge to his direction.   (II.iii.623-27)

Having listened to Tamburlaine's assurances of martial victory,
Cosroe comments: "Thy words assure me of kind successe" (658),
and Tamburlaine takes his "winged sword" (649) to turn promises
into reality. However, the success that Tamburlaine seeks is for
himself, not for others. Dying by Tamburlaine's hand, Cosroe
says, "death arrests the organe of my voice" (859), significantly
believing the loss of his voice to be as crucial to him as the torments
of his soul. Theridamas's assurance that Tamburlaine's actions
will "stay" Cosroe's "speech" has ironically come true. Cosroe is
silenced.

Comparable to Cosroe's death is the fate of Agydas. When
Agydas tries to win Zenocrate's thoughts from the "vile and barbarous" Tamburlaine, his rhetoric is insufficient. Zenocrate
commands him: "leaue to wound me with these words, / And
speake of *Tamburlaine* as he deserues" (III.ii.1011, 1020-21). But
Agydas persists, exhorting Zenocrate not to forget her first love,
the King of Arabia. Nevertheless, Tamburlaine has won Zenocrate with "those lookes, / Those words of fauour" (1046-47), and
Agydas is powerless. Unfortunately, Tamburlaine overhears
Agydas's arguments, and the stage directions suggest the outcome:
"*Tamburlaine goes to her* [Zenocrate], *& takes her away louingly by the*

hand, *looking wrathfully on Agidas, and sayes nothing"* (S. D., 1051).
Marlowe is obviously underlining the power of Tamburlaine's
facial expression. Agydas immediately understands the look:
"Vpon his browes was pourtraid vgly death" (1057); and Techelles
enters soon after with a *"naked dagger"* sent from Tamburlaine.
Agydas continues:

> I prophecied before and now I prooue,
> The killing frownes of iealousie and loue.
> He needed not with words confirme my feare,
> For words are vaine where working tooles present
> The naked action of my threatned end.   (1075-79)

Tamburlaine forces him to commit suicide in order to silence him.
Tamburlaine's winning looks which seduced Zenocrate and
Theridamas have changed, and his appearance is perhaps here
a just index to his savagery. His viciousness is set off against the
bravery of Agydas, who, even Usumcasane and Techelles admit,
was "manly" and "honorable", and they resolve to "craue his
triple worthy buriall" (1097). Tamburlaine has gone beyond
language, and we are able to witness his naked action, not clothed
in glittering words, against a man who has dared to speak what
Tamburlaine does not wish to hear. Dissent is not permitted. The
progress from Theridamas, through Cosroe, to Agydas is a movement
from refined rhetoric to brutality.

Tamburlaine's language is a major element throughout the
play, and this is not simply because he is a protagonist of 'poetic
drama', which demands that its chief personages speak eloquently.
As we have just seen, Marlowe emphasizes again and again
Tamburlaine's skill with language reinforced by an unusually
striking appearance. Moreover, his speeches are not idle bombast
in the tradition of the Braggart Warrior. It seems rather that the
most important use of language for Tamburlaine is as a façade
behind which to hide the excesses of his martial violence. What
the Soldan of Egypt characterizes as "theft and spoile", Tamburlaine dignifies, at the siege of Damascus, with his high astounding
terms:

> I will not spare these proud Egyptians,
> Nor change my Martiall obseruations,

> For all the wealth of Gehons golden waues,
> Or for the loue of *Venus*, would she leaue
> The angrie God of Armes, and lie with me.
> They haue refusde the offer of the liues,
> And know my customes are as peremptory
> As wrathfull Planets, death, or destinie.   (V.ii.1902-09)

The Egyptians prove that they are proud by their unwillingness to submit immediately to the invader, and because they have been thus "sinful", he feels justified in punishing them. The audience, on the other hand, may feel that he is projecting his own manifest pride upon the poor Egyptians who only offend by loyally defending themselves against an aggressor. Tamburlaine tries to turn the blame onto the blameless, but the playwright's irony should be apparent. Further, by using Biblical and classical allusions to suggest that nothing either earthly or heavenly can buy his clemency, by equating his will with the ultimate powers of fate, Tamburlaine attempts to obscure his own responsibility for his actions and the harshness of his refusal to change his mind.

In order to see more clearly what Tamburlaine is doing, we may compare just a portion of the speech of Shakespeare's Henry V before Harfleur:

> the fleshed soldier, rough and hard of heart,
> In liberty of bloody hand shall range
> With conscience wide as hell, mowing like grass
> Your fresh fair virgins and your flow'ring infants.
>
> (III.iii.11-14)[26]

Henry's language is aimed at frightening the citizens of Harfleur into a quick submission, and he concentrates on the precise details of martial brutality. His picture of a sacked city is realistic and effective for his purpose. Tamburlaine's speech is equally effective, but he consciously avoids detailed precision because his purpose is to apologize for the massacre he and his men are about to perform. Henry's speech may be brutal, but its purpose is merciful; Tamburlaine's is stuffed with allusions to hide the fact

[26] Alfred Harbage (ed.), *William Shakespeare: The Complete Works* (Baltimore, Maryland: Penguin, 1969).

that he has no mercy at all. There is an open discrepancy between Tamburlaine's controlled rhetoric and his devastating violence.

Language is used by Tamburlaine, then, as a propagandistic device, enabling him to create the proper atmosphere for his conquests. A major part of this linguistic façade is the religious terminology – which we have already seen used in *The Massacre at Paris*. In his first appearance, Tamburlaine claims:

> *Ioue* himselfe will stretch his hand from heauen,
> To ward the blow, and shield me safe from harme.
> See how he raines down heaps of gold in showers,
> As if he meant to giue my Souldiers pay ... .   (I.ii.375-78)

The playgoer is aware, of course, that Tamburlaine has stolen the gold, and the distance between his claim to divine sanction and the actuality of his theft indicates how we should view his assertion. Tamburlaine, however, continues throughout to insist that he is divinely inspired. After he is cursed by Bajazeth, he replies:

> The chiefest God first moouer of that Spheare,
> Enchac'd with thousands euer shining lamps,
> Will sooner burne the glorious frame of Heauen,
> Then it should so conspire my ouerthrow.   (IV.ii.1452-55)

He is, he continues, the "Scourge and Terrour" of the "maiestie of heauen" (1475-76), and two scenes later, he claims power "from the Emperiall heauen" (1668). Since the action of the play takes place entirely within the realm of nature (as opposed to that of grace), there is no possible way Tamburlaine can be certain about the divine will. His certitude in this matter is not so much self-deception, however, as part of the verbal wizardry which allows him to influence the vision of others.

Tamburlaine's rather violent piety is, in fact, questioned by his own words. If Tamburlaine recurrently claims divine approbation for his wars, he just as often threatens the gods themselves with military invasion:

> *Ioue* sometime masked in a Shepheards weed,
> And by those steps that he hath scal'd the heauens,
> May we become immortall like the Gods.
> Ioine with me now in this my meane estate,
> ...

And when my name and honor shall be spread,

...

Then shalt thou be Competitor with me,
And sit with *Tamburlaine* in all his maiestie.

(I.ii.394-97, 400, 403-04)

The speech savors of the blasphemous as well as the ridiculous, for Tamburlaine apparently conceives of himself as a kind of martial Christ. A few lines later, he promises friendship to Theridamas until death, "Vntill our bodies turne to Elements: / And both our soules aspire celestiall thrones" (431-32). Again the aspiration seems more military than religious. While bragging to Cosroe about the power of his army, he asserts:

Our quiuering Lances shaking in the aire,
And bullets like *Ioues* dreadfull Thunderbolts,
Enrolde in flames and fiery smoldering mistes,
Shall threat the Gods more than Cyclopian warres.

(II.iii.616-19; cf. II.vi.812-15)

Tamburlaine's assertions of his will against divinity, seen from a skeptical point of view, become comic. We know from experience that men do not invade heaven, and when a character seriously suggests that he will, we must either pity him for a madman or laugh at him for a fool. Tamburlaine may be subject to both reactions. But however the case may be, Tamburlaine's blasphemy forms a verbal pattern which competes with the more pious assertion of divine favor. There is no resolution of these two competing patterns, and Marlowe undoubtedly intended none. Both blasphemy and piety are to be included under the larger aspect of Tamburlaine's language, for both of his attitudes toward divinity are governed by his desire to impress and to control others.

This kind of verbal manipulation is not Marlowe's attempt to whitewash his protagonist, but simply the recognition of a certain power which words have over vision. How we feel about an action is, in great part, determined by how that action is described. Is Tamburlaine's conquest of Egypt the 'will of Jove' or 'unprovoked aggression'? While we accept Tamburlaine's own account of his exploits, we naturally accept him as a glorious and all-powerful conqueror. But when we are unwilling to accept his speeches at

their face value, when we begin to notice the discrepancies between allusions, metaphors, high astounding terms, and what is
actually happening on stage, then we see Tamburlaine as he
is.[27] In this context, it is interesting that both Tamburlaine and
Bajazeth should come to feel the limitations of language; and their
realizations, near the end of a play preoccupied with words and
their use, indicate that a full interpretation must take more than
verbal qualities into account. Sir Walter Raleigh may be our
guide at this point:

> *as the fruit tels the name of the Tree; so doe the outward workes of men (so farre*
> *as their cogitations are acted) giue vs whereof to guesse at the rest. Nay, it were*
> *neere the life: did not craft in many, feare in the most, and the worlds loue in all,*
> *teach euery capacity, according to the compasse it hath, to qualifie and maske ouer*
> *their inward deformities for a time. Though it be also true,* ... No man can long
> continue masked in a counterfeit behauiour: the thinges that are forced
> for pretences, hauing no ground in truth, cannot long dissemble their own
> natures.[28]

We must examine Tamburlaine's "outward workes".

The action of the play is built upon a series of interrelated
successes which Tamburlaine achieves as a military leader, and
these successes form an instructive progression. His first victories
come easily, and form a kind of prologue to his conquest of kingdoms.
Here we must review some familiar territory. Both Zenocrate and
Theridamas are rapidly assimilated into Tamburlaine's camp.
Travelling from her uncle's land of Media home to Egypt, Zenocrate is waylaid; her jewels and treasure are confiscated; and she
in the end willingly yields to her conqueror. Following her,
Theridamas also renders himself and his worldly possessions – in
this case "a thousand horse" – to Tamburlaine. Tamburlaine's
first conquests then are won by his eloquence. He appeals to the
vanity and pride of both the woman and the man; and both seem
content to sell themselves for his flattery. Nevertheless, he has not

[27] Cf. Montaigne's comment on language in *The Essayes*, trans. by John Florio
(London, 1603), p. 83 (STC 18041): "I see not one of these petty-ballad-makers,
or prentise-dogrell rymers, that doth not bumbast his labors with high swelling
and heaven-disimbowelling wordes ... . It is naturall, simple, and vnaffected
speach that I love."

[28] Sir Walter Raleigh, *The History of the World* (London, 1614), sig. A1ᵛ (STC
20637.2).

physically hurt anyone as far as we have seen on stage. His conquests have been bloodless, and clearly this man must have something. At the same time, we may not conclude that what he has
is morally good. As commentators have remarked about Milton's
Satan, to be effective, evil must be attractive. Zenocrate and
Theridamas are indices of just how effective and attractive
Tamburlaine can be.

Tamburlaine's successes with Zenocrate and Theridamas are
paralleled by Cosroe's bloodless assumption of the Persian crown.
Like Tamburlaine, Cosroe promises his supporters, who seem to be
mostly military men lacking "both pay and martiall discipline" under
the soft rule of Mycetes, that he will "cause the souldiers that thus
honour me, / To triumph ouer many Prouinces" (I.i.155, 180-81).
Cosroe gains his military support by promises which must, if they
are to be kept, be implemented with deeds. Therefore he hastens to the
army of Theridamas for military aid. By seeking Theridamas, he
finds Tamburlaine and makes him his commander-in-chief: "Now
worthy Tamburlaine, haue I reposde, / In thy approoued Fortunes
all my hope" (II.iii.599-600). In a way, Cosroe also becomes one
of Tamburlaine's conquests – here metaphorically, later actually.

Following these bloodless turns of fortune is the double victory
over the Persians. First, there is the rather humorous defeat of
Mycetes, the fatuous ruler of Persia. In II.iv, he enters comically
lamenting the hazards of battle. When safe in his palace, he
easily sent Theridamas against Tamburlaine and was pleased with
the contemplation of horrendous bloodshed. Now, having seen
the effects of battle, he says that the man who "inuented war" did
not realize the powerful effects of the cannon. Mycetes' defeat is
no political loss for Persia. In the first scene of the play, he reveals
himself as totally unable to rule, foolishly dictatorial, unwise in
his use of men, a failure. Even if we regret that such a man must
pay for his ineptitude with his life, we cannot doubt that Cosroe
will be a more accomplished ruler, and because of this understanding, we cannot feel too morally outraged that Tamburlaine
removes Mycetes from the throne. Their confrontation is comic
rather than tragic, and Marlowe is careful not to dramatize
Mycetes' death. It is passed over in silence.

Tamburlaine's victory over Cosroe is a somewhat different matter. We are not extremely troubled by Tamburlaine's breaking faith with him, since Cosroe is himself a usurper who has been willing to gain the crown by the death of his incompetent brother. Although Cosroe may call Tamburlaine a "grieuous image of ingratitude" (II.vi. 841), the playgoer may feel that the man who has been crowned by the murderer of his brother has little right to complain of another's moral principles. Cosroe is the usurper usurped, and before his death, Tamburlaine explains to him, in an oft-quoted and justly famous speech, why he has revolted:

> The thirst of raigne and sweetnes of a crown,
> That causde the eldest sonne of heauenly *Ops*,
> To thrust his doting father from his chaire,
> And place himselfe in the Emperiall heauen,
> Moou'd me to manage armes against thy state.
> What better president than mightie *Ioue*?
> Nature that fram'd vs of foure Elements,
> Warring within our breasts for regiment,
> Doth teach vs all to haue aspyring minds:[29]
> Our soules, whose faculties can comprehend
> The wondrous Architecture of the world:
> And measure euery wandring plannets course,
> Still climing after knowledge infinite,
> And alwaies moouing as the restles Spheares,
> Wils vs to weare our selues and neuer rest,
> Vntill we reach the ripest fruit of all,
> That perfect blisse and sole felicitie,
> The sweet fruition of an earthly crowne. (II.vi.863-80)

The aspiration for "celestiall thrones" which Tamburlaine had earlier espoused has undergone a radical change; and the shift in attitude indicates the system of values which truly motivates his quest. Although Cosroe may decry Tamburlaine's statement of faith, he himself is similarly motivated. In defeating Cosroe, Tamburlaine defeats a lesser version of himself.

[29] For a more conventional view of nature's function, see, e.g., *Sermons of Master Iohn Caluin, Vpon the Booke of Iob*, trans. by Arthur Golding (London, 1574), p. 314 (STC 4444): "when wee behold Gods workes both aboue and beneath, is it not to the end that his goodnesse, his wisedome, his rightfulnesse, and all his vertues should be knowne? ... let his workes which he sheweth vs & are neerest vnto vs, leade vs continually higher vnto him."

The first two acts of the play, in which Cosroe gains a crown and loses it, mirror Tamburlaine's rise to power; only the conclusion is changed. Cosroe speaks boldly and efficiently, acts with force after consolidating a strong faction, and achieves the throne of Persia. In these things, he is like Tamburlaine, and his fall suggests what MAY HAPPEN to the Scythian. There is a tension built up between his minor tragedy and the main action, which recapitulates the minor tragedy only so far – and then allows Tamburlaine to defy retribution.

Tamburlaine's next encounter is with the Turks under Bajazeth. Mycetes and Cosroe have been minor opponents. With Bajazeth a balance is struck, a balance symbolized in their parley before the battle: they evenly trade boasts of vengeance; each has three followers who speak in turn. Both Tamburlaine and Bajazeth address their wives and receive uxorial encouragement. And as the battle rages, the wives and their servants trade insults. This formal balance in the rhetoric suggests that Tamburlaine has met in Bajazeth an equal, and since Bajazeth is also a conquering warrior, he is a more complete mirror of Tamburlaine than Cosroe.

But Bajazeth is the rightful ruler of Turkey, not a usurper, and when we meet him in III.i, he is in control of a well-ordered besieging operation. Although he may be no less cruel, Bajazeth is a Tamburlaine whose power is traditional and orderly. Thus, Tamburlaine's victory over him is a victory over a civilized version of himself. His treatment of the captured Bajazeth and Zabina is unreasonably barbaric, and this barbarism suggests what his conquest of the Turks has meant. The kind of forbearance we associate with civilization is lost. Bajazeth had sent his Bassoe to Tamburlaine saying, "I am content to take a truce" (III.i.949). But Tamburlaine is unwilling to give any quarter, and from his victory over Bajazeth until the end of the play, the kind of moderation embodied in Bajazeth is gone. Of course, Bajazeth must not be overemphasized as a symbol of civilization, for as the mighty opposite of Tamburlaine, he embodies some of Tamburlaine's worst qualities.

Tamburlaine's treatment of the royal Turks results in a reversal of our estimation of him. First, he refuses to set a ransom on Bajazeth:

What, thinkst thou *Tamburlain* esteems thy gold?
Ile make the kings of *India* ere I die,
Offer their mines (to sew for peace) to me,
And dig for treasure to appease my wrath.   (III.iii.1360-63)

Tamburlaine makes it evident that wealth is not UNimportant to him, but he feels that he can extort riches from others without ransoming the Turks. His unwillingness to free Bajazeth and Zabina is linked with his former unwillingness to set a ransom on Zenocrate and her attendant lords. To the lords, he says:

Thinke you I way this treasure more than you?
Not all the Gold in *Indias* welthy armes,
Shall buy the meanest souldier in my traine.   (I.ii.280-82)

And to Zenocrate:

Thy person is more woorth to *Tamburlaine*,
Than the possession of the Persean Crowne,
Which gratious starres haue promist at my birth.   (286-88)

The present passage, explaining precisely why Tamburlaine refuses ransom, casts an ironic light over his apparent magnanimity with Zenocrate and her followers. He is not concerned with intrinsic human worth. It is simply that the people he holds captive are more valuable to him as captives than as possible adversaries should they be granted freedom.

Second, Bajazeth is placed in a cage like an animal, and Zabina is enslaved as Zenocrate's maid. Their enslavement is the culmination of a theme announced earlier. In his second speech of the play, Tamburlaine asserts that one of his main principles is "to liue at liberty" (I.ii.222); the wealth he steals must maintain his "life exempt from seruitude" (227). In their initial confrontation, he promises Bajazeth "that those which lead my horse, / Shall lead thee Captiue thorow Affrica" (III.iii.1170-71), and he is echoed by Bajazeth who promises Zabina to "bring this sturdy *Tamburlain*, / And all his Captains bound in captiue chaines" (1212-13). The point of this emphasis on servitude and enslavement seems to be that, in Tamburlaine's world, one is either slave or free. Tamburlaine feels, with a good deal of justice, that for

him to be at liberty, his competitors for power must be dead or
enslaved. Bajazeth's cage becomes a symbol of the absolute subordination which Tamburlaine must demand if he is to have
absolute sovereignty. For him, liberty apart from sovereignty does
not seem to exist.

The tragedy of Bajazeth and Zabina is worked out in three
scenes (IV.ii, IV.iv, and V.i), with the destruction of Damascus as
a backdrop. The tragedy of the city reflects the tragedy of the
royal couple, and, in a sense, the cold-blooded murder of the
Virgins looks forward to the suicides of Bajazeth and Zabina. As
Tamburlaine's tents change their color from white (clemency), to
red (selective execution), to black (total annihilation), so his
treatment of the Turk becomes increasingly harsh, until Bajazeth
is driven to despair. Sending out the Virgins to plead with Tamburlaine for clemency, the Governor of Damascus hopes:

> that their vnspotted praiers
> Their blubbered cheekes and hartie humble mones
> Will melt his furie into some remorse:
> And vse vs like a louing Conquerour.   (V.i.1801-04)

But the Governor's hopes have already been discounted by
Tamburlaine's inability to accept Zenocrate's pleas for the city's
safety, and his words ring hollow and ironic. In the same way,
Tamburlaine has been unable to respond sympathetically to the
plight of Bajazeth and Zabina. His progressive cruelty toward the
Damascans, imprisoned within their walls, and toward the captive
Turks forces us to lose sympathy for this character who refuses to
acknowledge the suffering of others. He is the portrait of brutal
egocentricity.

In considering the background material, we have already
noticed how deeply Zenocrate is moved by the death of Bajazeth
and Zabina. Tamburlaine may triumph, but his mistress somehow
finds these triumphs less than morally or spiritually satisfying.
While Zenocrate grieves for the dead Turks and contemplates her
own and Tamburlaine's mortality, he actively pursues his conquests, this time against Zenocrate's former lover and her father.
His soldiers having dispatched the Arabian king, Tamburlaine
surveys the carnage:

Millions of soules sit on the bankes of *Styx*,
Waiting the back returne of *Charons* boat,
Hell and *Elisian* swarme with ghosts of men,
That I haue sent from sundry foughten fields,
To spread my fame through hell and vp to heauen:
...
The Turk and his great Emperesse as it seems,
Left to themselues while we were at the fight,
Haue desperatly dispatcht their slauish liues:
With them *Arabia* too hath left his life,
Al sights of power to grace my victory:
And such are obiects fit for *Tamburlaine*,
Wherein as in a mirrour may be seene,
His honor, that consists in sheading blood,
When men presume to manage armes with him.

(V.ii.2245-49, 2252-60)

Obviously Zenocrate and Tamburlaine do not share the same vision: she finds in the scene a thought of worldly impermanence and human evil, while he views the slaughter with moral obtuseness. Perhaps we may be justified in again using the Renaissance distinction between nature and grace, and saying that Tamburlaine has no vision of any world but the 'natural' one, a world red in tooth and claw. For him, there is no moral dimension, and in his language, the realm of grace becomes merely an extension of his martial world. In the deaths of his adversaries, there is only the nebulous quality of "honor".

"Honor" is a word used throughout the play, twenty-eight times according to Crawford's concordance (as opposed to seventeen in Part II). Its recurrence, especially in the mouth of Tamburlaine, forces us to evaluate what kind of honor Tamburlaine actually has. In the final acts, Tamburlaine's "honor" is interpreted through the eyes of the Soldan of Egypt, who, as Zenocrate's father and as a legitimate and competent ruler, must be viewed as a spokesman of some merit. In two scenes, he comments on the conduct of the Scythian leader: first, hearing of Tamburlaine's practise of using the colors white, red, and black to indicate his degree of clemency and ferocity, the Soldan says:

Mercilesse villaine, Pesant ignorant,
Of lawfull armes, or martiall discipline:

> Pillage and murder are his vsuall trades.
> The slaue vsurps the glorious name of war.   (IV.i.1436-39)

In the second scene, the Soldan thinks of Tamburlaine and his army as a type of Hydra:

> A monster of fiue hundred thousand heades,
> Compact of Rapine, Pyracie, and spoile,
> The Scum of men, the hate and Scourge of God,
> Raues in *Egyptia*, and annoyeth vs.
> ... it is the bloody *Tamburlaine*,
> A sturdy Felon and a base-bred Thiefe,
> By murder raised to the Persean Crowne,
> That dares controll vs in our Territories.   (IV.iii.1577-84)

In the Soldan's view, Tamburlaine is a proud and "presumptuous Beast" (1585). The military honor, in which he glories, lacks all qualities of the truly honorable.[30]

The Soldan's evaluations of Tamburlaine form an ironic parenthesis around Tamburlaine's own contention that he is "the chiefest Lamp of all the earth" (IV.ii.1480). The Soldan's comments set off this self-praise far enough for us to see it as darkly humorous. The man who calls himself the light of the world is its rampant destroyer; and, of course, the irony increases when we remember that, for an Elizabethan audience, the "Lamp of all the earth" was Christ, the Saviour.

In the final scene, the Soldan, standing over the body of Arabia, his friend and proposed son-in-law, eulogizes the military success of Tamburlaine:

> Mighty hath God & *Mahomet* made thy hand
> (Renowmed *Tamburlain*) to whom all kings
> Of force must yeeld their crownes and Emperies,
> And I am pleasde with this my ouerthrow:
> If as beseemes a person of thy state,
> Thou has with honor vsde *Zenocrate*.   (V.ii.2261-66)

---

[30] L'Espine, pp. 20ᵛ-21ʳ, sigs. D7ᵛ-D8ʳ, distinguishes between two kinds of honor. First there is "a good and laudable testimonie, which we ought to purchase among men" (p. 20ᵛ). "But the honour which they [worldly men] speake of, and which is vsuallie vnderstood of them, rather it is vaineglorie purchased by meanes partly vnlawfull, and partlie ridiculous" (p. 21ʳ). The second kind of honor belongs to Tamburlaine.

And he pretends to be satisfied by Tamburlaine's assurance that no "blot of foule inchastity" stains his daughter (2268). Although we may have leave silently to question Zenocrate's virgin state, we are possibly more puzzled by the Soldan's reversal. The "base-bred Thiefe" is now accepted as a new son-in-law – "a person of thy state" – literally over Arabia's dead body. Some readers may catch a touch of irony in the Soldan's speech, but the scene readily suggests the way of the Marlovian world. The Soldan honors Tamburlaine for his material success; evil has, of necessity, been accepted as good. Material power is ultimately triumphant, and there appears to be no other yardstick extant for the measurement of achievement.

The last action of the play is the crowning of Zenocrate; it is a symbolic climax. Imaginatively her coronation leads us back to the emphasis on crowns which pervades the play. As we have already seen, Tamburlaine publicly announces that Nature teaches "vs all to haue aspyring minds" so that we never rest "Vntill we reach the ripest fruit of all, / That perfect blisse and sole felicitie, / The sweet fruition of an earthly crowne" (II.vi.871, 878-80). That man's soul which strives after infinite knowledge should be contented with an earthly crown seems strangely perverse, and the playgoer may see this speech as a piece of irony undercutting Tamburlaine's excessive materialism. J. D. Jump, one of the recent editors of the text, feels quite otherwise:

In the age of Marlowe ... intelligent men did not commonly think the exercise of political and military power an unworthy employment for the highest human abilities. Very few contemporary playgoers can have felt surprise at his introduction of crowns, the traditional symbols of supreme power on earth, as the natural objects of the aspiring mind and consequently as the central symbols of [Marlowe's] play.[31]

Jump overstates his case. In any age, most intelligent men realize the limitations of material attainment; and while in their public lives Elizabethans may have wished for political power, few Renaissance men would have admitted that the highest achievement of their inmost nature, the faculties of the soul, could be the

---

[31] John D. Jump (ed.), *Tamburlaine the Great: Parts I and II*, p. xvii.

attaining of an earthly crown. Although it was written too late for Marlowe to have read, the following comment suggests how some contemporaries would have looked at the "introduction of crowns":

all *Earthly* and *Sublunary* things whatsoever, all carnall desires, and delights; the *concupiscence* of the *Eyes*, *concupiscence* of the *Flesh*, and *pride* of *Life*; all the pleasures, profits, and preferments of this present evill world, with the best of earthly contents; yea, the whole lustre and glory of the world, such as *Sathan* shewed our *Savior*, with all the unsanctified Pleasures that ever any seemingly *inioyed*, or superficially *ioyed in*, with which the heart of man hath beene bewitched, and insnared; ... are not all of them, of any validity, or sufficiency, to give any true Comfort and contentation, ... to the heart and soule, and spirit of a man.[32]

The author's "maine Poinct" is that *"no earthly Vanitie satisfies mans heavenly Soule"*.[33] For at least part of the Renaissance audience, the attainment of an earthly crown was not a thing of cosmic importance.

The emphasis on the crown reaches its high point in Tamburlaine's victory banquet. Presenting his men with crowns, Tamburlaine asks: "here are the cates you desire to finger, are they not?" (IV.iv.1747-48). Roy Battenhouse has suggested that the crowns are sweetmeats molded into the shape of crowns, molded dessert, which Tamburlaine's three men can actually devour, thus emphasizing their unnatural appetite for power.[34] However, the same objective is attained by the substitution of real crowns for food. It seems most likely that the crowns are supposed to be those taken from Bajazeth's contributory kings, and thus that Theridamas, Techelles, and Usumcasane have unnaturally put a desire for power in the place of the normal desire for food. Unnatural thirst and hunger form a significant motif ("That fiery thirster after Soueraintie" – II.vi.842), which reaches a climax in the banquet of power. Tamburlaine's feast is a celebration, not of social unity as the feast is in Shakespeare's plays, but of material values.

[32] R. H., *The Arraignement of the VVhole Creature*, p. 13, sig. C3ʳ.

[33] R.H., p. 13, sig. C3ʳ.

[34] Battenhouse, *Marlowe's Tamburlaine*, p. 155, goes on to contrast Tamburlaine's feast of crowns with the Last Supper, another suggestion that Marlowe thought of Tamburlaine as an anti-Christ.

Zenocrate's coronation ties these threads together. Theridamas, Techelles, and Usumcasane help to crown her, as they helped Tamburlaine conquer Asia; and the coronation makes Zenocrate not only the queen of Persia but also of "all the kingdomes and dominions / That late the power of *Tamburlaine* subdewed" (V.ii.2290-91). If we see Zenocrate as the epitome of beauty and love in the play – as she is perhaps the only spark of goodness – her coronation is the symbolic overthrow of her function. She is subdued by the material values inherent in the crown; and she becomes the captive queen of conquered lands. Tamburlaine sets his seal on her brow.

Although J. D. Jump contends that "Marlowe's purpose is to prevent conventional moral judgments, and humanitarian and Christian feelings, from compromising the almost unbounded admiration that he wishes to excite for his hero's prowess",[35] the preceding discussion points in a different direction. Marlowe provides an increasingly wider context in which to judge Tamburlaine's actions, and our humanitarian feelings are very much engaged as Tamburlaine becomes more brutal and savage in his quest for power. At the beginning of the play, his conquests are bloodless or he is set against lesser characters, who, because of their moral weaknesses, hardly evoke a sympathetic response. In Bajazeth, Tamburlaine fights an adversary equal to himself, and in defeating him, reveals his full savagery. Placing Bajazeth in a cage, mistreating Zabina, refusing to grant Zenocrate's pleas for clemency, slaughtering the Damascan Virgins, killing Arabia – these acts put Tamburlaine in an increasingly worse light. From a presumably young shepherd-soldier, he has become progressively a thief, a usurper, a murderer of women, and a sacker of cities. It is difficult not to see in this degenerative movement a dramatic comment on Tamburlaine's character, and we should perhaps recall the words of Lord Acton about the absolute corrupting force of absolute power. There is an inverse ratio between Tamburlaine's accumulation of worldly goods and might and the playgoer's positive response to his actions. As Spenser puts it, "Regard of

[35] Jump, p. xviii.

worldly mucke doth fowly blend, / And low abase the high heroicke spright."[36]

To claim that we can ignore Tamburlaine's brutality because of his verbal ability is to ignore what the play is saying about language. Tamburlaine, of course, endeavors to cover his savagery with his high-flown rhetoric, but as the play goes on, his attempts at propaganda are less and less effective. Standing among the corpses of the characters he has slain, he can hardly convince the sensible or sensitive playgoer that he is a divinely appointed minister. His drive has not been toward godhead, but toward the golden round of sovereignty which he has, from the beginning, equated with ultimate happiness. "If this is the kind of materialism you respect", Marlowe is, in effect, saying, "then Tamburlaine is indeed your hero, and his world, where evil is accepted as good, has become yours also." In an age when Machiavelli could set up his picture of the prince as a political ideal, Marlowe's warning had to be taken seriously. In the twentieth century, we need only remember Hitler to see how relevant the play is for us.

[36] *Faerie Queene*, II.vii.10.

VI

2 TAMBURLAINE

As many critics have recognized, when Marlowe finished *1 Tamburlaine*, he had exhausted most of the conventional material at hand. Battenhouse, for example, writes: "It is true that Marlowe, now [in Part Two] without the aid of historical material, has to invent almost all the action."[1] Although few would insist that Marlowe was incapable of inventing this action, there are indications that Part Two was thoroughly researched. The evidence has been painstakingly compiled by Ethel Seaton and John Bakeless, and it appears that Marlowe went far afield consulting a variety of sources for his new play. From our vantage point, Part Two may be seen as more of a synthesis than a creation *ex nihilo*.

I. BACKGROUND

Marlowe immersed himself in the historians. The first scenes of the second part are taken from Turkish history of the period immediately following Tamburlaine's death in 1405. The Turko-Hungarian treaty was violated by the Hungarians, and at the Battle of Varna (1444), the promise-breaking Hungarians were beaten and their king was killed. Although Marlowe may have found accounts of the incident in short histories such as Coelius Curio's *A Notable History of the Saracens*, translated by Thomas Newton (1575), Bakeless believes that Marlowe used Antonius

---

[1] Battenhouse, *Marlowe's Tamburlaine*, p. 149.

Bonfinius's *Rervm Vngaricarvm Decades Qvatvor* (1581), supplemented with Callimachus's *De Clade Varnensi* (1519). The latter is available in Philipp Lonicer's collection, *Chronicorvm Tvrcicorvm* (1578, 1584).[2] Ethel Seaton also traces Marlowe's description of the Zoacum tree (II.ii.2940-45) to Lonicer's compilation, though her case is here weakened by her emphasis on the significance of spelling (which in Renaissance printing was more often compositorial than auctorial).[3] In Belleforst's *Cosmographie Universelle* (1575) or in Jacobus Fontanus's *De Bello Rhodio* (1556), Marlowe may have found the germ from which the first section of the Olympia subplot grew.[4] It is further possible that Marlowe found a reference to Tamburlaine's three children in one of these scholarly histories, since the more popular accounts mention only two. Laonicus Chalcocondyles, a Byzantine historian, translated into Latin and published by Sigismundus Feyrabendius (1577), writes: "Temiri nati sunt filii, Sachruchus, Paiangures, & Abdulatriphes."[5]

[2] John Bakeless (*The Tragicall History of Christopher Marlowe* [Cambridge, Mass.: Harvard University Press, 1942], I, 232-36), following and elaborating Ethel Seaton ("Marlowe and His Authorities", *TLS* [16 June 1921], 388). See also Curio Coelius, *A Notable History of the Saracens*, trans. by Thomas Newton (London, 1575), p. 130[r], sig. Mm4[r] (STC 6129). I have consulted the 1569 Basil edition of Antonio Bonfini, and the Callimachus in Lonicer's compilation (Frankfort, 1578), II, 1-83. The story was used in the pamphlets dealing with the French Civil Wars. See *The Contre-Guyse* (London, 1589), sigs. E4[v]-F1[r] (STC 12506), and *The Restorer of the French Estate* (London, 1589), p. 9, sig. G1[r] (STC 11289). Although the historical Callapine did not war with Sigismund, there is a suggestion that some Renaissance authors thought that he did. See, e.g., Stephen Batman, *Batman Vppon Bartholome, his Booke De Proprietatibus Rerum* (London, 1582), p. 252[v], sig. Vv6[v] (STC 1538), and Robert Allott, *Wits Theater of the Little World* (London, 1599), p. 184[r] (STC 382).

[3] Ethel Seaton, "Fresh Sources for Marlowe", *RES*, 5 (1929), 385-88.

[4] Seaton, "Fresh Sources", pp. 394-95, and Bakeless, *Tragicall History*, I, 209. Fontanus may be found in Lonicer, II.113-83. Cf. Nicholay, *Navigations*, p. 16, sig. C4[r].

[5] Sigismundus Feyrabendius (ed.), *Historia Rervmin* [sic] *Oriente Gestarvm ab exordio mvndi et orbe condito ad nostra haec vsqve tempora* (Frankfort, 1587), p. 241[r]. Feyrabendius (or Feyerabend) was a publisher interested in Eastern materials. Chalkokondyles was translated into French by Blaise de Vigenere, *L'Histoire de la decadence de l'empire Grec, et establissement de celvy des Turcs ... par* Nicolas Chalcondyle [sic] (Paris, 1577). This version reads: "Il auoit trois enfans entre autres, dont il faisoit estat; Sacruch, Abdulatriph, & Paiamgur" (p. 217, sig. Ee1[r]).

Of course, the names of Tamburlaine's children have been changed, but even the changes indicate an increased familiarity with the histories. Seaton suggests that the names "Calyphas" and "Amyras" were selected by Marlowe from Eastern titles of dignity, while the name "Celebinus" is one of the several names given to Bajazeth's son Callapine.[6] Orcanes and Gazellus as well as Frederick, Baldwin, and Sigismund are also names taken from Eastern history.[7] In Part Two, there are few names like "Meander" which bulk out the *dramatis personae* of Part One and which are drawn from other than Eastern sources. The place names, moreover, indicate Marlowe's increased knowledge of learned sources. As Seaton points out, Part One has relatively few geographical references, even though Marlowe's awareness of geography is suggested by Tamburlaine's metaphor of "blind Geographers" (*1 Tamburlaine*, IV.iv.1715). Part Two, in contrast, is replete with exact geographical details – exact by Renaissance standards – and Seaton has demonstrated that most of the movements of both Turk and Scythian can be traced on Abraham Ortellius's maps in *Theatrum Orbis Terrarum* (1570).[8]

Marlowe also became more knowledgeable about military tactics between the writing of Part One and Part Two. In the first part, he is content to use indefinite descriptions of military actions, but in Part II, he turned to Paul Iue's *Practise of Fortification* (1589) in order to replace rhetoric with the facts of Renaissance warfare. Tamburlaine's description of fortifications is very close to those in Iue, a work which Marlowe may have consulted in manuscript.[9] Again, Marlowe's movement is toward a more detailed knowledge of his subject.

Further, the playwright must have become interested in the history of Scanderbeg, the Albanian military leader; for Scander-

---

[6] Seaton, "Fresh Sources", p. 388.

[7] See, e.g., Knolles, *The Generall Historie of the Turkes*, pp. 179, 267, 527, *et passim*.

[8] Ethel Seaton, "Marlowe's Map", *E&S*, 10 (1924), 13-35.

[9] Paul Iue (*The Practise of Fortification* [London, 1589], STC 14289), bound with his translation of *Instructions for the Warres*, stands behind III.ii.3245-80. F.-C. Danchin ("Études critiques sur Christophe Marlowe", *Revue germanique*, 8 [1912], 23-33) first noted the parallels. The fact that Marlowe turned to a study of fortification suggests something about the temper of Part Two.

beg's final victory over the Turk's armies parallels Tamburlaine's
second defeat of Callapine. Scanderbeg's soldiers

> passed on ouer the plaines vntyll they came to the ryuer named Cliro.
> Then a certaine of the Turckes which were on the other syde of the riuer
> making garde (as sone as they sawe them) knewe them to be of Scanderbegs
> souldiours, and maruelling at their sudden aryuale, called vnto them
> asking where Scanderbeg was, it was aunswered that he was in Alessio,
> and that the morning folowing he wolde loke vpon them, where vpon the
> Turckes repared to their Captaine Hamathbeg.[10]

The Turks spend the night in battle array and flee the next day,
marching "awaye in exceding great feare" and looking "often
tymes behind them yf that they mought se Scanderbeg to folowe
them, and had determined, yf they had seen him comme, to fall
vpon their knees, & to yelde vnto him".[11] During this time,
Scanderbeg was terminally sick with a "feruant feuer".[12] Tamburlaine also is afflicted with "accidentall heat" (V.iii.4476) as his
final battle approaches, and like Scanderbeg, he forces the Turks
to flee by his "royall presence" (4504). The parallels suggest that
Marlowe appropriated the story of Scanderbeg's final days as a
fitting conclusion for his play.

There is ample evidence that Marlowe did not create Part
Two out of whole cloth, but, after the success of the initial play,
went in search of new material, reading widely and especially in
the historians. Given this evidence, it may be possible – and I will
argue in the next paragraphs that it is – that Marlowe found in
his voracious reading of history a fresh account of Tamburlaine
which gave him ideas for some of the main themes and actions of
the second part.

My argument rests on the resemblance of Part Two to Jean Du
Bec-Crespin's *Histoire dv grand Tamerlanes*, the prefatory material
of which is dated 23 March 1594 – or too late for Marlowe to have

---

[10] [Demetrius Francus], *Tvvo Very Notable Commentaries*, trans. by John Shute
(London, 1562), pp. 40ᵛ-41ʳ, sigs. Ee2ᵛ-Ee3ʳ (STC 4470). The Harvard Catalog
attributes the second commentary (on Scanderbeg, i.e., George Castriota) to
Francus. I tentatively follow the attribution.

[11] Francus, p. 41ʳ, sig. Ee3ʳ.

[12] Francus, p. 40ʳ, Ee2ʳ.

consulted.[13] Thus former critics of *Tamburlaine* have passed by
Du Bec with either a brief comment or in complete silence.[14]
Nevertheless, Du Bec claims that the history which he is printing
in 1594 has been in his hands since his "voyage into the East
Countrey" (p. 1, sig. A3r). At some undesignated date, he had
travelled "en Égypte et en Palestine, recueillant des médailles et
des manuscrits".[15] Presumably we must date this journey before
1578 when he became Abbot of Mortemer in the diocese of Rouen,
since the completed history is dated from there. Although Du Bec's
biography is admittedly sketchy, given these facts, his story of the
reception of the history has some degree of plausibility. Since he
was unable to read the history in the original language, he says,
it was "interpreted vnto me by an Arabian, who did speake
Frank" (p. 2, sig. A3r). From this Arabian translator, Du Bec
heard the original story, which was apparently written in Arabic
by an author named "*Alhacen*". Supposedly Du Bec's history
comes from this retelling: "I tooke therof as much as I coulde in
his language" (p. 2, sig. A3v). If we may grant the truth of Du
Bec's statement (and the fact that he is a churchman may be a
point in favor of our believing so), then this history of Tamerlane
had some currency in the East.[16] On the other hand, Du Bec

---

[13] Jean Du Bec-Crespin, *Histoire du grand Tamerlanes, ov sont descrits les rencontres,
escarmouches, batailles ... tirée des monumens antiques des Arabes* (Lyons, 1602). I have
been unable to obtain a copy of the 1594 edition. The English translations here
used are taken from *The Historie of the Great Emperovr Tamerlan. VVherein are
expressed, encounters, skirmishes, battels, ... Drawen from the auncient Monuments of the
Arabians*, trans. by H. M. (London, 1597), STC 7263, and have been checked
against the French. The Britwell Court Catalogue attributes the translation to
Humphrey Mildmay. For convenience, references to the translation are placed
in the main text.

[14] See, e.g., Una Ellis-Fermor (ed.), *Tamburlaine the Great in Two Parts* (New
York: Dial, 1930), p. 34.

[15] *Dictionnaire de Biographie Française*, XI, 886, s.v. Du Bec-Crespin (Jean), 1540-
1610.

[16] Hookham (*Tamburlaine the Conqueror*, p. 230) relates an attempted assassination
of Tamburlaine: "An assassin in the garb of a darvish, with two young assistants,
was sent into the Tatar camp and managed to gain access to the imperial tents.
There they drew suspicion on themselves and when searched, were found to have
poisoned daggers concealed in their boots. The false monk was killed with his
own dagger." Du Bec relates a similar attempt by Arsanibei (pp. 162-63), and
this accuracy in a minor detail may suggest that Du Bec indeed had access to
primary material about Timur.

protests a bit too much that he is not "writing any thing of these times" (p. 3, sig.A4ʳ), and it is difficult to believe that he has not slanted his story to comment on the troubles of civil-war France. But whatever the origins of Du Bec's story, there are parallels between it and Marlowe's play.

According to the subtitle of *2 Tamburlaine*, one of its major themes is Tamburlaine's "*fourme* of exhortation and discipline to his three *sons*". The histories which Marlowe followed in writing Part One say nothing about this education and only mention Tamburlaine's children in passing. Du Bec's Tamerlane, on the other hand, explicitly considers the education of his eldest child, the heir apparent. Tamerlane

forbad from hence forward they should suffer him to weare any thing vpon his head, & himselfe did hang a bowe about his necke, saying aloud, that they which from their birth were called vnto soueraignties, should bee vsed both vnto cold and heate, and should be exercised in Armes betimes, and not brought vp delicately and easily …. If he [the son] be not borne (said he [Tamerlane]) for to be strong in Armes, he will not be worthy to succeed me: for hee must not bee an effeminate Prince that shall preserue the Parthian Empire. (p. 219, sig. O8ʳ)[17]

Later in the history, Tamerlane desires that all his youthful subjects be brought up to warlike enterprise rather than to courtly dalliance. For Tamerlane, a rigorous martial education is important.

In the play, the theme of martial education is introduced in I.iv, where Tamburlaine urges his son to follow him in arms: "If thou wilt loue the warres and follow me, / Thou shalt be made a King and raigne with me" (2616-17). And immediately after the death of their mother, Zenocrate, Tamburlaine decides to begin their education in earnest:

> But now my boies, leaue off, and list to me,
> That meane to teach you rudiments of war:
> Ile haue you learne to sleepe vpon the ground,
> March in your armour throwe watery Fens,
> Sustaine the scortching heat and freezing cold,
> Hunger and thirst right adiuncts of the war. (III.ii.3243-48)

---

[17] The suggestion of effeminacy here may be related to Marlowe's treatment of Calyphas, the effeminate son.

Tamburlaine wishes all three of his sons to learn "to beare couragious minds, / Fit for the followers of great *Tamburlaine*" (3333-34).
Marlowe and Du Bec are obviously quite close in this aspect;
both their protagonists emphasize the necessity of a rigorous military training if the sons are to be worthy of the fathers.

But there are more interesting parallels in action. Marlowe's
play is built around the attempted revenge of the Turks for the
defeat of their leader Bajazeth in Part I, and revenge is one of
the leading motifs. The Turks attempt a league with a Christian
king of Hungary, and Callapine gains his liberty by making his
Egyptian keeper, Almeda, King of "*Ariadan*, / Bordering on *Mare
Roso* neere to *Meca*" (III.v.3632-33). Callapine fights two battles
with Tamburlaine and is defeated in both, but in neither is he
captured. During the second engagement, which follows Tamburlaine's siege of Babylon, the old conqueror becomes ill and consults
his astrologers, who warn of certain critical days. After the battle,
Tamburlaine makes Amyras mount the royal chariot, "That I
may see thee crown'd", he says, "before I die" (V.iii.4572). He
says that he is called from above: "In vaine I striue and raile
against those powers, / That meane t'inuest me in a higher throane,
/ As much too high for this disdainfull earth" (V.iii.4513-15). The
play ends with a speech by Tamburlaine's son.

One may find analogues to these incidents in Du Bec's history,
although the arrangement is somewhat different. By the final
part of Du Bec's account – after Tamerlane's war in Egypt and
Persia – the conqueror is depending a good deal on Prince Axalla
to command his troops:

Prince Axalla, ... being returned from *Babilon*, whither hee went vpon
some reuolt, gaue the Emperour [Tamerlane] to vnderstand that the
Ottamans hauing knowledge of the death of the Emperour *Baiazet* ..., had
chosen his second sonne called *Calepin*, and that they gathered together,
a great Armie for to conquer all *Natolia* againe.   (p. 239, sig. Q2ʳ)

After hearing of Calepin's plans, we are told that Tamerlane has
"complanied these 3. moneths of a paine in his reines" (p. 241,
sig. Q3ʳ). He consults his astrologers, one of whom says "that he
should giue a battel vnto all the East, and that he should be
victorious", and a second who warns him of "the third day of the

Moone, of the ninth moneth". This day, we suppose, will be critical for his health. Though sick, Tamerlane realizes that he must "roote out for euer the Empire of the *Ottomans* ... to assure his estate, and settle the foundation of his glory" (p. 242, sig. Q3ᵛ). In the meanwhile, Calepin prepares for the war. He reaches an agreement with the Christian Emperor of Greece and is joined by the Egyptian "*Soldan*" who "had bin entised by *Calepin*, & had entred into this league vpon hope that if his affaires had good successe, he [Calepin] would giue him aide for the recouering of *Syria* and *Egypt*" (p. 246, sig. Q5ᵛ). Before encountering the army of Tamerlane, Calepin is careful to put his army in charge of a "*Bassa*" so that he will not be captured as was his father (p. 244, sig. Q4ᵛ).

With full details, Du Bec recounts the story of Axalla's campaign and victory against the Turks in Natolia. Two days before his death, Tamerlane is "brought newes of the happie successe of two battailes wonne in *Natolia*, by the Armie led by Prince *Axalla*, victorious ouer *Calepins* forces" (p. 262, sig. R5ᵛ). To make sure that the transfer of power is carried out smoothly at his death, Tamerlane places "his seale" in the hands of his son as a sign of inheritance (p. 262, sig. R5ᵛ). He announces that he is "called by a greater then himselfe, and vnto a more happie conquest, seated in a more high place, whither he must needs go" (p. 263, sig. R6ʳ). After Tamerlane's very quiet death, Sautochio, his heir, assembles the army and makes "an oration vnto the Captaines and soldiers" (p. 265, sig. R7ʳ). Du Bec closes his history with a few perfunctory comments on the collapse of Tamerlane's empire through fraternal quarrels. In Marlowe's play and in the relevant sections of Du Bec's history, the major action is Tamburlaine's struggle with the second generation Ottomans.

If we are willing to admit that these correspondences indicate some kind of relationship between the works, then we must try to establish what that relationship may be. Since Du Bec's history was printed four years after Marlowe's play, the first possibility to face is that Du Bec used Marlowe's plot as the basis for the latter part of his story. The evidence seems to militate against this conclusion, since the early parts of Du Bec's history differ greatly from *1 Tamburlaine.* Tamerlane is not a poor shepherd, but the son of a chieftain. One of his first acts is to fight against the Muscovites, one of the few groups of people Marlowe's Tamburlaine does not attack, or think of attacking. If Du Bec were using Marlowe as a source, we would expect him to use elements from Marlowe throughout, especially since both parts of *Tamburlaine* were published in one volume in 1590. It does not seem plausible, then, that the history is derived from the plays.

Two major possibilities remain: (1) Marlowe consulted the same basic material as did Du Bec, or (2) Marlowe read Du Bec's account before writing *2 Tamburlaine* and probably after writing Part One. The first possibility cannot be disproven, and it may well be that Du Bec is retelling Eastern stories of Emir Timur which were gaining currency in late sixteenth-century Europe. Histories of Tamburlaine written after Du Bec tended to use his material.[18] Richard Knolles in his *Generall Historie of the Turkes* carefully follows Du Bec,[19] and even though Purchas is somewhat skeptical that the humanistic elements are Eastern in origin, he has confidence in Du Bec's narrative.[20] It may be that Du Bec was the first visible spokesman for a growing tradition founded on quasi-historical sources. But however we may explain Du Bec's popularity, until we know more about the man and the genesis of his *Historie,* we should reserve our judgment. Marlowe may, or may not, have had an opportunity to read the sources from which Du Bec gathered his story – accepting, for the present time, that the story is not largely a fabrication.

---

[18] *The History of Tamerlan the Great Taken out of Alhacent,* by Lord de Sainctyon, trans. by D'Assigny (London, 1679), is in reality a translation of Du Bec. See Gerard Langbaine, *An Account of the English Dramatick Poets* (Oxford, 1691), p. 345. Nicholas Rowe in his play *Tamerlane* (London, 1702) follows Du Bec's history. In 1782, Du Bec was again translated (with omissions) into English, this time by Lyonell Vane (*The History of the Life of Tamerlane the Great* [London, 1782]).

[19] Knolles, pp. 210-28.

[20] Samuel Purchas, *Pvrchas his Pilgrimes, Part II* (London, 1625), III, N4ʳ-N4ᵛ (STC 20509): "*whether* [Alhacen was] *an exact Historian, euery where literally to be vnderstood; or whether in some part he be parabolicall, and presents a* Tamerlane *like* Xenophons Cyrus (*in some things rather what he should haue beene, and what the Authour could say, then what he was) I vndertake not to determine. The Abbot of* Mortimer *takes it for a wist Storie, and so doth Master* Knolls."

The second hypothesis apparently flies in the face of known facts, the dates of printing. But, as we have already seen in our previous discussions of Marlowe's source material, we cannot substitute with any confidence the 'printing date' for the 'date of publication' when studying Renaissance literature. Manuscripts circulated freely, and there is every indication that Marlowe did not confine his reading to printed texts.[21] Taking our conjectures one step further, if Du Bec's history were available in manuscript during the 1580's, Marlowe may well have read it. Admittedly the possible link is tenuous, but worth exploring.

Marlowe was in France sometime during the 1580's, and he possibly visited Rheims for an unknown length of time. Probably disguised as a Catholic convert, Marlowe was carrying out some undesignated mission for Elizabeth's government.[22] Beyond these meager details and conjectures, we know almost nothing of his movements. Whether he met Du Bec while in France or had a chance to read his manuscript history, we have no right to guess – but Marlowe's shadowy journey allows us to entertain the possibility.

Another possible point of contact is Richard Knolles, who must have spent a great deal of his life working on Eastern history. Hugh Dick has traced the probabilities of a connection between Knolles and Marlowe through Sir Roger Manwood (1525-92), known to them both.[23] Since Knolles used Du Bec's history and seems to have been a Francophil, it seems likely that, if Du Bec's manuscript were in circulation before 1594, he would have known it and perhaps possessed a copy. If Marlowe read the manuscript while in England, rather than in France, he was most likely introduced to it by Knolles. Or, perhaps Knolles introduced him to the Eastern stories (if indeed there were such) upon which Du Bec's history is based. We do not know. And in the end, it must be admitted that the foregoing paragraphs are a tissue of conjecture meant to suggest possible ways in which Marlowe may have had

[21] See, e.g., Battenhouse, pp. 178-92.
[22] See Boas, *Christopher Marlowe*, pp. 21-28.
[23] Hugh Dick, *SP*, 46 (1949), 154-66. Knolles was the translator of Jean Bodin, *Six Bookes of a Commonweale* (London, 1606).

contact with material that provided him with ideas and incidents for Part Two.

But Du Bec's history is important to the critic of Marlowe's Tamburlaine even if the playwright never saw it; for the history allows us to see how another Renaissance author of the same period, although of a different country, handled the same story. A comparison of the two should help us more clearly to define Marlowe's conception of the conqueror. Du Bec's Tamerlane is a model humanist, a philosopher king. Although a successful general, he understands the evils of war. Du Bec writes:

I wil not forget to declare, that when as this Prince [Tamerlane] did behold so many thousands of men lie dead on the ground where the battaile was fought, he turned himselfe vnto one of his familiars, lamenting the condicion of them who command ouer Armies, & commending the profession of the Emperour his father, he counted him happie, for that hee had sought rest, acknowledging humaine miserie, the which in destroying his owne kind, procured his glorie. That for his part such tokens of victory were sorrowful eue vnto his hart.   (p. 13, sig. B1ʳ)

To a group of Chinese ambassadors, Tamerlane explains that "the endes of the warres, were for the most part enterprises for to come vnto peace, and to make those vnderstand reason, that refused the same" (p. 93, sig. G1ʳ). War is not an instrument of personal ambition.

Again and again, Du Bec underlines Tamerlane's mercy to conquered peoples: "Now in our Prince there was not any thing noted but curtesie vnto the conquered, insomuch as this made him admired and honoured" (p. 61, sig. E1ʳ). He "did mislike of nothing more thē cruelty" (p. 103, sig. G6ʳ). He is often found in prayer (p. 70, sig. E5ᵛ), but he is not a religious bigot:

Now he had all religion in reuerence, so as it did worship one onelie God, creator of all things. He often said, that the greatnes of Diuinitie cōsisted in the sundry kindes of people which are vnder the coape of heauē, who serued the same diuerslie, nourishing it selfe with diuersitie, as the nature was diuers where it had printed his image, God remaining notwithstanding one in his essence, not receiuing therin any diuersitie. This was the reason that mooued him to permit and graunt the vse of all religions within the Countries of his obedience.   (p. 20, sig. B4ᵛ)

Sympathy for the human condition, mercy, piety, and tolerance are the leading personal qualities of the French Tamerlane. In the humanistic tradition, Du Bec uses history to present a mirror for princes.

Tamerlane's English counterpart has none of these good qualities. He never broods over the bodies of the slain, puts whole cities to the sword without mercy, never prays to God, and, after a particularly blasphemous speech, expresses his cosmic skepticism. If Purchas saw Du Bec's Tamerlane as a model ruler, Marlowe's Tamburlaine would have been for him the other side of the coin. Although some critics, like Harry Levin, have argued that Marlowe was following the French humanistic portrait of Tamerlane, a detailed comparison points in another direction.[24] Marlowe is emphasizing the limitations of his character, Tamburlaine's inability to be both conqueror and humanist ruler. In Part Two, it becomes increasingly apparent that Marlowe does not hold Tamburlaine up for admiration.

That Marlowe is underscoring the limitations of Tamburlaine is also seen by a comparison of the conclusions of the history and the play. The final episode of Du Bec's story, a defensive campaign against Callapine, is expanded by Marlowe to provide the action of the entire play. From the aggressor of Part One, where each of the battles is initiated by him, Tamburlaine becomes a ruler who must defend himself against a new generation of Turks. Like Du Bec's Tamerlane, he comes to depend increasingly on his lieutenants. Balsera is besieged and captured, not by him, but by Techelles and Theridamas. When he reviews his conquests at the end of the play, he claims those of his subordinates as his own. But the final irony of Tamburlaine's aspiration for world dominion is his second victory over Callapine, for it is a victory purchased with his own death. At a crucial moment in the progress of his disease, a disease which is literally burning him up inside, Tamburlaine exerts his final fury which disperses the Turkish army, but which

---

[24] Levin, *The Overreacher*, p. 33. See Loys le Roy, *Of the Interchangeable Covrse, or Variety of Things*, p. 108ᵛ, where Tamerlaine denies the "insatiable couetise of conquering countries, or enlarging his dominions". Contrast Marlowe's Tamburlaine.

also proves disastrous to his own health. Ultimately, Tamburlaine's rage is self-destructive. Although Du Bec's Tamerlane also dies after the defeat of the Turks, Du Bec does not indicate that there is any necessary connection of cause and effect. Marlowe, using the history of Scanderbeg, adds the irony of defeat-in-apparent-victory. Tamburlaine has reached the limit of his finite capabilities.

This limitation is further suggested by Tamburlaine's chariot drawn by captive kings. For this dramatic symbol, Marlowe again turns to the emblem tradition. The emblematic fable of Sesostris and his captive kings was often told in the Renaissance. It might be found in books of moral philosophy, like that of Matthieu Coignet:

Sundry writers make mention of K. *Sesostris*, that he made himselfe be drawen by foure Kings which he held captiues, and one of them euer vsed to turne his face backwarde, and being demaunded what he did so, aunswered, that in beholding the wheeles, howe the highest part became lowest, he remembered the condition of men: with which aunswere the same *Sesostris* became a great deale the more ciuill.[25]

Or it might be seen in emblem books, like that of Henry Peacham:

> FOWER Captiue Kinges, proud *Sesostris* did tie,
> And them compeld his charriot to draw,
> Whereof the one, did ever cast his eie
> Vnto the wheele: which them the Tirant saw,
>   And ask'd the cause, the chained King repli'de,
>   Because heerein, my state I haue espi'de.
>
> For like our selues, the spoke that was on high,
> Is to the bottome, in a moment cast,
> As fast the lowest, riseth by and by,
> All humane thinges, thus kind a change at last:
>   The Tyrant fearing, what his hap might be,
>   Releas'd their bandes forthwith, and set them free.[26]

---

[25] Coignet, *Politiqve Discovrses Vpon Trveth and Lying*, p. 178, sig. M3ᵛ. Cf. Barckley, *A Discovrse of the Felicitie of Man*, p. 147, sig. L2ʳ: "The king *Sesostris* was aptly taught the vncertainty of humane thinges .... when ambition and desire of hauing hath possessed a mans mind, what soeuer is sweete and pleasant in this life, is lost."

[26] Henry Peacham, *Minerva Britanna, 1612*, p. 76, appeared too late for Marlowe's

But no matter the source, the meaning was the same: one should come to realize one's human limitations and by this realization treat others humanely. Although Tamburlaine's chariot is also a symbol of earthly change (V.iii.4623-26), he will not acknowledge that it may break from his control. Unlike Sesostris, he refuses to SEE the inevitability of change: whom the gods will destroy, they first make blind. To the playgoer, it should be perfectly clear that Tamburlaine stands in violent contrast to the humanistic tradition with its emphasis on insight and self-analysis.

II. THE PLAY

The second part of *Tamburlaine* is a sequel which concludes the adventures of Tamburlaine, and as with many Elizabethan two-part plays, the sequel is a mirror of the first play.[27] The careful and thoughtful preparations of the Turks at the beginning of Part Two reflect invertedly the witless preparations of Mycetes. Further, both plays begin with a civil conflict (the first between Mycetes and Cosroe, the second between Orcanes and Sigismund), following which Tamburlaine defeats the victors, Cosroe and Orcanes. The episodes are further related because Sigismund essentially assumes, in Part Two, the role of Tamburlaine in the early scenes of Part One. Just as Tamburlaine, taking counsel with his captains, betrays Cosroe in order to win the Persian crown, Sigismund decides to attack Orcanes while his back is turned. In the first part, Tamburlaine wins; in the second, Sigismund is defeated and dies acknowledging his wrongdoing. When Tamburlaine defeats Cosroe, he overcomes a self-seeking usurper; when he defeats and enslaves Orcanes, he overcomes a man who may be as cruel as himself, but who has proved an able warrior in defeating Sigismund. Callapine, Bajazeth's son, takes the place of his father

---

use, but suggests a Renaissance way of looking at the story. Cf. Robert Cockcroft, "Emblematic Irony: Some Possible Significances of Tamburlaine's Chariot", *RMS*, 12 (1968), 33-55, who points to another, wider context.
[27] See Hunter, *RES*, 5 (1954), 236-48.

as Tamburlaine's chief antagonist, and when the armies of
Callapine and Tamburlaine meet, there is the same kind of
stylized verbal warfare we noted in Part One. Again, Tamburlaine
is successful in battle, treating the captured Turks like animals.
In place of the siege and razing of Damascus, there is the conquest
of Babylon, followed by a final battle in which Tamburlaine is
victorious. Like the Soldan of Egypt in Part One, Callapine
escapes from this battle with his life. Marlowe is at some pains
to connect the action of the two plays, and an exploration of the
themes of Part Two should suggest why he built these parallels.

In many ways, the Tamburlaine of the second play is the same
character as the Tamburlaine of Part One. The thematic patterns
which earlier distinguished him re-emerge here. Tamburlaine
still proclaims that he can make war against heaven. As he is dying,
he blusters:

> What daring God torments my body thus,
> And seeks to conquer mighty *Tamburlaine*,
> Shall sicknesse prooue me now to be a man,
> That haue been tearm'd the terrour of the world?
> *Techelles* and the rest, come take your swords,
> And threaten him whose hand afflicts my soul,
> Come let vs march against the powers of heauen,
> And set blacke streamers in the firmament,
> To signifie the slaughter of the Gods.   (V.iii.4434-42)

Concurrently, he still claims divine sanction for his actions: "Thus
am I right the Scourge of highest *Ioue*" (IV.iii.4003), and makes
the metaphor literally true by scourging the pampered jades of
Asia with his whip (3980). We find him still using the high astounding terms to cover his less than virtuous deeds: both Apollo
and Hercules are invoked to hide the barbarous act of hitching
men to his chariot (3986-95). In his final battle, as in his first, his
"royall presence" dismays "the enemy" (V.iii.4504-05). Tamburlaine's appearance remains a vital force.

But there are significant changes in emphasis, and as we have
seen in our exploration of the background, the theme of education,
for the first and the last time in Marlowe's drama, becomes an
important part of the action. Since education is usually linked

with permanence and continuity, it is ironic that the education
theme here suggests the impermanence and limitation of human
achievement. As one of his chief objectives Tamburlaine wishes to
educate his three sons[28] so that they are able to take his place as
Conqueror of the World. "Be al a scourge and terror to the world,
/ Or els you are not sons of *Tamburlaine*" (I.iv.2632-33). But
Calyphas, the recalcitrant and effeminate oldest son, finds his
father's warlike teaching less than palatable. To his father's
exhortations, he replies:

> But while my brothers follow armes my lord
> Let me accompany my gratious mother,
> They are enough to conquer all the world
> And you haue won enough for me to keep.   (I.iv.2634-37)

Cowardly perhaps, Calyphas displays a facet of humanity that
Tamburlaine cannot comprehend. Calyphas realizes a certain
moderation in his desires; "enough" is sufficient for his happiness.
Tamburlaine's response:

> Bastardly boy, sprong from some cowards loins:
> And not the issue of great *Tamburlaine*,
> Of all the prouinces I haue subdued
> Thou shalt not haue a foot,   (I.iv.2638-41)

represents his immoderate response to all stimuli. His own im-
perviousness to fear possibly makes Calyphas appear even more
cowardly than he is.

---

[28] Although there is a hint of recurring triads in *1 Tamburlaine*, Part Two appears
to have a greater emphasis on groupings of three. As the play begins, the Turks
are presented by Orcanes, Gazellus, and Vribassa; they are met by the three
Hungarians, Sigismund, Fredericke, and Baldwine. When Tamburlaine and
Zenocrate first appear, they are accompanied by their three sons, and are met by
their three returning henchmen. In the next scene, the three Hungarians re-
appear; and in the next, the three Turks (II.i, and II.ii). After the Turko-
Hungarian battle, Zenocrate appears surrounded by her three physicians, the
three henchmen, and her three sons. Apparently the three physicians return at
Tamburlaine's illness (V.iii). Olympia, her husband, and her son form a family
of three; Callapine has three tributory kings; and so on. The recurring triads
suggest a formal balance in the play, and we may believe that their appearance
here is planned. The point is that few of these groups are left undisrupted.
Sigismund is killed, disrupting the Hungarian triad; the Turks are captured and
enslaved by Tamburlaine; Tamburlaine kills one of his sons; Olympia and her
family die. The perfection implicit in the triad is set up only to be destroyed.

At the same time, Calyphas ironically undercuts his father's belligerent speeches. After Tamburlaine describes all the martial activities he will teach his sons how to perform, Calyphas skeptically and realistically notices:

> My Lord, but this is dangerous to be done,
> We may be slaine or wounded ere we learne.   (III.ii.3283-84)

His initial "My Lord" sounds almost like an exclamation of disbelief, and indeed the situation is potentially comic. Calyphas is using his father as a 'straight man'. In one way, the wide-eyed innocence of his reply may remind us of the simpleton Mycetes, but in another, his realistic evaluation of military honor reminds us of Falstaff on the fields of Shrewsbury.

Tamburlaine is again driven to question his son's parentage; and to teach him that a wound is "nothing", Tamburlaine cuts his own arm, declaring that "Blood is the God of Wars rich liuery" (III.ii.3305-06). He demands that the boys "search" the self-inflicted wound with their fingers and "wash" their hands in his blood, while he will "sit smiling to behold the sight" (3316-18). The scene may remind us of Shakespeare's *Julius Caesar* where the conspirators wash in Caesar's blood, or possibly of *Titus Andronicus* where Lavinia is poetically turned into a fountain of blood, but on another level of reference, it should remind us of Christian myth, of purification through sacred blood, of Thomas's searching Christ's wound, of ritual redemption. In contrast, the ritual celebration here is one of initiation into martial life: it is part of the warrior's education in bloodshed and destruction. As a young man who had studied theology, Marlowe must have understood this contrast between Tamburlaine and Christ, and, in any case, it is suggestive. If Christ came to save, Tamburlaine comes to destroy. Celebinus and Amyras respond positively to their father's wound: "giue me a wound father" (3322), while Calyphas has a confused, but human reaction: "I know not what I should think of it. Me thinks tis a pitifull sight" (III.ii.3320-21). Calyphas misinterprets his father's lesson. As Tamburlaine explains, the wound should "Teach you my boyes to beare couragious minds, / Fit for the followers of great *Tamburlaine*" (III.ii.3333-34). But to a certain type of sensibility, a wound may not excite valor or blood lust.

Before the initial battle with Callapine, Calyphas's brothers try to persuade him to take part in the fight. His answers clearly indicate the sensuous aspect of his nature, but they also point to a latent humanitarianism. To the warlike Amyras, he says:

> I know sir, what it is to kil a man,
> It works remorse of conscience in me,
> I take no pleasure to be murtherous,
> Nor care for blood when wine wil quench my thirst.
>
> (IV.i.3700-03)

Calyphas gives a civilian answer to a military mentality. Again, the juxtaposition of "blood" and "wine" may underline a theological dimension, and it certainly stands for the difference between death and life. Calyphas functions to remind the playgoer of the part of human existence which Tamburlaine does not understand and cannot tolerate. His inability to deal with Calyphas in a positive way is a severe but not surprising limitation. After he has put Callapine to flight, Tamburlaine addresses his sons:

> Stand vp my boyes, and I wil teach ye arms,
> And what the iealousie of warres must doe.   (IV.i.3777-78)

Having decided that Calyphas is unteachable, he kills him in cold blood.[29] Obviously this solution to the problem of 'unteachable students' has a very limited application. Or, at least, we hope so.

One critic has claimed, however, that the teaching pattern in

---

[29] Kocher (*Christopher Marlowe*, p. 263) defends Tamburlaine's stabbing of Calyphas as part of military discipline. Iue's translation of *Instructions for the Warres* contains a list of military offenses punishable by death. One is: "Whoeuer shall disobey the cryes that the Drummes and Trumpets shall make: specially if the said cries be made vpon paine of the heart, or vpon paine of death" (p. 263, sig. T4ʳ). Apparently Calyphas is guilty of this offence. However, another rule of war reads: "Whoeuer shall rauish any woman" shall be punished by death (p. 263, sig. T4ʳ). If Tamburlaine strictly follows the code in condemning his son – a place where the rules might be relaxed somewhat – he should also follow it in not giving the Turkish women up to his common soldiers (IV.iii.4060-64). In any case, Tamburlaine's murder of Calyphas is not presented as an act of justice.

Part Two is Marlowe's personal endorsement of the humanistic emphasis on education.[30] According to humanists like Ascham, education when used properly was a deterrent to the 'effeminacy' of the Italianate Englishman. Since Tamburlaine is trying to educate his sons, and since he decries the effeminacy of Calyphas, it may be argued that he is following a humanistic credo. But the argument overlooks, or must gloss over, some pertinent details. As far as we see in the play, the education which Tamburlaine wishes for his sons is purely military, an education designed to make them conquering soldiers, not philosopher kings. Although the sons may be able to read several languages, Tamburlaine never asks them to read a book. If we may again use Du Bec's Tamerlane as a model of the humanist prince, we can easily see that the education proposed by Marlowe's protagonist has little or nothing to do with Renaissance humanism.

The major flaw in his program of education is that it excludes any comparison and teaches that the student must, in himself, become an absolute. To teach each of the three sons this doctrine is shortsighted, for ultimately they must destroy each other vying for supremacy. Although Tamburlaine's teaching is not presented as completely self-destructive in the play, we know from the histories which Marlowe read that Tamburlaine's empire collapsed after his death because of the internecine struggles of his sons.[31] The thoughtful playgoer, who cares to contemplate what may be the outcome of Tamburlaine's actions, will find the seeds of dissolution in his misguided form of education. Tamburlaine has educated his sons for absolute war, but has done nothing to prepare them for the arts of peace. If anything, then, the educational pattern in the play is ironic; the purpose of education is continuity, ordered change, survival; it should, if it is humanistically oriented, stress the social duties, what one owes to his fellow men.

---

[30] T. M. Pearce, "Tamburlaine's 'Discipline to His Three Sonnes': An Interpretation of *Tamburlaine, Part II*", *MLQ*, 15 (1954), 18-27.

[31] See, e.g., Whetstone, *The English Myrror*, p. 82, and Thomas Fortescue (trans.), *The Forest or Collection of Historyes*, by Pedro Mexia (London, 1576), p. 87ʳ (STC 17850).

Tamburlaine's failure to change Calyphas through his brand of education is linked with another thematic pattern: unfaithfulness. Tamburlaine interprets the recalcitrance of Calyphas as a form of treachery: "traitor", he calls him, "to my name and maiesty" (IV.i.3764). This is a new experience for Tamburlaine. In Part One, no one had proved unfaithful to him; all had obeyed his command; no one had failed him. In the second part, the failure to obey extends even to his son. The first traitor to Tamburlaine, however, is Almeda, Callapine's jailor, who releases the young Turk to gain a kingdom: "Shall I be made a king for my labour?" (I.iii.2553-54). Callapine assures him that he shall, and the price is right for betrayal:

> as I am *Almeda*,
> Your Keeper vnder *Tamburlaine* the great,
> (For that's the style and tytle I haue yet)
> Although he sent a thousand armed men
> To intercept this haughty enterprize,
> Yet would I venture to conduct your Grace,
> And die before I brought you backe again.   (2558-64)

The scene mirrors Tamburlaine's seduction of Theridamas in Part One. The reversal, with Callapine as seducer, suggests the inability of Tamburlaine to control the action with his former ease and initially makes us feel that Callapine will be a worthy opponent.

Of course, as we follow the fortunes of Almeda through the play, we come to realize that they do not fully parallel those of Theridamas, who successfully betrayed his master. When he confronts Tamburlaine, Almeda cowers beneath his scorn, and comically asks permission to accept the crown proffered by Callapine. After Callapine's first defeat, Almeda disappears from the play. He is not another Theridamas, but a lesser character, just as Callapine does not, finally, rival Tamburlaine in his abilities or his desires. The new men desire the earthly crown, not universal dominion; they are controlled by their limitations; they will not destroy the world in their lust for power. Almeda's failure to attain even his limited aspiration, only a kingdom, is part of the pattern of failure that marks the play.

This pattern of treachery and failure is foreshadowed in the first and second acts by Sigismund's decision to attack Orcanes after having given him an oath that he would not: "By him that made the world and sau'd my soule / The sonne of God and issue of a Mayd, / Sweet Iesus Christ, I sollemnly protest, / And vow to keepe this peace inuiolable" (I.ii.2458-61). Sigismund's counselors, Fredericke and Baldwine, however, encourage him to break this vow in order to "worke reuenge vpon these Infidels" (II.i. 2807) for past defeats. They argue that Christians should not keep oaths to Pagans: "what we vow to them should not infringe / Our liberty of armes and victory" (2834-35), and that "tis superstition / To stand so strictly on dispensiue faith" (2843-44). When Sigismund attacks the weakened Turkish army, the Moslem Orcanes rather ironically appeals to Christ for victory, a victory which follows shortly. Sigismund interprets his defeat as God's "thundered vengeance from on high, / For [his] accurst and hatefull periurie" (II.ii.2923-24), and dies repentant. Although Gazellus calls him "the periur'd traitor *Hungary*" (2933), and Orcanes envisions him in hell, Marlowe gives no clear indication of his posthumous fate. Nonetheless, Sigismund has come to a realization about moral causation, and his death at the beginning of the play may adumbrate Tamburlaine's death at the end.

By beginning Part Two with these incidents of unsuccessful treachery, Marlowe points to a quality of the new dramatic world. Although the Marlovian world is always one of evil action and idea, here we see the failure of evil from the start. Evil is introduced as self-destructive. Furthermore, the straightforward military conquests of Part One modulate into the deceit and treachery of Part Two. Very subtly Tamburlaine's world has changed, and with it, Tamburlaine's good fortune.

The second part might, with some degree of accuracy, be called "Callapine's Revenge". Callapine is obsessed with the idea of revenge on Tamburlaine. He ends his first scene with the promise: "Now goe I to reuenge my fathers death" (I.iii.2569), and when we see him with his warriors, he again threatens to make Tamburlaine bear "the vengeance of our fathers wrongs" (III.i.3128). Through most of his first confrontation with Tamburlaine,

Callapine remains silent while Tamburlaine rants; but during a hiatus in the fustian, he reiterates: "Raile not proud Scythian, I shall now reuenge / My fathers vile abuses and mine owne" (III. v.3592-93). Although Callapine's first attempt to revenge himself ends in failure, the audience awaits, with some anticipation, Callapine's next attempt. As he and his subordinate, the King of Amasia, prepare for another assault on Tamburlaine's army, Callapine again contemplates vengeance:

> When I record my Parents slauish life,
> Their cruel death, mine owne captiuity,
> My Viceroies bondage vnder *Tamburlaine*,
> Me thinks I could sustaine a thousand deaths,
> To be reueng'd of all his Villanie.   (V.ii.4352-56)

We have already noted that Callapine and his army flee from Tamburlaine's very appearance on the battlefield. But, at the same time, Tamburlaine is unsuccessful in recapturing him: "could I but a while pursue the field, / That *Callapine* should be my slaue againe" (V.iii.4510-11). No longer is Tamburlaine able to hold his slaves in absolute bonds, and Bajazeth's son remains alive to nurse his obsessive vengeance against Tamburlaine's children.

The revenge motif suggests a quality of the action. Callapine's determination to revenge his dead parents puts Tamburlaine on the defensive, in contrast to his offensive wars in Part One. Although he is able to hold the kingdoms he has collected under his aegis, Death proves to be a monarch who cannot be held at bay as Callapine is. The revenge plot leads us back, then, to what we have sensed as a central element of Part Two: the comparative passivity of Tamburlaine, who is not the initiator of action, but the character against whom the action is initiated. The revenge plot, furthermore, introduces a suggestion of moral cause and effect. In Part One, Zenocrate felt that Tamburlaine's savage treatment of Bajazeth and Zabina might call forth a moral reaction, but in the first part, there is none. Callapine, by emphasizing that his revenge is motivated by Tamburlaine's mistreatment of his parents, becomes a symbol of the necessary reaction to Tamburlaine's evil.

Nevertheless, revenge is a wild kind of justice, not calculated to bring order and sanity in its wake. Basically, the world of the play is geared to destruction, and this destructive quality is perhaps most adequately suggested by the imagery of fire. Although Marlovian scholars and critics have noticed his penchant for flames,[32] 'fire' is as particularly pertinent here as in *Dido*. Fire provides not only the metaphor, but also the means for destroying. When Zenocrate dies, Tamburlaine irrationally vows:

> This cursed towne will I consume with fire,
> Because this place bereft me of my Loue:
> The houses burnt, wil looke as if they mourn'd.   (II.iii.3105-07)

The stage directions suggest that some attempt was made to simulate a burning city, but in any case, Tamburlaine describes what we are to image:

> So, burne the turrets of this cursed towne,
> Flame to the highest region of the aire:
> And kindle heaps of exhalations,
> That being fiery meteors, may presage,
> Death and destruction to th'inhabitants.   (III.ii.3191-95)

A fire also blazes at the death of Olympia's husband and son. She tells Theridamas that she has burnt their bodies, and later begs:

> Take pitie of a Ladies ruthfull teares,
> That humbly craues vpon her knees to stay,
> And cast her bodie in the burning flame,
> That feeds vpon her sonnes and husbands flesh.   (III.iv.3480-83)

As at the end of *Dido*, a funeral pyre dominates the stage.

After his first battle with the Turks, Tamburlaine promises to "vtterly consume" their cities and palaces, and "with the flames that beat against the clowdes / Incense the heauens, and make the starres to melt" (IV.i.3867, 3869-70). And though we do not witness him carrying out this threat, he later has the Koran burnt on stage: "let there be a fire presently" (V.i.4289). Fire, with all its suggestions of destruction and aspiration, is Tamburlaine's

---

[32] See, e.g., Marion Bodwell Smith, *Marlowe's Imagery and the Marlowe Canon* (Philadelphia, 1940), p. 41.

element. It is therefore highly appropriate, in the scheme of moral causality, that he should be burnt up from within: "Your vaines are full of accidentall heat", his physician tells him, "Whereby the moisture of your blood is dried" (V.iii.4476-77). "The liuely spirits which the heart ingenders / Are partcht and void of spirit" (4486-87).[33] The man who has destroyed by fire dies in "burning agony" (4602).

It is one of the final ironies of the play that Tamburlaine places his son Amyras in his chariot with the admonition:

> As precious is the charge thou vndertak'st
> As that which *Clymenes* brainsicke sonne did guide,
> When wandring *Phoebes* Iuory cheeks were scortcht
> And all the earth like *AEtna* breathing fire:
> Be warn'd by him .... (4623-27)

The fate of the father may well foreshadow the fate of the son. The allusion subtly indicates that Amyras, like Phaeton, does not have the control necessary to guide the chariot of fire, and his inability will lead to destruction for both the charioteer and his world.

The series of minor *de casibus* tragedies, which give unity to Part One, did not closely touch Tamburlaine and his associates. These tragedies formed steppingstones in their rise to power. But in the second part, a personified Death broods over the action. Olympia invokes him, almost as a lover, to take her and her son:

> Death, whether art thou gone that both we liue?
> Come back again (sweet death) & strike vs both:

---

[33] Thomas Adams (*Diseases of the Sovle* [London, 1616], STC 109) suggests a relationship between physical and spiritual diseases. "There is a disease in the bodie called *immoderate thirst*; ... By this I would (I suppose not vnfitly) expresse that *spirituall* disease, Ambition, a proud soules thirst, when a draught of honour causeth a drought of honour. ... The disease is caused in the body, through abundant heate drying vp moysture; and this is done by hot, cholericke, or salt humours engendred in the stomacke, or through Feuers burning or Ecticke. ... The *cause* of Ambition is a strong opinion of honour; how well he could become a high place, or a high place him. ... Hee professeth a new quality, called the art of climbing: wherin he teacheth other by patterne, not so much to aspire, as to break their neckes" (pp. 39-40, sigs. F4ʳ-F4ᵛ). Although too late for Marlowe to have seen in print, this passage forms an apt commentary on Tamburlaine's fever.

One minute end our daies, and one sepulcher
Containe our bodies: death, why comm'st thou not?
Wel, this [i.e., a knife] must be the messenger for thee.
Now vgly death stretch out thy Sable wings,
And carie both our soules, where his [her husband's] remaines.

(III.iv.3422-28)

Moreover, Part Two brings death closer to the core characters –
to Tamburlaine and Zenocrate, to their three sons, and to their
three captains.

In II.iii, Zenocrate sickens and begins to die. Although Tamburlaine insists that the glories of the earth have been made only "To
entertaine deuine *Zenocrate*", when he asks, "how fares my faire
Zenocrate?" she replies:

I fare my Lord, as other Emperesses,
That when this fraile and transitory flesh
Hath suckt the measure of that vitall aire
That feeds the body with his dated health,
Wanes with enforst and necessary change.   (II.iii.3010-14)

Zenocrate is not deluded by the extravagance of Tamburlaine's
language; she understands too well that humans are mortal, and
that change is inevitable no matter how much we strain after
permanence. Tamburlaine's answer, "May neuer such a change
transfourme my loue" (3015), reveals his basic failure to recognize
that he and his must accommodate themselves to universal
necessity. His vision is limited and thus darkly comic. After
Zenocrate's death, he attempts to deny, or perhaps even to control,
change by embalming her body "with Cassia, Amber Greece and
Myrre", and placing the corpse "in a sheet of gold" which shall
be carried with him (3098-3100). Without commenting on the
morbidity of his conception, we understand that Tamburlaine
cannot preserve life, but only the dead carcass, the empty shell.
His vaunted mastership of death has been a fable; he has been
able only to take life, not to restore it. He may not have reached
the limits of destruction, but he quickly reaches the limits of
restoration.

These same limits are suggested in Olympia's story. Longing
for death so that she may follow her dead family, Olympia tells

Theridamas that no "discourse is pleasant" to her ears, but "tha
where euery period ends with death, / And euery line begins witl
death againe" (IV.ii.3927-29). Nevertheless, she promises Theri
damas that she will give him a present which will allow him to
transcend human frailty, to resist change:

> An ointment which a cunning Alcumist
> Distilled from the purest Balsamum,
> And simplest extracts of all Minerals,
> In which the essentiall fourme of Marble stone,
> Tempered by science metaphisicall,
> And Spels of magicke from the mouthes of spirits,
> With which if you but noint your tender Skin,
> Nor Pistol, Sword, nor Lance can pierce your flesh.
>
> (IV.ii.3940-47)

Her claim is entirely specious. In this play, in contrast to Ariosto's
Orlando Furioso from which the incident is derived, there is no
simple against mortality.[34] However, Theridamas, like Tambur-
laine, will not be easily convinced of the inevitable. When Olympia
volunteers to show him the efficacy of the magic fluid, he does not
hesitate to strike her with his sword. His lament over her dead
body parallels Tamburlaine's for Zenocrate:

> Now Hell is fairer than *Elisian*,
> A greater Lamp than that bright eie of heauen,
> From whence the starres doo borrow all their light,
> Wanders about the black circumference,
> And now the damned soules are free from paine,
> For euery Fury gazeth on her lookes:
> Infernall *Dis* is courting of my Loue.
>
> (3968-74)

In his comparable speech, Tamburlaine laments:

> *Zenocrate* that gaue [the sun] light and life,
> Whose eies shot fire from their Iuory bowers,
> And tempered euery soule with liuely heat,
> Now by the malice of the angry Skies,

---

[34] John Payne Collier (*The History of English Dramatic Poetry to the Time of Shakespeare: and Annals of the Stage to the Restoration* [London, 1879], II, 497-98) first noted the source. In *Orlando Furioso*, the eponymous hero is immune to physical injury.

Whose iealousie admits no second Mate,
Drawes in the comfort of her latest breath
All dasled with the hellish mists of death.
...
For amorous *Ioue* hath snatcht my loue from hence,
Meaning to make her stately Queene of heauen.

                                    (II.iii.2976-82, 3075-76)

Both ladies are the lights of this world, and after their deaths, all
is darkness. Olympia's death at Theridamas's hands may, however, be a kind of darkly comic scene which contrasts with the
serious death of Zenocrate. A sophisticated playgoer could hardly
restrain himself from grinning at Theridamas's incredulous "What,
haue I slaine her?" (3963). The two scenes tend to reinforce each
other as well as the theme of human limitation. But there is also
the view, more pronounced in Tamburlaine's lament, that the
divinities of the world envy man's felicity, that there is a kind of
divine malevolence operating in death.

In contrast is Olympia's view of death. Although death is
horrible enough to her, she does not see it as basically evil. Through
death, she will be reunited with her husband. Before her capture
by the Scythians, she asks her son:

Tell me sweet boie, art thou content to die?
These barbarous Scythians full of cruelty,
...
Will hew vs peecemeale, put vs to the wheele,
Or els inuent some torture worse than that,
Therefore die by thy louing mothers hand,
Who gently now wil lance thy Iuory throat,
And quickly rid thee both of paine and life.   (3429-30, 3432-36)

"Sweet mother strike", he answers, "that I may meet my father"
(3441). Like his mother, the child emphasizes the positive aspects
of dying, and in context his death at his mother's hands should be
seen as an affirmation of faith. Neither Olympia nor her son sees
death as a limitation imposed by an envious or angry god, but as
a needed and merciful limit on human existence. Theirs is a
rational acceptance of the inevitable.

Moreover, Olympia's sacrifice of her son forms a parallel to

Tamburlaine's murder of Calyphas, his unwarlike son. Since Calyphas has not lived up to his father's expectations and has continued to question his military values, Tamburlaine in a kind of inverted religious rite kills him:

> Here *Ioue*, receiue his fainting soule againe,
> A Forme not meet to giue that subiect essence,
> Whose matter is the flesh of *Tamburlain*,
> Wherein an incorporeall spirit mooues,
> Made of the mould whereof thy selfe consists,
> Which makes me valiant, proud, ambitious,
> Ready to leuie power against thy throne,
> That I might mooue the turning Spheares of heauen,
> For earth and al this aery region
> Cannot containe the state of *Tamburlaine*.   (IV.i.3785-94)

At this point, Tamburlaine dispatches Calyphas and continues his ranting speech by assuring God that He has procured, in sending Tamburlaine's "issue such a soule" (3796), a greater enemy than the rebellious Giants. Tamburlaine shakes a warning finger at God.

The Turkish prisoners are shocked by the blasphemous murder, and Orcanes voices their reaction: "Thou shewest the difference twixt our selues and thee / In this thy barbarous damned tyranny" (3812-13). The difference between Tamburlaine and the rest of humanity is also underscored by Olympia's prayer after she has killed her child:

> Ah sacred *Mahomet*, if this be sin,
> Intreat a pardon of the God of heauen,
> And purge my soule before it come to thee.   (III.iv.3442-44)

Tamburlaine's proud (and ridiculous) threatening is set against the humility of Olympia. She kills her child to save him from pain; Tamburlaine kills his because he believes the child unworthy of the father. The positive and the negative aspects of death are again juxtaposed. Tamburlaine and his men are the same negative destructive forces they were in Part I, but here their power becomes self-destructive, turns inward. Tamburlaine kills his son; Theridamas kills his love. The pattern of death prepares for the final death: Tamburlaine's. The personified Death, invoked by Olympia, comes uncalled to stalk Tamburlaine. "My slaue", says

Tamburlaine, "the vglie monster death / Shaking and quiuering, pale and wan for feare, / Stands aiming at me with his murthering dart" (4459-61). In the course of the final scene, he comes to recognize that Death, not Tamburlaine, is the "Monarke of the earth" (4609). Like Agydas in Part One, Tamburlaine, at his master's command, destroys himself in a final fury of action, burnt up from within.

Most critics, I believe, would agree that the second part of *Tamburlaine* is concerned with human limitations;[35] but they might very well disagree on how to interpret this theme. Roy Battenhouse, for example, feels that lines 4290-4329 are crucial to an interpretation of Tamburlaine's death. Here Tamburlaine declares that there is no God of love, but a divinity "full of reuenging wrath" whose "Scourge" he is (V.i.4294-96), thus implicitly denying the Christian ethos. He continues by denying "*Mahomet*" (4309), and desires his followers to adore the "God that sits in heauen, if any God" (4312). The touch of skepticism – "if any God" – possibly reveals the basis for his religious liberalism. For his blasphemy, Battenhouse suggests, Tamburlaine becomes ill sixteen lines later: "I feele my selfe distempered sudainly" (4329). The argument is that Tamburlaine's pride and cruelty are causally connected with his final sickness and that this sickness is part of a divine judgment on Tamburlaine's career.

In reply to this kind of argument, J. D. Jump argues that there is nothing at all to indicate that Tamburlaine's final illness is caused by his challenge to divinity; and though "certain incidents in Part II serve to define the limits of Tamburlaine's power", we cannot call these limitations "'setbacks'" for Tamburlaine:

In Part II, then, the self-assertive, ambitious man confronts the limits imposed upon his power by the natures of the persons involved and the mortality to which all are subject. Within these limits, however, Tamburlaine continues to carry everything before him and is at the most victorious immediately before his death.[36]

---

[35] See, e.g., Helen Gardner, "The Second Part of *Tamburlaine the Great*", *MLR*, 37 (1942), 18-24, and Susan Richards, "Marlowe's *Tamburlaine II*: A Drama of Death", *MLQ*, 26 (1965), 375-87.

[36] J. D. Jump (ed.), *Tamburlaine the Great*, pp. xix-xx.

Although we may wish to qualify Jump's final assertion, we may yet recognize that his overall interpretation is a possible one for the play. Perhaps no dramatic judgment is intended by the emphasis on limitation.

The two interpretations clearly point in opposite directions, toward a negative view of Tamburlaine as a type of anti-Christ and toward a positive view of him as a glorious military leader. The limitations have been built into the play either as a sign of auctorial censure or as merely some kind of natural boundary within which the hero is contained. But no matter how we wish to see the boundary, because of its presence in the play, the hero is limited, restrained. Tamburlaine, however, declares recurrently that he is not subject to mortal limits: he is the favorite of an angry god, or an unconquerable Titanic rebel against divine omnipotence. And the human frailty that he exhibits, no matter how much he may claim that he is free, indicates that his bluster is merely bluster. Materially he may be as powerful as he says: he may conquer the world, or embalm the dead body of his wife and so preserve the flesh from which the soul has fled; but he cannot coerce heaven, nor can he retrieve the soul departed from the body. The contrast between his boasted power and his actual inability to control the most essential events of human existence is an implied comment on his frailty. The aspirer is subject to material limits, especially when he sets those limits by his own materialism.

Blind to moral and spiritual facts, Tamburlaine takes the egocentric position to its psychotic extreme. Looking at the sky, he sees the heavenly bodies designed to entertain his wife. The assertions of his centrality in the universal system are not new to the second part; from the beginning, he is the mouthpiece of human *braggadocio*. But here the contrast between his words and his failures takes the place of the contrast between his rhetoric and his brutal deeds which we have seen in Part One. Zenocrate dies; Almeda betrays him; Calyphas refuses to obey; Callapine remains an uncaptured opponent; and in the end, Tamburlaine dies. The bragging must be measured against the failures. The theatrical illusion, by which many are taken in, that Tamburlaine is the center of his universe is a Marlovian irony. It is the illusion which Tamburlaine himself tries to project, but which is constantly undercut by the reality of his weakness, by his inability to make his world in his own image. He may attempt the godlike act of creation, but he achieves only self-destruction. He is ultimately absurd. Posturing feebly before infinity, he is comic in his exaggeration of his finite powers, the ancestor of Fielding's Jonathan Wild, a cosmic clown.

But we must return briefly to the relationship of the two parts of the play. In the first part, Tamburlaine initiates a series of destructive actions, each one implementing his power and prestige. As he increases in military strength, he loses proportionally a degree of audience sympathy. Each of the deaths he causes is more poignant, demanding more sympathy for the sufferer and less for the perpetrator. Finally, when Tamburlaine places the crown of blood on Zenocrate's head amid the slaughtered bodies of Turks, Egyptians, and Arabians, a sensitive playgoer can hardly be expected to applaud his valiant conquests. Tamburlaine has won, but he has become an emblem of man's inhumanity to man, and we see the price of military greatness.

The second part clarifies the meaning of the first. Tamburlaine's destructive actions bring about their own destructive reactions, and Marlowe emphasizes the limitations of human power. If the central idea of Part One is that absolute power corrupts absolutely, then perhaps that of Part Two is that human power is ephemeral, a loan, never a permanent possession. All living creatures, even those with the greatest pretensions, ambitions, and conquests, will come to THIS. The playgoer is asked to view the career of Tamburlaine through the skeptical eyes of Montaigne, who saw, with that morose Biblical Preacher, that "there is no constant existence. ... And we, and our judgment, and all mortal things else do incessantly roll, turn, and pass away."[37] Or, as Peele put it: "Tamburlaine triumph not, for thou must die / As Philip did,

---

[37] Montaigne, *An Apology of Raymond Sebond,* in *Selected Essays of Montaigne in the Translation of John Florio,* ed. by Walter Kaiser (Boston: Houghton Mifflin, 1964), p. 244.

Caesar, and Caesars peeres."[38] Part Two is a *memento mori* for
Renaissance conquistadors. Even the greatest of conquerors will
die.

[38] Peele, *The Battle of Alcazar*, I.ii.224-25, in *The Dramatic Works of George Peele*
(New Haven: Yale University Press, 1961), II, 304. Cf. R. H., *Arraignment of
the VVhole Creatvre*, p. 248, sig. Ii4ᵛ.

VII

DOCTOR FAUSTUS

After a century of intensive criticism, *Doctor Faustus* has undoubtedly revealed most, and perhaps all, of its esthetic secrets. Possibly
the most that the critical Johnny-come-lately may hope for is to
put some of this accumulated knowledge in his own words and to
provide a new context. For this study, *Faustus* is the final member
of a trilogy on power, and, at the same time, it is Marlowe's third
attempt (counting the two parts of *Tamburlaine*) at a monodrama
in which the protagonist dominates the action. Here the aspirations
which were confined to the natural world in *Tamburlaine* take on
metaphysical dimensions. Faustus wishes to enter and to control
the world of spirits. If we see the two parts of *Tamburlaine* as
experimental, in the sense that in them Marlowe first discovered
and used the kind of drama for which he is best known, then
Faustus turns experiment into subtlety. If *Tamburlaine* is a brass
band, *Faustus* is a delicate flute.

Nonetheless, this chapter begins with a bleak outlook for origi-
nality, but then *Faustus* is a basically bleak play for all its humor
and movement. The learned Doctor Faustus does very little to
alienate the audience; he commits no murders, no actual robberies.
He may delude a peasant or two (with various tricks centered
around hay rather than corn), and he certainly proves spiteful
toward the kind Old Man who tries to save his soul; but these
actions come after a life which is virtually harmless. Faustus is in
the main a simple trickster. His pranks played on the Pope and
Cardinals would hardly antagonize a Protestant English audience,
and he is properly dutiful to all Christian rulers. The bleakness
of the play results from Faustus's damnation, his selling his im-

mortal jewel to become a comedian and the outcome of that sale. The deaths of Tamburlaine and the Guise were hardly calculated to make us bewail their undeserved ends, but with Faustus, there is an apparent difference.

But perhaps the difference is only apparent; and the playgoer may be as deluded about the harmlessness of the German wizard as the wizard himself is deluded about his pact with the devil and, indeed, about the nature of his universe. Faustus firmly believes (in his diabolical faith) that he will inherit the grandeur of the earth, that he will (to use his words):

> be great Emperour of the world,
> And make a bridge, through the mouing Aire,
> To passe the Ocean: with a band of men
> I'le ioyne the Hils that bind the *Affrick* shore,
> And make that Country, continent to *Spaine*,
> And both contributory to my Crowne.   (B 329-34)[1]

Rather subtly through the voice of the Chorus, Marlowe has already warned us that these deeds which Faustus imagines for himself will not be realized:

> Not marching in the fields of *Thrasimen*,
> Where *Mars* did mate the warlicke *Carthagens*,
> Nor sporting in the dalliance of loue
> In Courts of Kings, where state is ouer-turn'd
> Nor in the pompe of proud audacious deeds,
> Intends our Muse to vaunt his heauenly verse.   (B 2-7)

Faustus will not be like Marlowe's earlier plays, chronicles of love and war. The playgoer will not be astounded by Faustus's "audacious deeds", and though the playgoer may be deceived, he has been forewarned.

---

[1] The text used throughout this chapter is W. W. Greg (ed.), *Marlowe's Doctor Faustus, 1604-1616: Parallel Texts* (Oxford: Clarendon, 1950). The letter A refers to the 1604 text; B, to the 1616. Most citations made here are to the B text which both Greg and Leo Kirschbaum (ed.), *The Plays of Christopher Marlowe*, pp. 461-64, have notably defended. In the prose passages, Greg's slash marks indicative of line endings are deleted. The plot of the play is based on the *Historia von D. Johann Fausten*, perhaps in English translation, *The Historie of the Damnable Life, and Deserued Death of Doctor Iohn Fausten* (London, 1592), STC 10711. A modernized, but convenient version of this translation has been published by William Rose (ed.) (Notre Dame: University of Notre Dame Press, 1963).

The delusion of Faustus begins in the first scene where he examines the various disciplines of learning which he may adopt as his life-long vocations. To a Renaissance man who took religion and religious life seriously, the choice of a vocation was not simply a matter of personal preference. It had spiritual overtones of everlasting consequences. As Jean de L'Espine writes: "God hath commanded euery man to be careful and vigilant in matters appertaining to his charge and vocation."[2] We must at the same time "in all our actions haue a charitable regard of our neighbours", since the vocation is not only a personal but a social obligation.[3] The "passion and perturbation of the minde" which hinders us from effectively following our calling is "Curiositie". This "infectious and diseased humour" entices us "to be importunate to know but vnprofitable and vnnecessary matters, and to interpose our selues in many things either cleane contrarie, or quite beside our vocation and calling."[4] Curiosity is engendered partly from ambition, partly from covetousness, and partly from envy. But there are other factors involved:

This is also a great cause of our curiositie, when as we disdain and contemne our callings, as esteeming them too base and too vile for vs: though that in deede, there is no trade so bad, which will not maintaine him that vseth it ... and which will not enrich a man, if he be sufficiently painefull and industrious therein.[5]

Human pride gets in the way. Nevertheless, Christ's example should teach us humbly to accept our vocation. He "tooke vpon him the shape of servaunt, and made him selfe like vnto men; for whome in the ende he was crucified, after that with wonderfull humilitie and lowlinese he had washed many of their feete and legges".[6]

Before ending his chapter on the evils of Curiosity, L'Espine feels it expedient to "touch ... briefly & in a word that wicked & profane curiositie, wherby divers mē are wonderfully stirred vp

---

[2] Jean de L'Espine, *A Very Excellent and Learned Discovrse*, p. 120ᵛ, sig. R3ᵛ.
[3] L'Espine, p. 125ᵛ, sig. R8ᵛ.
[4] L'Espine, p. 120ᵛ, sig. R3ᵛ.
[5] L'Espine, p. 133ʳ, sig. S8ᵛ.
[6] L'Espine, p. 134ʳ, sig. T1ʳ.

to know such things either of God, of nature, or of their neigh-
bors, as are most secret, difficult, dangerous, & wholy inpertinēt
vnto thē".

And this kind of humor doth oftentimes exceedingly torment such as haue
reaching and aspiring minds, who contēning the study of meane things,
as an exercise too base & contēptible for them, wil needs sore aloft & apply
thēselues to that which is very rare & farre frō the knowledge of euery
common personage: as though it were an easie matter to flie vp to heauen
without wings ....[7]

L'Espine goes on to discuss those who pervert their vocation.
Some men devote themselves to dabbling in alchemy, while others
"write whole bookes of Magicke and Nigromancie", and yet
others pervert the study of law and divinity.[8]

  L'Espine's commentary gives us a position from which to watch
Faustus's initial choice of vocations. Faustus surveys the various
disciplines open to him as a scholar: logic, medicine, law, and
theology. From each of these he expects more than is intrinsically
possible and rejects each in turn as beneath his abilities. It is
important to notice that one of his chief desires is eternal existence
in one form or another. By medicine, he may "be eterniz'd for
some wondrous cure" (B 43); his fame will last as long as the
history books. And then comes the sharp realization: "Yet art
thou still but *Faustus*, and a man" (B 50):

> Couldst thou make men to liue eternally,
> Or being dead, raise them to life againe,
> Then this profession were to be esteem'd.   (B 51-53)

The allusion to bringing men back to life is to Christ's resurrection
of Lazarus, but it is submerged because Faustus does not realize
its application. Where medicine fails, religion ideally succeeds;
for while the body may die, the soul may live.

  After rejecting law as a subject fit for a "Mercenarie drudge"
(B 61), Faustus turns directly to divinity, which he immediately
says is "best" (B 64). But he is primarily interested in the eternal

---

[7] L'Espine, p. 135ᵛ, sig. T2ᵛ.
[8] L'Espine, p. 136ʳ, sig T3ʳ.

life promised by religion, and he ponders the possibility of such a phenomenon by using two partial quotations from the Bible: "The reward of sin is death" (B 67) from Romans 6:23, and "If we say that we haue no sinne / We deceiue our selues" (B 69-70) from 1 John 1:8.[9] From this evidence, Faustus concludes: "Why then belike we must sinne, / And so consequently die" (B 71-72). Here his self-delusion depends on fragmentary quotation (as it often does in literary criticism), because the completion of the first quotation from Romans is a guarantee of life everlasting through religious faith: "but the gift of God is eternall life through Jesus Christ our Lord". And the next verse from the first epistle of St. John reads: "If we acknowledge our sinnes, he [God] is faithfull and iust, to forgiue vs our sinnes, and to clense vs from all vnrighteousnesse" (1:9). Faustus fails to realize that in the universe in which he lives eternal life is a product of the proper religious action, and on the contrary he concludes that all men "must die, an euerlasting death" (B 73). Thus, Faustus bids divinity adieu and turns to black magic: "These Metaphisicks of Magitians, / And Negromantick bookes are heauenly" (B 76-77). The imaginative leap from the denial of theology as worthy of study to the acceptance of magic as "heauenly" is beyond the realm of human logic, and ironically Aristotelean logic is the first discipline rejected by the would-be magician.

Although an apparently logical rejection of false arts, Faustus's arguments are based on improper assumptions about human activities.[10] He wishes logic to perform miracles, and medicine to keep men alive forever. Law must do more than deal with the legal problem of man in society. But logic, medicine, and law are by their natures not miraculous, but practical; and, on the other hand, religion should not be practical but miraculous.

---

[9] *The Bible: Translated according to the Ebrew and Greeke* (London, 1586), Geneva version (STC 2145).

[10] Cf. Henry Cornelius Agrippa, *Of the Vanitie and Vncertaintie of Artes and Sciences*, trans. by James Sanford (London, 1569), p. 2^r, sig. B2^r (STC 204): "all Sciences be as well naught as good, and ... bringeth to vs, aboue the limite of Humanitie, none other blessing of the Deitée, but that perchance, which that auncient Serpent promised to our firste parents, saiynge, *Ye shalbe as Goddes, and shall know good and ill.*"

Nevertheless, through his juggling of quotations from religious writ, Faustus makes practical nonsense rather than miracle of religion. His first speech, a tissue of flawed arguments, suggests that he is a character ready to be fatally deluded. Faustus has fallen into the blindness of human pride described by L'Espine, and in his blindness he has turned things upside down.

That Faustus is ripe for self-deception becomes a certainty as the play progresses. His power over the forces of evil is, of course, his greatest delusion, for, in fact, Faustus gives Evil power over him. The reversal is immediately apparent in scene 3 (B I.iii), where Lucifer and four of his devils enter and wait for him to begin his conjuring. His self-assurance is ironic:

> I see there's vertue in my heauenly words.
> Who would not be proficient in this Art?
> How pliant is this *Mephostophilis?*
> Full of obedience and humility,
> Such is the force of Magicke, and my spels.   (B 255-59)

When he asks Mephostophilis about the power of his conjuring, the devil honestly tells him that his magic was the cause of his coming, "but yet *per accident*" (B 272). That is, the devils have come "in hope to get" Faustus's "glorious soule" (B 275), which he has endangered by abjuring the Trinity. However, even after this admission by Mephostophilis, Faustus is not convinced that he lacks the power to command devils. He still believes that he can bargain his soul for that power and that through this bargain he can get all that he demands. It is only near the end of the play that he learns how he has been duped. Mephostophilis explains:

> 'Twas I, that when thou wer't i'the way of heauen,
> Damb'd vp thy passage, when thou took'st the booke,
> To view the Scriptures, then I turn'd the leaues
> And led thine eye.   (B 1989-92)[11]

---

[11] Vaughan, *Golden-groue*, sig. Aa1r: "for the coniurer or magician, it is almost impossible that hee should be conuerted, by reason that the Diuell is alwayes conuersant with him, and is present euen at his very elbow, and will not once permit him to aske forgiuenesse. Experience whereof Doctor Faustus felt, who was at last torne in peeces by the Diuell." One wonders if perhaps Vaughan saw Marlowe's play.

Faustus is led to his choice by forces outside his control.

On the other hand, Faustus makes his decision to bargain with the devil because he has DELUDED HIMSELF about two aspects of eternity: first, the nature of damnation, and second, the nature of grace. These delusions follow hard upon those of his first illogical arguments in scene one. Faustus tells Mephostophilis: "This word Damnation, terrifies not me, / For I confound hell in *Elizium*" (B 284-85). He wishes to pass quickly to more important matters than "these vaine trifles of mens soules" (B 287). With a manifestation of divine wrath standing before him, Faustus's assertion that hell does not exist is purposefully delusive. Upon questioning, Mephostophilis admits that he is "for euer damn'd with Lucifer" (B 298), and gives his memorable speech on the quality of spiritual alienation:

> Why this is hell: nor am I out of it.
> Think'st thou that I that saw the face of God,
> And tasted the eternall Ioyes of heauen,
> Am not tormented with ten thousand hels,
> In being depriu'd of euerlasting blisse?   (B 301-05)

Echoing Faustus's line (B 287), Mephostophilis asks him to "leaue these friuolous demandes, / Which strikes a terror to my fainting soule" (B 306-07). The effect of this exchange is intensified by later repetition. Mephostophilis moans: "Hell hath no limits, nor is circumscrib'd, / In one selfe place: but where we are is hell" (B 513-14), and Faustus still replies: "I thinke Hel's a fable" (B 519). The hell which Faustus is able to dismiss as a classical legend is felt by Mephostophilis as the supreme reality; and where Faustus believes the soul to be a vain trifle, Mephostophilis knows that the very discussion of damnation strikes terror into his. Marlowe sets up a recurring contrast between the deceived theorist and the experienced realist, between the blind scholar and the damned angel.

Beyond doubting the existence of eternal punishment (alienation from God), Faustus believes that he has already "incur'd eternall death, / By desperate thoughts against *Ioues* Deity" (B 313-14). He imposes his own limitation on divine grace and mercy; and by setting this limit, by excluding himself from the realm of

grace, he dismisses any idea of life everlasting. The very thing he
had desired, seen as a *summum bonum* in both medicine and theology,
he now willfully and ironically rejects in a series of rejections
which marks his progress toward complete damnation. First
Faustus turns away from the fundamental employments of social
man in order to engage in anti-social magic, and then stepping
beyond the social context into the universal, he rejects what is
apparently the basic metaphysical structure of the play's world.
These rejections of reality point to Faustus's distorted vision. He
turns from the real so that he may more firmly believe in his own
universal importance: "I'll be great emperor of the world." As
Faustus sees greater and greater vistas opening before him, he
feels divine power growing less and less. If there is no salvation,
there is also no damnation. The end of man is death, and only
his physical pleasure here on earth is of importance to him.

The following scenes illustrate the emptiness of Faustus's power,
because there are certain things which, unfortunately for Faustus,
Mephostophilis cannot perform. Faustus's desire for a wife is
answered by the devil's "talke not of a wife" (A 590), and when
Faustus begs, Mephostophilis brings in "*a woman deuill*" (S. D.,
B 536). The point is that marriage is a sacrament, and since
Mephostophilis cannot deal in divinity, he cannot provide Faustus
with a real wife. As he says, "Marriage is but a ceremoniall toy,
/ And if thou louest me thinke no more of it" (B 540-41). If
Faustus, like Tamburlaine, by willful choice has rejected the
creative power of the universe, the devil is limited by the power of
God from participating in creativity; he may only destroy. Later
when Faustus commands Mephostophilis to tell him who made
the world, he answers: "I will not" (B 637). He can only speak of
what "is not against our Kingdome" (B 641), the kingdom of
Hell. Faustus has allied himself with the destructive forces of the
universe, and from these forces, he had expected to reap the fruits
(Marlowe's metaphor) of temporal happiness. Instead, he gains
the inconsequential and the trivial; and he is able to create nothing
of lasting value – except, perhaps, an exemplum for preachers.

The chief dramatic symbol for his lack of real power is the show
he presents to the Emperor Charles. The Emperor announces:

> We would behold that famous Conquerour,
> Great *Alexander*, and his Paramour,
> In their true shapes, and state Maiesticall,
> That we may wonder at their excellence.   (B 1264-67)

Attempting to overgo the request, Faustus prefaces the appearance
of Alexander and his lover with Alexander's defeat of Darius.
But, when the Emperor rises to embrace them, Faustus quickly
stops him: "These are but shadowes, not substantiall" (B 1304).
His art is the art not of actualized power, but of illusion. It is one
of the supreme ironies of the play that the deluded sorcerer is the
master of illusions. He deludes, as he is deluded, with insubstantial
pageants.

The progress of Faustus's movement from Pope, to Emperor,
to Duke is a movement downward in the social scale, but it is also
a progress toward triviality. In each case, Faustus visits the famous
man, performs a piece of magic, and then vents his spite. However,
it is not so much the parallels, but the differences which indicate
Faustus's degeneration. When he visits the Pope, he confronts his
alter ego, for the Pope also claims the omnipotent powers which
Faustus feels he has received from Lucifer. Disputing with the
captive Bruno, a rival Pope created by the Emperor Charles, the
Pope asks rhetorically:

> Is not all power on earth bestowed on vs?
> And therefore tho we would we cannot erre.
> Behold this Siluer Belt whereto is fixt
> Seuen golden seales fast sealed with seuen seales,
> In token of our seuen-fold power from heauen,
> To binde or losse, lock fast, condemne, or iudge,
> Resigne, or seale, or what so pleaseth vs.   (B 960-66)

The Pope treats Bruno as Tamburlaine treats Bajazeth, using him
as a footstool (B 904-05). Both his speech and his action are clear
enough indications that he lacks any kind of religious humility.
That the Pope appears as a bumptious ass should be a warning to
Faustus, though it is not.

Apparently the Pope is helpless before the power of Faustus and
Mephostophilis, although, as we have seen, this power is something
less than awesome. Because Faustus is here pitted against an opponent no stronger than himself, he accomplishes something. Bruno

is released by a magical stratagem, and according to Mephostophilis, he posts "hence, / And on a proud pac'd Steed, as swift as
thought, / Flies ore the Alpes to fruitfull Germany, / There to
salute the wofull Emperour" (B 1017-20). Here Faustus frees an
innocent man whose only sin appears to be his bravery in the face
of the Pope's self-assertion. Looking forward in the action, we find
an inverted parallel in Faustus's meeting with the Old Man, who
tries to force him to see the truth about himself. In retaliation,
Faustus has him tortured by devils and, although Greg would
disagree, torn to pieces.[12] It is an instance of Faustus's degeneration
that he becomes as vindictive as the Pope, his former opponent.
His viciousness grows along with his own spiritual sufferings and
the increasing possibility that he himself will be drawn by devils
to hell. Although there are suggestions of Faustus's spite in his
beating the Friars and flinging fireworks among them (B 1125),
for the moment we can only applaud his freeing of Bruno.

At the Emperor's court, Faustus's actions are less worthy of
applause. From insulting the Pope, he comes to ingratiate himself
with the Emperor, who welcomes him warmly:

> Wonder of men, renown'd Magitian,
> Thrice learned *Faustus*, welcome to our Court.
> This deed of thine, in setting *Bruno* free
> From his and our professed enemy,
> Shall adde more excellence vnto thine Art,
> Then if by powerfull Necromantick spels,
> Thou couldst command the worlds obedience.   (B 1237-43)

In context, Charles's speech is ironic, and his last lines appear to
question Faustus's ability to command the world with his magic
power. Faustus's reply unveils another side of the here-to-fore
proud wizard:

> These gracious words, most royall *Carolus*,
> Shall make poore *Faustus* to his vtmost power,
> Both loue and serue the Germane Emperour,
> And lay his life at holy *Bruno's* feet.   (B 1250-53)

Although the playgoer may feel that this reply is spiced with a

[12] Greg (ed.), *Doctor Faustus*, p. 125. Many of the play's themes focus on the Old
Man.

good deal of irony, the words are not those of a man who believes, as he once believed, that he will be emperor of the world. His present servility is striking.

In contrast to his freeing of Bruno is his transformation of the skeptical Benvolio into the semblance of Actaeon. His first venture releases a man from the clutches of spiritual pride; his second is a practical joke – with serious consequences – on a young man who has scoffed at his magic. The comparison reveals further points on the graph of Faustus's degeneration. As with the Pope's contemplated revenge on Bruno, it is possible to see the present multiple revenge related to larger concerns in the play. Faustus's first revenge – giving Benvolio horns which are soon removed at the Emperor's request – leads to Benvolio's plot, which is foiled by Faustus, and which in turn leads to his further revenge: physically punishing Benvolio and his accomplices and giving them permanent horns. At the Papal Court, Faustus, although indulging himself in practical jokes, which seem to delight him, was aloof from this kind of long-range, nasty vengefulness. Now he has accepted the idea of vengeance, and the Benvolio affair leads irrevocably to Faustus's command to Mephostophilis:

> Torment sweet friend, that base and aged man,
> That durst disswade me from thy *Lucifer*,
> With greatest torment that our hell affoords.   (B 1857-59)

The Benvolio episode brings us again to Faustus's relationship to the Old Man. We might parody Marlowe's own line by asking of Faustus, was this the man who had a thousand hopes to conquer all the world? His ambition to be more than human has led to his becoming less than humane. The man who initially wants power so that he can protect Germany with a wall of brass and help its students by clothing them in silk ultimately focuses all his vengeance and hate on an innocent old man whose only sin was to attempt to save Faustus from damnation.

The third episode in this progressive degeneration is Faustus's visit to the Duke of Vanholt. It is the winter of his magical career, and his tricks are becoming less and less amazing. Desiring to be of service to the pregnant duchess, he asks her if she longs for any food which he may by his magic provide. "Were it now Summer", she answers, "as it is Ianuary, a dead time of the Winter, I would request no better meate, then a dish of ripe grapes" (B 1655-57). When Mephostophilis returns with the desired fruit, the Duke says: "This makes me wonder more then all the rest" (B 1663-64). The trick, Faustus explains, is accomplished by a swift spirit who goes to another part of the world where grapes are in season and returns with them. And so, this feat which the Duke finds so astounding is hardly more than a matter of speed. For the man who has disrupted the papal feast with his invisible presence and has produced Alexander and his lover, this is minor magic. But then, so is the hypnotic show which follows.

The show stands in relation to the release of Bruno and the feud with Benvolio: it is one of the personal byproducts of Faustus's visit to a political dignitary. In plotting the course of Faustus's degeneration, we should realize that, in releasing Bruno, he was dealing with matters of international importance, the struggle between Church and State in Europe. In fighting with Benvolio, he is involved in an affair of much less consequence, but he is at least confronting a nobleman who has laid a plot for his life. At the Duke of Vanholt's court, however, Faustus is playing with drunken clowns, and even at this he feels that he must ask permission from the Duke: "I do beseech your grace let them come in" (B 1695), and when the Duke replies: "Do as thou wilt *Faustus*, I giue thee leaue" (B 1697), Faustus humbly thanks him. The man who gave his soul for complete temporal power now thanks a Duke for giving him permission to banter with clowns before he hypnotizes them into silence. The progress from Pope to Duke is a chronicle of growing triviality, and from our point of view, this chronicle is ample evidence of Faustus's delusion. In fact, his belief that he will control the world is slowly transmuted into the spiritual knowledge of his own damnation. There is the greatest irony in the Duke of Vanholt's final line: "His Artfull sport, driues all sad thoughts away" (B 1773). Faustus's own thoughts have been less jocose. Two scenes earlier (IV.v), when the Horse-courser claims that he is "a made man for euer" (B 1544-45), Faustus asks himself:

What art thou *Faustus* but a man condemn'd to die?

> Thy fatall time drawes to a finall end;
> Despaire doth driue distrust into my thoughts.   (B 1546-48)

Although others may take joy from his delusive art, the master of illusion comes to understand the reality of his position.

But before we discuss his final realizations, we must look at several thematic patterns which contribute to the total impact of Faustus's delusion and transformation. One of the most interesting of these is the servant-master relationship, which includes that of the master and student. The play begins with Faustus as a novitiate in the art of conjuring. Although a master in the other branches of knowledge, he needs Cornelius and Valdes to instruct him in magic. They have the greatest respect for their student. Valdes tells him: "First I'l instruct thee in the rudiments, / And then wilt thou be perfecter then I" (B 183-84). There is an implied reversal in the lines, and it is not an oversight which makes Marlowe drop the names of Cornelius and Valdes from the play after the next scene. Faustus himself has assumed their roles; the student becomes the master magician.

The problem of servant-master is more complex when Faustus begins to make his overtures to Lucifer. Since Mephostophilis appears after his invocation, Faustus gloats: "How pliant is this *Mephostophilis?* / Full of obedience and humility, / Such is the force of Magicke, and my spels" (B 257-59). When the devil reappears dressed as a Franciscan friar, Faustus says: "I charge thee waite vpon me whilst I liue / To do what euer *Faustus* shall command" (B 262-63). Mephostophilis's reply, "I am a seruant to great *Lucifer*, / And may not follow thee without his leaue" (B 266-67), shatters any belief that Faustus may control the devil. As it turns out, Faustus must become the servant of hell before he can gain the service of Mephostophilis, and, since this is so, Faustus is content: "There is no chiefe but onely *Beelzebub*: / To whom *Faustus* doth dedicate himselfe" (B 282-83). Although he signs the pact which contains the condition "*that Mephostophilis shall be his seruant, and be by him commanded*" (B 489-90), he can have or do nothing that is against the kingdom of hell to which he is sworn servant, and this is indeed a severe limitation on any concept of masterhood. Faustus later admits to himself:

> The God thou seru'st is thine owne appetite
> Wherein is fixt the loue of *Belzebub*,
> To him, I'le build an Altar and a Church,
> And offer luke-warme bloud, of new borne babes.   (B 398-401)

In a sense, the evil that Faustus projects onto the devil is within himself; his reason has lost control, and he is governed by that universal wolf, appetite. Faustus is an anti-type of the Biblical 'suffering servant', who gives himself for others.[13]

As Faustus himself realizes, the god he serves is his own sensual appetite, and this turns out to be a fair insight into his nature. A large aspect of the Faustian character is sensuality. "O", he exclaims in ecstasy over black magic, "what a world of profite and delight, / Of power, of honour, and omnipotence, / Is promised to the Studious Artizan?" (B 80-82). Out of this list of attributes, it is "delight" which echoes through the play. When Faustus balks at signing his soul to the devil, Mephostophilis immediately decides: "I'le fetch him somewhat to delight his minde" (B 470), and the first in a series of diabolic entertainments ensues. Several devils enter giving crowns and "*rich apparell*" (B 472) to the recalcitrant diabolist; and they then entertain him with a dance. When the delighted but puzzled Faustus asks the meaning of the pageant, Mephostophilis answers: "Nothing *Faustus* but to delight thy mind, / And let thee see what Magicke can performe" (B 476-77). The "nothing" stands out: the pageant is meaningless, a toy which gives Faustus pleasure and keeps him from questioning essentials. After he has signed the agreement with the devil, he feels "wanton and lasciuious" (B 533), and Mephostophilis offers the consolations of sin:

> I'le cull thee out the fairest Curtezans,
> And bring them euery morning to thy bed:
> She whom thine eye shall like, thy heart shall haue,
> Were she as chaste as was *Penelope*;
> As wise as *Saba*, or as beautifull
> As was bright *Lucifer* before his fall.   (B 542-47)

---

[13] The theme of servant-master is related to the theme of free-slave in *1 Tamburlaine*. Faustus's mastership and Tamburlaine's freedom are equally limited. Contrast Michael Quinn, "The Freedom of Tamburlaine", *MLQ*, 21 (1960), 315-20.

The last line is another example of Mephostophilis's recurrent undercutting of the powers of hell, but the passage in the main points toward Faustus's carnal desires. He is completely satisfied with the diabolical alternative to marriage, which, in turn, means that for him marriage is chiefly a physical relationship, not (in Shakespeare's ideal world) a marriage of true minds. Strangely and perhaps ironically, Faustus the scholar is not half so moved by the true pleasures of the mind and spirit as by the promises of bodily gratification.

In the next scene, Faustus is already repenting, though quite selfishly, that he has sold himself to Lucifer. He informs us that he would have committed suicide long before "Had not sweete pleasure conquer'd deepe despaire" (B 594): THIS from the man who had desired immortal life and absolute power. But to occupy his mind, Faustus determines to question Mephostophilis. Comparable to his inability to supply Faustus with a legitimate wife, Mephostophilis cannot name the creator of the universe. When he remains obstinately silent, Faustus commands himself, as is his wont: "Thinke *Faustus* vpon God, that made the world" (B 643). When Lucifer and Belzebub appear on the scene to admonish him, Faustus is commanded to "Thinke on the deuill" (B 663), and Belzebub cannot resist a pun: "And his dam [dame and damn] to" (B 664). Again the diabolic powers propose to woo Faustus from his heavenly thoughts with a pageant, this time the Seven Deadly Sins. "That sight will be as pleasant to me, as Paradise was to *Adam* the first day of his creation (B 673-74), says Faustus. Meant to be ingratiating, the comment is not well received: "Talke not of Paradice or Creation, but marke the shew" (B 675-76). The whole exchange is potentially comic.

Nevertheless, such black humor usually has a serious basis. To compare Paradise and the Seven Deadly Sins is to join completely antithetical ideas: creation and destruction. Through his sinful quest for greater knowledge, Adam lost his place in Paradise, and his primal innocence was destroyed. By linking Eden with the Sins, Faustus reveals his own inverted sense of values, and I suggest at this juncture (hoping to prove the point thoroughly in the course of this chapter) that Faustus takes a good deal of pleasure in destruction, that destruction rather than genuine creation is his mode. "O", he exclaims ecstatically, as he had first exclaimed over his contemplation of black magic, "how this sight doth delight my soule" (B 731). "But *Faustus*", Lucifer interrupts, "in hell is all manner of delight" (B 732). If he finds a pageant of Deadly Sins delightful, what indeed may not hell offer him? In any case, until his time to become a permanent part of these diabolical pleasures, he resolves:

> My foure and twenty yeares of liberty
> I'le spend in pleasure and in daliance,
> That *Faustus* name, whilst this bright frame doth stand,
> May be admired through the furthest Land.   (B 862-65)

He hopes to gain a certain kind of eternization through sensuality.

In the following scenes, Faustus becomes the master of illusion, the giver of delight, the servant of great men, who produces the diabolic shows which formerly kept him from despair and repentance. For his students, as he is nearing death, he produces Helen – "that peerelesse Dame of *Greece*" (A 1281-82). Following this show, Faustus's last performance, the Old Man encourages him to forego his diabolical pact, and Faustus finally says:

> I do repent, and yet I doe despaire,
> Hell striues with grace for conquest in my breast:
> What shall I doe to shun the snares of death?   (B 1844-46)

By threatening him with physical dismemberment, Mephostophilis easily brings Faustus to "repent" his momentary slip from diabolism, and Faustus confirms his pact, apparently rewriting the agreement in blood. After begging punishment for the Old Man – the kind of punishment with which Mephostophilis has threatened him – he asks the devil to give him "delight" which will keep him faithful to Lucifer:

> One thing good seruant let me craue of thee,
> To glut the longing of my hearts desire,
> That I may haue vnto my paramour,
> That heauenly *Hellen*, which I saw of late,
> Whose sweet embraces may extinguish cleare,
> Those thoughts that do disswade me from my vow,
> And keepe my vow I made to *Lucifer*.   (B 1863-69)

The apparition of Helen is the climax of the series of delusive entertainments given Faustus by the devils, and it is neatly juxtaposed to the very real torments (*pace* Greg) of the Old Man. At the same time, as Mephostophilis leads us to feel, both of these experiences are merely physical. Although he will surely torment the Old Man, he says: "His faith is great, I cannot touch his soule; / But what I may afflict his body with, / I will attempt, which is but little worth" (B 1860-62). By extension, the playgoer may feel that Faustus's experience with Helen is just as worthless, a passing physical pleasure with no extrinsic value.

Or, the experience may be genuinely destructive. Because of the romantic connotations of Helen and the story of Troy, most critics have not carefully examined the implications of Faustus's salutation to his paramour:

> Was this the face that Launcht a thousand ships,
> And burnt the toplesse Towers of *Ilium?*
> ...
> I will be *Paris*, and for loue of thee,
> In stead of *Troy* shall *Wittenberg* be sack't,
> And I will combat with weake *Menelaus*,
> And weare thy colours on my plumed crest.
> ...
> O thou art fairer then the euenings aire,
> Clad in the beauty of a thousand starres:
> Brighter art thou then flaming *Iupiter*,
> When he appear'd to haplesse *Semele:*
>
> (B 1874-75, 1881-84, 1887-90)

The emphasis is on destruction, on destructive rather than creative love. Jupiter, to whom Helen is compared, consumes Semele with his fire. The burning of Troy and the death of Paris are compared to the offered sack of Wittenberg, Faustus's city, and the implied death of Faustus himself. By his longing for Helen, Faustus involves himself in the destruction for which she is a symbol.[14] Ironically,

---

[14] Cf. *Dido*, II.i.587-95; Edgar Wind, *Pagan Mysteries in the Renaissance*, pp. 167-68; and Cole, *Suffering and Evil in the Plays of Christopher Marlowe*, p. 222. In *Euphues* (1578, 1579), Lyly sees Helen as evil. Merritt Lawlis (ed.), *Elizabethan Prose Fiction* (New York: Odyssey, 1967), pp. 119, 125, 127, 177, 183. See *The Lyfe of the Most Godly ... Iasper Colignie Shatilion*, sig. C3ᵛ, "as *Helene* was to the *Troianes,*

he asks her to make him "immortall with a kisse" (B 1876), but after the kiss is given, he says: "Her lips sucke forth my soule, see where it flies. / Come *Hellen*, come, giue me my soule againe" (B 1877-78). Nonetheless, his ravished soul convinces him that "heauen is in these lippes" (B 1879). But as the playgoer easily sees, the speech is a series of ironic juxtapositions. The figure before him is not Helen, but a devil in her form, a succubus. Hell, not heaven, is in her lips, and what he has here attained is illusive. "And none but thou", he swears, "shalt be my Paramour" (B 1893). His values have now been completely inverted, as he accepts illusion as his greatest reality and finds his only heaven in a piece of hell. The sensualist has become immersed in the delusive glories of this world.

Looking at the plight of the Old Man who is left on stage to be tortured by the entering devils, a deluded playgoer might easily feel that Faustus, even though Helen is diabolic, has gotten the better of the immediate bargain. But Marlowe is again playing with a reversal. Faustus attains earthly pleasure, but at the price of his soul; the Old Man, expecting torture, can see that Faustus is the genuinely miserable man (A 1377). His last speech makes the point:

> Sathan begins to sift me with his pride,
> As in this furnace God shal try my faith,
> My faith, vile hel, shal triumph ouer thee,
> Ambitious fiends, see how the heauens smiles
> At your repulse, and laughs your state to scorne,
> Hence hel, for hence I flie vnto my God.   (A 1381-86)

The contrast set up between Faustus and the Old Man, with the Old Man trying to save Faustus's soul and Faustus seeking to destroy the Old Man's body, is part of contrasting ideas which underlie the play: the infinite joys of heavenly beatitude, and the finite sensations of the body, which, if followed exclusively, lead to spiritual destruction.

The contrast between heaven and hell is, of course, a common-

---

so the Duke of *Gvyse* was to the *Frenchmen* the cawse of all the greate miseries that befell them".

place Christian thought, but as we have noticed, Faustus is at some pains to doubt what everyone ought to know: "I thinke Hel's a fable." What is interesting to notice is not that Marlowe espouses the traditional manner of contrasting the two modes of existence after death, but that Marlowe's Faustus, after he comes to accept hell as a reality, thinks of the diabolic torments in physical terms as if they were finite sensations. He cannot understand why Mephostophilis says he is damned, and even after the devil has carefully described the spiritual torture of divine alienation, Faustus still determines to consider hell a physical state. When he asks Mephostophilis to torment the Old Man, he apparently still has not grasped the distinction between spirit and flesh. Although Mephostophilis has learned through suffering, Faustus is blinded to the obvious by his own desires. He denies his chance at true immortality, infinite union with the godhead, for a transitory union with Helen. Although Romantic critics found a great deal of nobility in this act, we are perhaps more aware that what appears to be nobility may be three-quarters self-delusion.

Faustus's sensuality is underlined by the motif of eating and feasting.[15] We have examined how Marlowe uses the unnatural hunger after power in *1 Tamburlaine*, and the idea carries some of its former meaning here. In the Prologue, we are told that Faustus is "glutted now with learnings golden gifts" and "surfets vpon cursed Necromancie" (B 24-25). The image of eating knowledge is just startling enough to give it added emphasis and to alert us to the idea of eating in the play. There is the suggestion that Faustus is a glutton, desirous of more food than is good for his health, in this case, spiritual health. Before being instructed by Valdes and Cornelius in the black arts, he extends an invitation: "Then come and dine with me, and after meate / We'le canuase euery

---

[15] Although too late for Marlowe to have seen in print, *Two Guides to a Good Life* (London, 1604), sigs. F1ᵛ-F6ᵛ (STC 12466), gives a conventional picture of the gluttonous man. "Gluttony may bee called the Deluge or inundation of the soule, because it is a rauenous desire to feed and fill the stomach, beyond the rule and bounds of nature" (F1ᵛ). Faustus's gluttony is a sign of his unnatural desires. Cf. Pierre Boaistruau, *Theatrum Mundi*, trans. by John Alday (London, 1574), p. 41, sig. D5ʳ (STC 3169), on the "Belligods" who "shall one day be made a pray for Diuels".

quidditie thereof" (B 185-86). One cannot help observing that
with Faustus food comes before magic. When he is visited by the
Seven Deadly Sins, Gluttony has one of the longest speeches, and
Faustus's reply: "Choke thy selfe Glutton" (B 724), may be ironically reflexive. In Rome, Mephostophilis and Faustus attend St.
Peter's feast, and Faustus is promised that they will make bold with
the Pope's "Venson" (B 831). After desiring to "be cloyd / With
all things that delight the heart of man" (B 860-61), Faustus,
rendered invisible by Mephostophilis, eats freely at the papal
feast. Later, in a comic version of Faustus's passion for food, the
Carter relates:

As I was going to *Wittenberge* t'other day, with a loade of Hay, he met me,
and asked me what he should giue me for as much Hay as he could eate;
now sir, I thinking that a little would serue his turne, bad him take as
much as he would for three-farthings; so he presently gaue me my mony,
and fell to eating; and as I am a cursen man, he neuer left eating, till he
had eate vp all my loade of hay.   (B 1600-07)

The comedy reflects what is, in the main action, deadly earnest.
   As Faustus prepares to be taken to hell, he feasts his former
students with a banquet served by devils. Taking a conventional
view, Wagner is deluded: "if death were nie, he would not frolick
thus: hee's now at supper with the schollers, where ther's such
belly-cheere, as *Wagner* in his life nere saw the like" (B 1781-83).
The action draws to a close with Faustus eating. When he tells
his students that he "must dye eternally" (B 1925), they reply,
"Tis but a surfet sir" (B 1931) – a comic, though obvious conclusion from the facts. Faustus's response: "A surfet of deadly sin,
that hath damn'd both body and soule" (B 1933-34), suggests
that his overeating is symbolic of his complete commitment to the
sensual as opposed to the spiritual. Of course, there is also the
submerged idea that Faustus's last feast is the opposite of Christ's
Last Supper. In one case, man is redeemed from sin; in the other,
Faustus is snared by his own appetite. As Christ symbolically
distributes himself to his disciples, Faustus after his diabolic feast
is literally torn to pieces. And "for the vaine pleasure of foure and
twenty yeares hath *Faustus* lost eternall ioy and felicitie" (B 1959-
61). His hunger for infinite power and knowledge is a manifesta-

tion of gluttony, suggesting the weight of flesh and fleshly desires which keeps the magician from any spiritual flights outside the realm of nature.

Dedicated as he is to the pleasures of the flesh, Faustus immediately withdraws from any threat of physical violence – at least when this physical violence is offered by the devils. When attacked by fellow mortals, he is, of course, protected from physical harm by his diabolic contract. During his first bout of repentance, the Bad Angel warns him: "If thou repent, deuils will teare thee in peeces" (B 650), and when Lucifer and the devils enter, Faustus returns to obedience. The pattern is repeated in Faustus's attempt at repentance before his fatal last scene. The Old Man advises Faustus to "call for mercy, and auoyd despaire" (B 1838), and he will be saved; but when Mephostophilis threatens, "I'le in peece-meale teare thy flesh" (B 1849), Faustus at once repents his apostasy. The fear of physical pain, which the Old Man can sustain because of his spiritual confidence, forces Faustus to elect the course of least resistance, continued worldly pleasure.

The dismemberment or mutilation which Faustus fears so much is a recurring idea in the play, and the motif is suggested by Faustus's pact with the devil, a pact which must be signed in blood. Here is the first hint that the physical pleasure that Faustus desires must be paid for ultimately by sacrificing himself. "I cut mine arme", he says, "and with my proper blood / Assure my soule to be great *Lucifers*" (A 494-95). In this scene, in which Faustus purposefully wounds himself to acquire the power of hell, we may again be reminded of Christ's sacrifice. The words *Consummatum est* 'It is finished', are used by Christ as he dies on the Cross (John 29:30), and by Faustus as he finishes writing the pact in blood. That Faustus and Christ share these words suggests that Marlowe wishes us to draw a contrast between selfless savior and egoistic magician. For the one, these words are the culmination of a life of religious piety; for the other, they are the end of comparative innocence. In this context, we should perhaps remember the passage from James 1:15-16: "sinne when IT IS FINISHED, bringeth forth death. Erre not" (emphasis mine). The signing of the pact looks forward inevitably to Faustus's death. The inscription which

appears on his arm, "*Homo fuge*" (B 465), also points to a New
Testament reading. In 1 Timothy 6:11, there is a warning against
evil: "But thou, O man of God, flee these things". It is possibly
this passage that Marlowe was thinking about when he placed the
inscription on Faustus's arm.[16] The playwright entreats the audience to recall the Christian concepts which stand behind
Faustus's pact with the devil and to compare this pact with the
sacrifice of Christ, which is, in its miraculous way, a general pact
between man and God. Faustus's pact is written in blood which
"congeales" (B 449) as he writes and must be warmed by fire, fire
which prefigures the hellfire of damnation toward which this pact
leads. God's pact with man is written in the life-blood of Christ,
readily available to those who ask for mercy and salvation.
"Christs blood streames in the firmament" (A 1463).

Although Faustus is threatened with dismemberment if he
should disobey the behests of the devil, the first dismemberment
of Faustus (symbolically staged) is Benvolio's revenge. Benvolio
strikes off his head, a "*false head*" as the stage directions inform us
(B 1412), and he and his fellow conspirators plan, in a darkly
humorous exchange, what they are going to do with the parts
of the severed head. The beard will be sold to a chimney-sweep
for a broom; the eyes will be plucked out and used as buttons to
keep the mouth closed. Martino chortles: "An excellent policie:
and now sirs, hauing diuided him, what shall the body doe?"
(B 1441-42). Although Marlowe's stage directions are absent from
the text at this point, it appears that the body begins to move.
Understandably the conspirators are shocked, but Faustus, again
intact, reminds them that he has a limited immortality while his
pact with the devil lasts:

> And had you cut my body with your swords,
> Or hew'd this flesh and bones as small as sand,
> Yet in a minute had my spirit return'd,
> And I had breath'd a man made free from harme.   (B 1449-52)

Their dismemberment of him could only be temporary. He commands the devils to punish the conspirators, apparently reserving

[16] Cf. Cole, p. 210.

the last and most vicious torment for Benvolio: he is flown to "some steepie rocke", where "rowling downe" he "may breake" his bones "As he intended to dismember" Faustus (B 1465-67).

In this scene there is an ironic foreshadowing of the final scene, with Benvolio playing the role of Faustus. It was generally thought during the Middle Ages and Renaissance that blasphemy, like the inverted rites of black magic, tore the body of Christ.[17] Faustus has performed these rites, and Mephostophilis tells him: "when we heare one racke the name of God, ... / We flye in hope to get his glorious soule" (B 273, 275). In the present scene, Benvolio tears the physical body of Faustus, as Faustus has torn the spiritual body of Christ. For this action, Benvolio is punished by the devils and receives a symbolic dismemberment in Faustus's description. In the play's final scene, these elements are present again: dismemberment, punishment, dismemberment. Benvolio is a dramatic analogue to Faustus.

But Faustus is dismembered once again before his last appearance. In the comic parallel to Faustus's dismemberment by Benvolio, the Horse-courser, who feels that he has been cheated by Faustus, comes upon him while he is sleeping. "Well", he says, "I'le go rouse him" (B 1557), and pulling on Faustus's leg to wake him up, he tears it off. Faustus pretends that he is wounded seriously, and the Horse-courser comically notes that he can now outrun Faustus who has but one leg. As in the former scene with Benvolio, Faustus's dismemberment is simply an illusion. The Horse-courser has pulled off a false leg as Benvolio has cut off a false head, and after he has gone, Faustus shows the audience (with a wink) that he "hath his leg againe" (B 1567). As with most comedy in serious Elizabethan plays, the scene intensifies rather than relieves the expectation inherent in the theme of dismemberment.

We have recurrently been drawn back to the Old Man, a focal character in the play's ideological scheme. From his dismemberment it should appear that neither the good nor the bad are

---

[17] See Vaughan, sig. G1ʳ: "What then shall be done with him that banneth and teareth in peeces the name of God, who is the King of Kings? Is hee not worthy of greater punishmēt, namely, to suffer both in body and soule."

exempt from fiendish attack and mutilation.[18] It logically follows that Faustus will be dismembered whether he repents and goes to heaven, or whether he despairs of grace and goes to everlasting damnation. The difference will be in his spiritual attitude at the end: despair or faith. The playgoer is fully prepared for the vision of *"Faustus* limbs, / All torne asunder by the hand of death" (B 2099-2100). But the Third Scholar objects to the euphemism of death's hand:

> The deuils whom *Faustus* seru'd haue torne him thus:
> For twixt the houres of twelue and one, me thought
> I heard him shreeke and call aloud for helpe:
> At which selfe time the house seem'd all on fire,
> With dreadfull horror of these damned fiends.   (B 2101-05)

What Faustus has endured in illusion throughout the play, he now experiences in reality.

There is another pattern in the play, that of transformation from a higher level in the scale of being to a lower,[19] which also culminates in this final scene. The pattern is especially evident in the comic episodes. When Robin asks Wagner if he will teach him how to conjure, Wagner replies: "I sirra, I'le teach thee to turne thy selfe to a Dog, or a Cat, or a Mouse, or a Rat, or any thing" (B 380-81). Robin is comically enthusiastic: "A Dog, or a Cat, or a Mouse, or a Rat? O braue *Wagner*" (B 382-83). He seems to feel that the ability to become a lower being demands an exclamation of praise. The comedy foreshadows the gift of Lucifer to Faustus two scenes later (II.ii). Giving Faustus a book of magic, Lucifer tells him: "peruse this booke, and view it throughly, / And thou shalt turne thy selfe into what shape thou wilt" (B 736-37). Like Robin the clown, Faustus is grateful: "Thankes mighty *Lucifer*:

---

[18] There is an ambiguity here. See lines B 651ff.: "Repent and they [the devils] shall neuer raise thy skin." The lines may support Greg's contention (derived from the source material) that the Old Man escapes without harm. Or, the lines may mean that if Faustus repents he will endure no essential harm, i.e., the lines are metaphoric.

[19] Cf. Hallett Smith, *Elizabethan Poetry* (Cambridge: Harvard University Press, 1952), p. 67, on Golding's Ovid: "The transformations or metamorphoses represent the subjection of men to fleshly appetites and their consequent internal resemblance to beasts."

This will I keepe as chary as my life" (B 738-39). Of course, Lucifer does not say that Faustus will be able to change himself into an animal, but the comic scene which precedes, as well as the ones which follow, implies as much.

In the next scene, Robin thinks he has mastered the black arts, and he threatens to put a fair "paire of hornes" (B 760) on Faustus's head. Apparently Robin contemplates literally changing Faustus into an animal, for it is Dick who turns this threat into a bawdy jest: "Thou needest not do that, for my Mistresse hath done it" (B 762-63). When Robin and Dick again enter, Robin mistakenly calls Mephostophilis who changes them into animals. Mephostophilis tells Dick:

> To purge the rashnesse of this cursed deed [i.e. calling him],
> First, be thou turned to this vgly shape,
> For Apish deeds transformed to an Ape.   (B 1168-70)

Robin responds with his usual enthusiasm: "O braue, an Ape?" (B 1171), while Mephostophilis says to him: "be thou transform'd to a dog, and carry him vpon thy backe; away be gone" (B 1173-74), to which Robin is equally enthusiastic. There are no stage directions on this passage, and one surmises that Mephostophilis puts an ape's head on Dick and a dog's on Robin.[20] In any case, these two comic scenes look forward to the horning of Benvolio, a transformation which occurs in the next sequence of scenes at the Emperor's court.

Here, because Benvolio is skeptical of magic, Faustus gives him animal horns: "See, see, my gracious Lord", Faustus cries, "what strange beast is yon, that thrusts his head out at window" (B 1319-20). At Charles's request, Faustus removes the horns, but the trick fires Benvolio's revenge plot, the failure of which we have already seen. Since Benvolio and his friends do fail, they are transformed; their "heads are all set with hornes" (B 1505). Benvolio resolves:

> I haue a Castle ioyning neere these woods,
> And thither wee'le repaire and liue obscure,

---

[20] See B 1630ff., where the Clown says that he was an ape.

Till time shall alter this our brutish shapes:
Sith blacke disgrace hath thus eclipst our fame.
We'le rather die with griefe, then liue with shame.   (B 1517-21)

His view offers a serious contrast to the comic happiness of Robin
at the prospect of being changed into an animal. Although he may
have acted irrationally (that is, like an animal) in taking umbrage
at the jest, Benvolio retains his human dignity. He would rather
die as a man, than live as an animal.

The semi-tragic scenes of Benvolio's transformation modulate
into the next scene (IV.v) in which the horse that Faustus sells
to the Horse-courser changes into a bottle of hay. The scene is
planned as a comic intensifier of the former action, for Faustus is
again (though this time comically) dismembered because of the
transformation. Part of this function we have already discussed in
tracing the pattern of dismemberment, but the full complexity is
realized only when we see that the transformation and dismemberment patterns are united in the Benvolio and Horse-courser
scenes. In their union, they look directly forward to Faustus's
death.

We have already examined the concept of man's transformation
into beast when Gaveston's bestial references in *Edward II* were at
issue. The idea of human degeneration was available to the early
Greeks, and was allegorized to mean that men who were controlled
by their sensual appetites soon became bestial. Spenser uses this
allegorization in the second book of *The Faerie Queene*, where
Acrasia changes men into beasts by appealing to their sexual lust.
Guyon, assuming the role of Odysseus and using both reason and
classical moderation, overcomes her and changes beasts back into
men – or most of the beasts. Spenser's Grill wishes to remain the
pig he has become.[21] The point seems to be that some men would
rather be bestial than human, and this point is relevant for
Faustus.

As Faustus approaches the hour in which he must render unto
Lucifer those things which are Lucifer's, he contemplates becoming
an animal:

[21] Spenser, *Faerie Queene*, II.xii.87.

Why wert thou not a creature wanting soule?
Or why is this immortall that thou hast?
Oh *Pythagoras Metemsycosis*; were that true,
This soule should flie from me, and I be chang'd
Into some brutish beast.
All beasts are happy, for when they die,
Their soules are soone dissolu'd in elements,
But mine must liue still to be plagu'd in hell.   (B 2072-79)

The man who has been able to transform others into animals now
wishes that he could do the same for himself; where Benvolio
prized his humanity, Faustus desires the oblivion of bestiality. If,
following Spenser, we consider wallowing in the senses as bestial,
then Faustus has led a bestial life, a life given not to the duties of
social man, but to animal pleasure. In man, however, sensuality
does not destroy the soul; it merely corrupts it, as it has done with
Faustus. Approaching the termination of his pact, he desires the
fullness of the animality which he has espoused. Readers of the
modern novel may think of Huxley's Jo Stoyte comically accepting
the prospect of apehood: "they look like they were having a pretty
good time. I mean in their own way, of course." Their way is his
way, and anything is better than death. But Faustus's world is
different. For him, death would be more desirable than eternal
damnation, and he longs for the oblivion that Stoyte shuns. In
the first scene, we saw Faustus deride medicine because it could
not offer man immortality; in his last thoughts, he realizes that
for some men immortality is less than a boon. He would now
willingly turn "into small water drops" (B 2086).

We have kept away from the comic scenes – that level of action
which Greg calls "farcical or clowning"[22] – as farcical as feasible, not
because they are excrescences, but because until recently their
value was virtually overlooked. Most modern critics see a quality
in these scenes which critics of, say, fifty years ago did not. Nevertheless, even in 1950, denying the integrity of the action, Greg
could write: "The tragic action is ... the essence of the play and
alone gives it interest and value."[23] He suggested that the scenes

[22] Greg (ed.), *Doctor Faustus*, p. 18.
[23] Greg (ed.), *Doctor Faustus*, p. 97, and cf. J. B. Steane's "fooleries" (*Marlowe:*

in question may have been written by another hand, possibly that
of Samuel Rowley.[24] Although I would not like to deny Greg's
position dogmatically, our study so far has indicated that it should
not be accepted without scrutiny. Part of the comic relevance has
already been indicated, but perhaps the best way to achieve an
impression of the total effect of the comic scenes is by looking at
them individually and in context, seeing how each fits into the
overall action.

Although the second scene of the play cannot be considered
totally comic, in it Wagner becomes a comic mirror of Faustus.
The two scholars wonder where Faustus has gone, for he was in
the past a prominent figure in the scholastic arguments of their
school; and when they ask Wagner, he plays with them by using
mock scholastic logic. "God in heauen knowes" where Faustus is
(B 194), he tells them. When they ask him if he does not know, he
answers: "Yes, I know, but that followes not" (B 196). The joke
is that Wagner denies the logic of the implied syllogism: God
knows where Faustus is; Wagner knows where Faustus is; therefore,
Wagner is God. The passage reflects on Faustus's assertion in the
preceding scene: "A sound Magitian is a Demi-god, / Here tire
my braines to get a Deity" (B 88-89). Where his servant comically,
albeit rationally, denies his divinity, Faustus egotistically feels that
he can make himself into a god. Wagner understands that KNOWL-
EDGE does not necessarily imply DIVINITY. He continues his logic-
chopping with the scholars – in mock analogy to Faustus's alogical
rejection of the humane disciplines in the first scene – finally
telling them what they want to know, that Faustus is at dinner with
Valdes and Cornelius.

Wagner's next scene (I.iv) is placed between the scene in which

---

A Critical Study, pp. 237-38). Robert Ornstein ("The Comic Synthesis in Doctor
Faustus", ELH, 22 [1955], 165-72) explained the function of the scenes, although
he has apparently changed his mind about the play in "Marlowe and God: The
Tragic Theology of Dr. Faustus", PMLA, 83 (1968), 1378-85. The most thorough
discussion is Charlotte Kesler, "The Importance of the Comic Tradition of
English Drama in the Interpretation of Marlowe's Doctor Faustus" (Unpublished
Dissertation, Missouri, 1954).
[24] Greg (ed.), Doctor Faustus, p. 133.

Faustus first calls Mephostophilis and that in which he signs the pact with Lucifer and supposedly obtains Mephostophilis as his servant. Again acting as a comic mirror to Faustus, Wagner obtains the services of Robin the clown. Wagner comments on his new-found servant: "I know the Villaines out of service, and so hungry, that I know he would giue his soule to the deuill, for a shoulder of Mutton, tho it were bloud raw" (B 347-49). But Robin denies the allegation: "Not so neither; I had need to haue it well rosted, and good sauce to it, if I pay so deere, I can tell you" (B 350-52). The passage, of course, reflects on the eating-gluttony pattern in the main plot; but it also mirrors Faustus's selling his soul to Lucifer. Robin will not give his soul for plain fare; it must be well cooked and seasoned. And this is precisely the view later espoused by Faustus. If the devil is to get his soul, "*Mephostophilis shall doe for him, and bring him whatsoeuer*" (B 491-92). By comically foreshadowing Faustus's agreement with Lucifer, Marlowe undercuts that agreement from the beginning. Faustus sells his soul for, in effect, nothing more than a well-sauced shoulder of mutton – a piece of sensual titillation.

In forcing Robin to accept the position as servant, Wagner threatens him with dismemberment: "if thou dost not presently bind thy selfe to me for seuen yeares, I'le turne all the lice about thee into Familiars, and make them tare thee in peeces" (B 359-61). In the main action, this situation is inverted. Although Faustus is the nominal master, he is threatened by his servant Mephostophilis with mutilation and dismemberment if he disobeys. Wagner calls Banio and Belcher, his devils, and Robin obediently submits, foreshadowing the recalcitrant Faustus frightened by the devils two scenes later (II.ii). But now that Robin has seen the power of black magic, he is anxious to learn: "but hearke you Maister, will you teach me this coniuring Occupation" (B 378-79). And Wagner here promises to teach him how to turn himself into an animal. The scene is filled with ideas which will become part of the ensuing main action, and it seems that the chief function of the comic scenes is to foreshadow and to establish a point of view. The Robin-Wagner relationship, initially mirroring the Mephostophilis-Faustus relationship, subtly (as well as comically) changes into something else. There is a suggested progression from Faustus, to Wagner, to Robin – each becoming less serious and ostensibly less intelligent in his ability to handle the magic in which he is dabbling. But the progression also reflects back upon Faustus, for he becomes only one member in a series of fools.

After this scene, Wagner disappears from the comic action, his place being taken by Robin and Robin's by Dick, another clown. Robin announces: "I haue gotten one of Doctor *Faustus* coniuring bookes, and now we'le haue such knauery, as't passes" (B 745-46). Dick enters to ask for Robin's help in walking the horses, but after some bawdy jesting, they go off to the tavern to eat and drink. The knavery which Robin contemplates promises to be rather low-keyed. The scene is placed directly after Faustus witnesses the pageant of the Seven Deadly Sins, and before he and Mephostophilis attend St. Peter's Feast in Rome. Dick and Robin provide a kind of comic analogue to the Sins, and their departure for the tavern leads into the action in Rome, which their next scene reflects. Immediately after the Friars curse Faustus and Mephostophilis for stealing the Pope's wine (B 1123), Dick and Robin enter with a cup stolen from the tavern. Apparently they too have been engaged in petty theft. As Faustus wishes to take part in the feast so "That this proud Pope may *Faustus* comming [i.e., cunning] see" (B 878), so when the Vintner comes to Robin to retrieve his cup, Dick says: "Now *Robin*, now or neuer shew thy cunning" (B 1135-36). Robin's stealing the Vintner's cup and Faustus's stealing the Pope's wine are on the same level of tomfoolery. Foolishness is foolishness, and Faustus's exploit is bracketed by clowning.

When the Horse-courser enters, Faustus has his first direct contact with the comic characters who have been foreshadowing and mirroring his actions. In our discussion of the main plot, we noticed that the elements of the play point to a progressive degeneration in Faustus, that as he becomes more deeply immersed in his diabolical way of life, he becomes less and less admirable. His connection with the low-life characters is another indication of his degeneration. When Faustus tampers with the Pope's feast, we recognize a conflict of equals; the pride of Faustus is set against the pride of the Pope. But when Faustus begins to play vicious pranks on the poor, we know that he has changed. The Horse-courser asks him to sell his horse at a bargain price, for, says the Horse-courser: "I am a very poore man, and haue lost very much of late by horse flesh, and this bargaine will set me vp againe" (B 1531-33).[25] But like Faustus's bargain with the devil, this one is also a thing made of straw. Since the horse is diabolic in origin, it cannot cross water,[26] and when the Horse-courser disobeys Faustus's injunction – "ride him not into the water" (B 1537-38) – the horse changes back into its prime element: straw. After Faustus dismisses the Horse-courser with another trick, Wagner enters with a message: "If it please you, the Duke of *Vanholt* doth earnestly entreate your company." And Faustus replies: "The Duke of *Vanholt's* an honourable Gentleman, and one to whom I must be no niggard of my cunning" (B 1571-75). There seems to be an intimate connection between Faustus as the tormentor of fools and Faustus the servant of great men. The emphasis is on the narrowness of his perspectives, the littleness of his soul.

In the following scene, the comic characters – Robin, Dick, the Horse-courser, and a Carter – meet in a tavern where they discuss the various tricks that Faustus has played upon them. Robin proffers this advice: "Hearke you, we'le into another roome and drinke a while, and then we'le go seeke out the Doctor" (B 1633-34). Having gotten themselves drunk, they miraculously appear at the Duke of Vanholt's court, where they provide a comic interlude. However, the episode is not without meaning. As each of the comic characters begins to accuse him, Faustus renders him speechless and sends him off before he can voice his accusation. The point is that Faustus refuses to listen to or to acknowledge what he has done and consequently become. Again we may be reminded of the Old Man's attempt to save him and his reward. Although the time of reckoning approaches, Faustus can still control the external situation and save himself from public shame. But, for the playgoer,

[25] Of course, we may wish to doubt the Horse-courser's veracity. He may be trying to trick Faustus into allowing him a bargain, and we have, in that case, an example of the trickster tricked, the reflexive action of evil.

[26] For the beliefs about diabolism and water, see Rossell Hope Robbins, *The Encyclopedia of Witchcraft and Demonology* (New York: Crown, 1959), pp. 492-94.

his subservience to Vanholt, at whose permission he performs hypnotic tricks, coupled with his lack of compassion for the poor, reveals the completeness of his fall.

The comic scenes are an integral part of the play. The comedy offers a perspective in which to see Faustus's actions, and when he is seen in this perspective, his accomplishments in diabolism may be evaluated for what they truly are. In reality, Faustus stands on the same ladder as Wagner, Robin, and Dick. The master and the servants are one, for, in a sense, Faustus's pretensions are as comic as the clowns'. What he performs with his magic does not seriously affect the world. He is an entertainer and a cheater of incompetents. His tragedy is that he sells his soul to become less than he was – a clown. In the end, Faustus reaches tragic reality through the comic mask.

The last lines of the play bring together its main ideas. The Bad Angel reveals a vision of hell: "There are liue quarters broyling on the coles" (B 2022), the bodies of dismembered sinners, and reminds Faustus that "He that loues pleasure, must for pleasure fall" (B 2032). The sensual Faustus, watching his time run out, remembers, ironically, a line from Ovid's *Amores:* "*O lente lente currite noctis equi*" (B 2045). In Ovid the line expresses the desire that the night may be prolonged so that the speaker may continue to enjoy his sexual pleasure.[27] Although the situations are radically different, Faustus uses the line in the same way; he, too, wishes the continuation of his sensual joys. He wishes time to stop; earlier, while waiting for midnight and Mephostophilis, he was impatient for time to pass:

> *Mepho:* come
> And bring glad tydings from great *Lucifer.*
> Ist not midnight? come *Mephostophilis.*
> *Veni veni Mephostophile.*
> (B 414-17)

The Latin summons reverberates with Faustus's Latin protest

---

[27] Ovid, *Amores*, I.xiii.40. Marlowe translated the line: "Then wouldst thou cry, 'Stay night, and run not thus.'" Millar MacLure (ed.), *Poems: Christopher Marlowe* (London: Methuen, 1968), p. 136. See Donald Baker, "Ovid and Faustus: The *Noctis Equi*", *Classical Journal*, 55 (1959), 126-28.

against the passage of time. In the end there is no call for the diabolical powers to come: "come not *Lucifer*, / I'le burne my bookes" (B 2091-92), but a vision of the possibility of salvation: "See see where Christs blood streames in the firmament, / One drop would saue my soule, halfe a drop, ah my Christ" (A 1463-64). Ironically, Faustus cannot accept Christ's offer; the devils may dismember him immediately. He is caught between desires, rendered immobile by his fears.

When he first met Mephostophilis, Faustus was eager to deny the existence of hell, of eternal alienation from God. Now, he can no longer be oblivious to the existential facts. At the beginning he is filled with confidence, longing for a field of knowledge which would grant freedom from death as well as life with pleasure. In his search for these things, he makes a pact with the devil, granting him both life and pleasure, but imposing a strict limitation on both: twenty-four years. In his eagerness for thoughtless sensuality, Faustus accepts unnatural limitation, and bargains eternal joy for what turns out to be servitude of the most obsequious sort. He becomes the plaything of great men, the court conjuror, and the fearful bondsman of Lucifer. If we look at him in this light, it is very difficult to see Faustus as a successful aspirer to universal power. He is a rather pitiful sensualist, caught in the toils of pleasure, and showing quickly the signs of his degeneration. As a master of shadows, Faustus commits himself to the uncreative, destructive elements of the universe, and in the end, he is destroyed by the very powers he has served. He has created nothing that survives, and leaves nothing behind but a mangled corpse.

Faustus is the climax of Marlowe's study of the aspiration for power and dominion. In the last four plays we have examined, Marlowe is exploring the various manifestations of human pride and presumption. The Guise is his Renaissance politician; Tamburlaine, his Renaissance conquistador; Faustus, his Renaissance scientist. All three refuse to accept natural limits. The Guise believes that he is capable of seizing France in a political coup; Tamburlaine feels that the world lies within the grasp of his military might; and, proudest of the three, Faustus looks forward to self-deification.

There is a progress of self-delusion from King to Emperor to God.

There is also a concomitant movement toward monodrama. Harry Levin's figures will help us to see what is happening.[28] Of the total number of lines in *The Massacre*, the Guise speaks only twenty-five percent. Tamburlaine, in Part One, speaks thirty-three percent, in Part Two, thirty-eight. Faustus is more difficult to calculate accurately because of the textual problems, but he speaks somewhere between thirty-eight and forty-seven percent. The figures help to confirm what we have already felt, that the central character becomes increasingly dominant. In *Tamburlaine*, Marlowe concentrates at least some of the play's interest on the minor characters, but in *Faustus*, the eponymous hero is everything.

Nevertheless, Harry Levin points out that the Jew of Malta speaks almost fifty percent of the lines in his play. What happens in *The Jew of Malta* is a union and consolidation of what Marlowe has learned about the monodrama. Barabas is the ultimate Marlovian character.[29] More fully than either Tamburlaine or Faustus, he is the clown, and his play, as Eliot saw, is a bloody farce.[30] Unlike the aspirers after power, Barabas does not seek to control his world. Indeed, he desires, like Mammon,[31] to build a world of his own, infinite riches in a little room; and when he fails to create his microcosm of wealth, he turns to destruction.

---

[28] Levin, *The Overreacher*, p. 186.

[29] Greg's contention (*Doctor Faustus*, p. 127) that one of Marlowe's chief characteristics is "moral earnestness" does not preclude his use of comedy, though Greg thought it did.

[30] T. S. Eliot, *Essays on Elizabethan Drama* (1932; rpt. New York: Harcourt, 1956), p. 62.

[31] An interesting analogue to Marlowe's Barabas is Spenser's Mammon, who concentrates infinite riches in his cave and tempts Guyon with his beautiful daughter, Philotime (*Faerie Queene*, II. vii. 3-65).

VIII

THE JEW OF MALTA

It is not difficult to see Faustian and Tamburlainean elements in *The Jew of Malta*.[1] The Maltese Jew in the manner of the German diabolist combines evil with comedy. There is almost as much black humor here as there is in *Faustus*, since, for all his evil, Barabas is essentially a comic character. At the same time, both he and Tamburlaine murder one of their children because that child differs from them in belief. After lives of successful worldly activity, they each die in a fire of their own creation – Tamburlaine burning himself up within, Barabas without. And since the cauldron into which Barabas falls may be seen as a symbol of hell,[2] we may also compare his end with the death of Faustus. There are other similarities, all of which suggest that Marlowe was perfectly aware, in writing this play, that he was bringing together the elements of earthly aspiration and metaphysical evil. If *Faustus* is the culmination of Marlowe's study of power, then *The Jew of Malta* is the highpoint of his monodrama.

In considering *1 Tamburlaine*, we saw that Zenocrate was

---

[1] While researching *The Massacre at Paris*, Marlowe may have learned about the practice of entering a city through the "common channels" (V.2092). Jean de Serres (*The Fourth Parte of Comentaries of the Ciuill Warres in France*, 4th Part, p. 55) writes: "There was at the walles of *Villeneuse* a hole, out of the which the water of the town, onely in the time of raine, runneth to purge the wayes and chanels: and the same had an yron grate before it. That hole this Souldier had viewed, and reported the same to be suche, that the barres of iron might easily be broken vp: through the which he affyrmed they might easily passe into the towne."

[2] G. K. Hunter ("The Theology of Marlowe's *The Jew of Malta*", *JWCI*, 27 [1964], 211-40) makes this point and explores the Judeo-Christan background of the play. He deals fully with the contrast between Job and Barabas (pp. 218-20) touched on later in this chapter.

essentially a figure of love and beauty who is unable to affect
the savage actions of the play. Barabas's daughter, Abigail, serves
a similar function here. She is as young as Juliet, scarcely fourteen,
says Mathias, and when we first meet her, she is weeping, not in
self-pity, as Barabas immediately assumes, but for him: "Father,
for thee lamenteth *Abigaile*" (I.463). Barabas, however, cannot
accept her protestation at face value. She must be grieving for
the loss of family wealth, he feels: "woman, moane not for a little
losse: / Thy father has enough in store for thee" (I.460-61). He
completely mistakes the source of her tears. The exchange is
brief, but the contrast between father and daughter is succinctly
drawn, and it points to a schism that will widen as the play goes on.

Unable to comprehend his daughter's motives, Barabas is ever
willing to use her for his ends, however much they may be at odds
with her personal ideals or feelings. For all his profession of love:

> one sole Daughter ... I hold as deare
> As *Agamemnon* did his *Iphigen*:
> And all I haue is hers.   (I.175-77)

the simile tells the story. Iphigeneia was sacrificed by her father
in order to assure a successful voyage to Troy. Later in the play,
to insure his own safety, Barabas promises: "I'le sacrifice her on a
pile of wood" (II.813). But he does not dispose of her until she
has helped him regain his lost gold and revenge himself on Ferneze.[3]

After his land and wealth have been confiscated by the Governor,
Barabas is prohibited from returning home, where he has hidden
"Ten thousand *Portagues*, besides great Perles, / Rich costly
Iewels, and Stones infinite" (I.478-79), since the house has been
immediately turned into a nunnery. Apparently Barabas has not
only been tricked by Ferneze, but inadvertently foiled as well.
However, he is infinite in the variety of his intrigues. Abigail must
become a convert to Christianity and desire to be a nun, thus
gaining access to the house and the hidden wealth. At this juncture,
Abigail is not a reluctant tool:

---

[3] Ferneze's name is probably derived from that of Alexander Farnese (1545-92),
Philip II's distinguished general in the Netherlands, who did not endear himself
to the English. See, e.g., *An Historicall Discovrse, or rather a Tragicall Historie of the
Citie of Antwerpe* (London, 1586), sig. F4ʳ (STC 691).

> Father, what e're it be to iniure them
> That haue so manifestly wronged vs,
> What will not *Abigall* attempt?   (I.509-11)

She still subscribes to the Hebrew ideal of retributive justice: an eye for an eye; and since Barabas's first scheme seems justified according to this ideal, she carries out the pretense. Later this initial pretense at conversion becomes ironic when she willingly adopts the ethic of love and rejoins the order for devout purposes. By using her as his agent here, Barabas gives her a chance to acquire a different, better set of values. Ironically, evil leads to good.

In the meanwhile, Barabas's reaction to his recovered gold indicates that his emotions for his daughter are closely associated with his attachment to money:

> Oh my girle,
> My gold, my fortune, my felicity;
> ...
> Oh girle, oh gold, oh beauty, oh my blisse!   (II.688-89, 695)

Using the images of the lark, he compares HIS MONEY BAGS, which he hugs in ecstasy, with the "young" of the bird (704). The easy emotive transference of affection for Abigail to affection for his money – a touch used by Shakespeare in *The Merchant of Venice* – points to the innate perversion of Barabas's emotions. He has confused the wealth of human love with the love of money. But then, money, unlike Abigail, is a tool which can be used without regard to its personal feelings.

By the play's fifth scene, Barabas has recovered his full wealth and is plotting the murder of Lodowicke, Ferneze's son. Using the jealousy of Mathias, the young man whom Abigail loves, Barabas plans to have Lodowicke killed in a duel; and Abigail must be the bait to set the trap. "It's no sinne to deceiue a Christian", he tells her:

> For they themselues hold it a principle,
> Faith is not to be held with Heretickes;
> But all are Hereticks that are not Iewes;
> This followes well, and therefore daughter feare not. –
>   (II.1075-78; cf. 994-95)[4]

---

[4] Cf. *2 Tamburlaine*, I.vi. 2805-53.

Nevertheless, Abigail submits to her father's plot only under compulsion: "Oh wretched *Abigal*, what hast thee done" (1085). Barabas has gone beyond any concept of retributive justice, and after learning that Mathias has been killed in a duel, Abigail re-enters the convent. The dissembling which has been forced upon her is contrasted with the sincerity of her elected religious life. As the friar (with a good deal of dark humor) laments, she remains true to her vows until death.

The two plots in which Abigail is Barabas's tool indicate something about the progress of the action.[5] From the daughter willing to aid her father in justly regaining his wealth, Abigail changes into a very unwilling accomplice, while Barabas moves from a man who simply wishes to reclaim his own, to a man who desires excessive revenge. Ironically, in pursuing his intrigue beyond rational bounds, he is forced (so he believes) to murder his daughter in order to preserve his secrets. What he takes from Ferneze, a child, he also takes from himself. His evil becomes reflexive.

In his change from rich merchant to murderous schemer, it seems almost as if the joy of plotting has taken the place of his love for money. The shift, although imperceptible to the playgoer, is too evident for some critics, who wish to see the second half of the play as a dramatic failure.[6] But the change in Barabas has its function and its meaning, and it has its counterbalance in the two conversions of Abigail, the false and the true. Abigail gains in moral stature; Barabas, like Tamburlaine and Faustus before him, degenerates.

The descent is marked by the child-substitute Barabas takes after he disinherits Abigail, an act which suggests his complete alienation from good. In the scene in which she begins to oppose her father's wishes, Barabas purchases Ithamore, a slave: "this is he / That by my helpe shall doe much villanie", Barabas informs us (II.897-98). Their relationship, based on a monetary exchange, is

---

[5] In 1 Samuel 25:24, Abigail calls herself a handmaid, a fact which apparently accounts for the popularity of the name in Renaissance England. In the play, her name suggests her function: a servant.

[6] See, e.g., T. S. Eliot, *Essays on Elizabethan Drama*, p. 62, and John Bakeless, *Tragicall History*, I, 334.

of questionable worth from the beginning. While the Spanish slave-traders are arranging their prisoners for sale, one of them comments: "Euery ones price is written on his backe" (764). Ostensibly he means the purchase price, but since the fourteenth century, English has had the idea that a *man's price* was the amount for which he is willing to sell his soul. The idea is not at all irrelevant to the relationship between Barabas and Ithamore. When Barabas substitutes Ithamore for his natural child, he also buys him:

> I here adopt thee for mine onely heire,
> All that I haue is thine when I am dead,
> And whilst I liue vse halfe; spend as my selfe;
> Here take my keyes, I'le giue 'em thee anon: (III.1345-48)

Of course, Barabas humorously withholds the final favor, the keys to the counting house, which would make the man as powerful as the master. But he makes sure that Ithamore understands what is involved in this adoption: "My purse, my Coffer, and my selfe is thine" (1396). And Barabas's protestations of love for his slave are comically ironic:

> Come neere, my loue, come neere thy masters life,
> My trusty seruant, nay, my second self;
> For I haue now no hope but euen in thee;
> And on that hope my happinesse is built: (III.1316-19)

The complete egotist, Barabas cannot be said to build his hope on anyone except himself; his insistence that he will base his future happiness on his less than intelligent slave is comic; and Barabas himself realizes the comedy of his words. However, when he tells Ithamore that he is his "second self", the irony is unconscious. On the surface, Barabas is attempting to deceive Ithamore by appealing to his vanity, but the playgoer can see that, in a sense, the egotist Ithamore is a second Barabas, the comic shadow of his master. When Ithamore betrays him, Barabas is symbolically betrayed by his own egotism, an extension of his own evil. The selfless Abigail who wills her father to "repent" his misdeeds (1307) is replaced by the purchased slave, the child of wealth.

To begin, Ithamore willingly takes Abigail's place as Barabas's tool, and there are parallels between the actions of Abigail and

Ithamore which are important to a reading of the play. First, Abigail's recovery of Barabas's money from the convent is related to Ithamore's poisoning of the nuns. Although Abigail pretends to be a devout convertite in order to gain access to the money, her action is relatively innocent. She merely recovers what her father must have to continue as a merchant. In contrast, Ithamore's pretended piety among the nuns, his delivery of the poisoned rice, is in reality mass murder (III.1378-84). Though Barabas claims to be legitimately revenging himself upon "False, credulous, inconstant *Abigall*" (1329), we cannot condone this action as we can the first. Poor Abigail may be credulous, but she is hardly as false and inconstant as her father, and the contrast between the true daughter and the adopted son indicates something about the degeneration of Barabas.

Second, there are parallels between the deaths of Mathias and Lodowicke, Barnadine and Jacomo, and Pilia Borza and Bellamira. All of these deaths are precipitated by Barabas's intrigue, but the first are prepared for without his intervention when Mathias and Lodowicke both fall in love with Abigail. Their deaths stem from their rivalry,[7] and Barabas's hands remain literally unsullied by their blood. Abigail is the decoy; Barabas writes the false challenges which lead to the fatal duel; but he, his daughter, and his slave are accessories before the fact, not the direct murderers. Abigail's murder is a consequence of Mathias's death; she is disposed of to ensure Barabas's safety.

The second two men, Barnadine and Jacomo, are brought to their deaths because of a combination of Barabas's crimes and their own greed. Since Abigail has confessed, the friars are fully aware that Barabas has planned, even if he did not execute, the first double murder. His involvement leads the friars to chide him for his crime and, in turn, forces him to plot their deaths to cover up his former murders. While the first murder plot is effected through jealousy, the second is based on the greed of the two friars, who are of different orders. Barabas promises to give his

[7] Molly M. Mahood (*Poetry and Humanism* [London: Jonathan Cape, 1950], pp. 79-80) suggests that the rivalry is motivated by greed. If so, they are even more closely related to the other doublet characters.

money, all of it, to the house of the friar who converts him; and he promises each friar that he will be THE ONE, in much the way that he promises both Lodowicke and Mathias that each will have his daughter. Unlike the first murders, however, Barabas and Ithamore are forced to strangle Barnadine themselves; this murder, it should be noticed, is the first Barabas performs on stage. The victim of deception, Jacomo is hanged for Barnadine's death. The second murders underline the fact that Barabas is being caught slowly in the web of his own plots.

The third murders develop out of the others and reflect them. Ithamore leaves his master for Bellamira, just as Abigail leaves her father for the convent. It may not be entirely fanciful to see a connection between the actual convent (with its unchaste nuns) and the metaphoric convent (Bellamira's bawdy house). If Abigail is motivated by love, Ithamore is drawn by lust. Bellamira invites him: "let's in and sleepe together" (IV.1848), and Ithamore replies with comic enthusiasm: "Oh that ten thousand nights were put in one, / That wee might sleepe seuen yeeres together" (1849-50). Because of his desire, Ithamore betrays his master to the greedy Bellamira and her pimp, Pilia Borza, just as Abigail, because of her filial love – "Couert my father that he may be sau'd" (III.1495) – inadvertently betrays Barabas to the greedy friars. The betrayals are certainly different in kind; but the consequences are very similar.

During this last crisis, however, Barabas no longer has a 'handmaid' or a slave to work his evil, and he must perform the murders by himself. Comparable to the poisoning of Abigail and the nuns is his poisoning of Ithamore and his two companions. The first poisoning is carried out by Ithamore, the comic slave; the second, by Barabas dressed as a comic French musician. Symbolically, Barabas takes on the identity of his comic servant, his "second self". In both poisonings, however, the victims do not die quickly enough to break the chain of cause and effect. As Abigail lives long enough to confess, Bellamira has her chance to inform Ferneze who plotted the death of his son. Both murder plots are ultimately unsuccessful in that they reveal rather than conceal Barabas's guilt.

Abigail and Ithamore, Mathias and Lodowicke, Barnadine and Jacomo, Bellamira (perhaps played by the same boy actor who played Abigail) and Pilia Borza are dual characters linked together in a complex pattern of degeneration. For Barabas, it is a trip downward from faithful daughter to faithless servant, from watching the death of a Governor's son to the actual poisoning of a common prostitute, from detached schemer to comically disguised murderer. It is the same kind of degenerative movement we have already seen in *Tamburlaine* and *Doctor Faustus*. As Barabas, like Tamburlaine and Faustus, becomes increasingly involved in the evils of his world, he becomes increasingly less the character to whom we are introduced at the beginning of the play.

But at this point, we must return to the beginning in order to explore certain thematic patterns which will help us define more specifically the Barabean world. Possibly the most important of these is the pattern of money. Money rather than love makes the world of Barabas go round: "The wind that bloweth all the world besides, / Desire of gold" (III.1422-23). The Prologue tells us that we are to see "the Tragedy of a Iew, / Who smiles to see how full his bags are cramb'd" (30-31), and five lines later, the first scene opens with "*Barabas in his Counting-house, with heapes of gold before him*" (S.D.). In his long soliloquy which follows, he plays variations on the theme of wealth, describing the rigid selection necessary to gather "Infinite riches in a little roome" (I.72). He has developed greed into an art. But Barabas is not the only character who aspires to material wealth, for greed motivates the public action of the play as well. The Turks, under Calymath, have come to Malta to demand the long-neglected tribute which the Knights of Malta owe them. The Christian Knights, who confiscate the wealth of the Jews, are equally greedy. Ostensibly needed to pay the tribute, this money is retained by Ferneze and his men at the suggestion of Martin Del Bosco, the Spanish Vice Admiral. Although Del Bosco offers to help the Maltese against the unbelieving Turks, he also has visions of gold. He may disguise his desires behind the façade of religion, but he basically wishes the Maltese to repudiate their Turkish alliance so that he may sell Turkish captives as slaves on the island. And the rest of the play, ironically, works out these tangled threads of greed.

That the prime motive of the play is greed tells us something about the world of Barabas. It is a small world, much smaller than the worlds of Tamburlaine and Faustus. The smallness of Greed is indicated in his allegorical speech in *Faustus*: "I am *Couetousnesse*: begotten of an old Churle in a leather bag; and might I now obtaine my wish, this house you and all, should turne to Gold, that I might locke you safe into my Chest: O my sweete Gold!" (B 691-95). There is no "thirst ... for Principality" or divinity in Barabas (I.173), and the quest for wealth, although it involves public action, is not comparable to the quest for ultimate physical or spiritual power. Greed is, in a way, a smaller vice; and Barabas is appropriately given a very limited, island background. "Infinite riches in a little roome."

It should be noticed, in transition, that the images and the language of wealth are used to indicate personal relations throughout. Barabas, for example, uses the code name "Diamond" for his daughter when discussing her with Lodowicke (II.810ff.). The substitution suggests that human worth has been replaced by monetary values. This confusion of values becomes a common feature in seventeenth-century English drama,[8] but it is equally evident in Marlowe, and it tells us that spiritual ideals have been subjected to material aspirations. The cash nexus has all but replaced the bonds of human love.

Nevertheless, as we have had opportunity to notice, all love is not dead on Malta. Abigail, in her love for Mathias and for her father, and Ithamore, in his passion for Bellamira, clearly manifest love, both unselfish and selfish. Although Mathias and Lodowicke are aware that Abigail is "the rich Iewes daughter" (I.608), the two young men seem interested in love rather than wealth. As Lodowicke tells Barabas: " 'Tis not thy wealth, but her that I esteeme, / Yet craue I thy consent" (II.1063-64). In contrast Bellamira admits that love, for her, is a means to wealth:

> Since this Towne was besieg'd, my gaine growes cold:
> The time has bin, that but for one bare night

8 See L. C. Knights, *Drama and Society in the Age of Jonson* (Harmondsworth: Penguin, 1962), pp. 145-50, *et passim*.

> A hundred Duckets haue bin freely giuen:
> But now against my will I must be chast.
> And yet I know my beauty doth not faile.
> From *Venice* Merchants, and from *Padua*,
> Were wont to come rare witted Gentlemen,
> Schollers I meane, learned and liberall.   (III.1150-57)[9]

She functions as a connecting link between love and money, just as the friars and nuns form a link between sexual love and religion. Although the religious characters are vowed to chastity, it is evident enough from the innuendoes that lust is not unknown in the convent.[10] As Ithamore asks with relish: "haue not the Nuns fine sport with the Fryars now and then?" (III.1254-55). If the desire for wealth is one dominant element in the play, it is both connected and contrasted with the longing for love and union.

But the love here is much like the love in *Dido* and *Edward II*. Creativity and unification, the qualities of love, are absent. The unnatural quality of love in the play is suggested by the prostitution of Bellamira and by the incontinence of the friars and nuns. The denial of true love suggests that we are in a world of death and divisiveness. Although children die, none are born. There are no marriages; and it is apparently a world of widows and widowers.

On Malta there are no permanent unions. Greed divides and leads ultimately to complete isolation – lonely death. On the public level, the division begins when the Turks insist that their tribute money be paid. Since both Maltese and Turks are interested in gaining or retaining wealth, the existing league between them is broken, and this broken league is the mirror before which Barabas acts out his dramatic destiny. Barabas underlines his own sense of isolation by contrasting himself with the "multitude" of Jews on Malta:

> You were a multitude, and I but one,
> And of me onely haue they taken all.   (I.411-12)

---

[9] The passage contains several examples of Marlovian punning. In "bare night", *bare* means both 'mere' and 'naked'. In "rare witted Gentlemen", *rare witted* means both 'extremely intelligent' and 'half-baked'. The idea that Marlowe was above this kind of wit should be disregarded.

[10] See, e.g., I.569-70, and III.1457, 1497.

After the multitude has departed, he claims that he is "fram'd of finer mold then common men" (453). As we see, Barabas uses his sense of individual distinction to assert his superiority. Like Faustus, he has no concept of the suffering servant who, through moral elevation, is isolated and yet helps his fellow man. When the Governor ironically suggests that "To saue the ruine of a multitude" (330), one man should suffer, Barabas implicitly rejects any such Judeo-Christian ideal. He cannot believe that the "priuate man" should perish for "a common good" (331-32). His isolation is spiritual as well as physical.

We have already noticed how Barabas is divided from his child and from his slave, and how the doublet characters are isolated by jealousy, greed, and death. But one further parallel may be used to illustrate how carefully Marlowe plotted this pattern of division and alienation. In Act I, after Calymath has gained the assurance that the Christians will pay the delinquent tribute, he grants them a month's grace and takes his leave: "Farewell great Gouernor, and braue Knights of *Malta*" (I.262). Ferneze gives the departing Turk his benediction: "And all good fortune wait on *Calymath*" (263). Near the end of the play when Barabas has temporarily become Governor, Calymath salutes him in leaving: "Farewell braue Iew, farewell great *Barabas*" (V.2121), and Barabas replies: "May all good fortune follow *Calymath*" (2122). The verbal echo is a signal that we should be alert to a parallel in action. What has taken place is a rather complex reversal. By his schemes, Barabas has been able to oust Ferneze, assume his power, and re-establish for the moment the league between Malta and Turkey. Ferneze is forced into the former role of Barabas: as the Christians have compelled the Jews to pay for their safety, now Barabas puts Ferneze and the Christians in the same position:

> What wilt thou giue me, Gouernor, to procure
> A dissolution of the slauish Bands
> Wherein the Turke hath yoak'd your land and you?
> What will you giue me ... ? (V.2177-80)

And Ferneze promises "Great summes of mony" (V.2189). If the plan succeeds, the Turks will again be deceived by the fair words of a Maltese Governor – this time more violently. But once again, the Governor of Malta is hoist with his own petard. As Ferneze is beaten, captured, and imprisoned by the Jew he has swindled, so Barabas is betrayed by the Christian Ferneze with whom he has joined against the Turks. Alone in his flaming cauldron, Barabas dies cursing, ultimately separated from those things he held most dear – his money and his life. But the play does not end with Barabas's death. The final lines focus on the betrayal of Calymath: his men have been blown up, and he is in the hands of the treacherous Ferneze, who promises to fight the Turks and to hold Calymath hostage until reparations are paid. As in *Dido*, there is no hope for union, only the promises of continued division.

This lack of human community which marks the play is underlined by the overt pattern of deceit and dissembling. And, as Howard Babb has carefully shown, deception is closely allied to the use of the word "policy" in the play.[11] "Policy" is first spoken by the Maltese knight who tells Barabas that it would be "simple policie" (I.392) not to keep the day of reckoning with the Turks. He means, intentionally, that it would be a foolish stratagem not to do so. But Barabas picks another meaning: "I, policie? that's their profession, / And not simplicity, as they suggest" (393-94). In his opinion, the Maltese have substituted Machiavellian policy for the ideal of Christian simplicity. But as Barabas himself comes to deal increasingly in intrigue, he increasingly emphasizes his own policy. He gains and must maintain his position by "firme policy" (V.2137); he will make a "profit" of his "policie" (2214); his "policie detests preuention" (2223); and he finally asks Ferneze to "partake" of his "policy" (2307). The word comes to mean a kind of cunning deception, and it is an index to Barabas's growing reliance on intrigue as well as his decreasing reliance on human ties.

The duplicity, which the word "policy" highlights, is reflected by the use of asides. Although the dramatic aside is a conventional Renaissance technique, Marlowe uses it to an extraordinary

---

[11] Howard S. Babb, "Policy in Marlowe's *The Jew of Malta*", *ELH*, 24 (1957), 85-94.

degree to emphasize the levels of action: that which is apparently
happening, and that which is actually happening. In certain
scenes, there are enough asides so that we have the effect of a
double play with separate streams of action. When Lodowicke and
Barabas are discussing the metaphoric "diamond", the playgoer
sees three levels on which the action is taking place:

> Lod. And what's the price?
> Bar. Your life and if you haue it. – Oh my Lord
> We will not iarre about the price; come to my house
> And I will giu't your honour – with a vengeance.
> *Aside.* (II.827-30)

In order to disguise their negotiations about Abigail, there is the
agreed upon code name; superficially, Barabas and Lodowicke
are buying and selling a jewel. One level deeper, which is still
a level of shared communication, they are talking about Lodowicke's marriage to Abigail, while on the lowest level, Barabas is
plotting a murder. On the surface levels, Barabas is the obsequious
merchant and the dutiful father making a good marriage for
his daughter, but the asides reveal the illusion. Shakespeare was to
use the same method with Shylock, and the aside became increasingly, in later drama, the conventional method of manifesting
this essential dualism between external appearance – the playing
of a role – and the reality which lies beneath the façade.

The deceptive façades of the Maltese world are almost as various
as the kinds of depravity thus hidden, and, as in Marlowe's earlier
plays, the most respectable of these façades is religion. Machiavel
introduces the dominant attitude toward religious faith in the
Prologue. Some men, he insists, will publicly decry his doctrines:

> Yet will they read me, and thereby attaine
> To *Peters* Chayre: And when they cast me off,
> Are poyson'd by my climing followers.
> I count Religion but a childish Toy,
> And hold there is no sinne but Ignorance. (Prologue, 11-15)

Religion may be used to conceal one's true feelings, but it is not
to be mistaken for a functional part of life.[12] However, Machiavel's

---

[12] Marlowe's personal comments on religion may have been directed against

statement should not be mistaken for the playwright's credo; if anything, the play explores the evils of such hypocrisy. Although Barabas hides his greed behind his Judaism as carefully as the Governor and his Knights hide theirs behind Christianity, he is quick to criticize this practice in the Christians. After listening to them quote John 11:50 and Matthew 27:25, he replies sharply:

> What? bring you Scripture to confirm your wrongs?
> Preach me not out of my possessions.
> Some Iewes are wicked, as all Christians are.   (I.343-45)

Ferneze and his men go far to justify Barabas's complaint.

The link between religion and money is suggested here by the double meaning of "profession". It is used to mean 'line of business' (353), 'religious faith' (378), and possibly both (393). Religion becomes, in the play's terms, a business, a way of gaining wealth. When Martin del Bosco is told that he cannot sell his Turkish slaves on Malta because of the existing league, he asks: "Will Knights of *Malta* be in league with *Turkes*, / And buy it basely too for summes of gold?" (II.733-34), and he goes on to emphasize the religious antagonism between Christians and Moslems. Ferneze quickly takes the cynical cue from Del Bosco and soon speaks with religious fervor of "these barbarous mis-beleeuing Turkes" (751). In the first Act, he had blessed Calymath and wished him good fortune. Now, as the scene ends, Del Bosco prepares to market his Turkish slaves, and Ferneze, with his eye on gold and under the color of religion, has found an excuse to keep the money he has extorted from the Jews. We should not miss the comedy of this scene, and we should be skeptical of genuine religious feeling in any of the characters.

If Barabas is correct in saying that some Jews are willing to prostitute their religion, he himself is one of these. He persuades Abigail to play a Christian convertite, while he feigns the outraged Jewish father. Later to save his skin, he pretends a desire for con-

---

the kind of religious attitude pictured here, where "all religion" is "but a deuice of pollicie" (Beard, *The Theatre of Gods Iudgements*, p. 147). There is no indication in the plays that he condoned religious hypocrisy or blasphemy.

version. We may see this deceptive conversion, if we wish, as a contrast to the final and heartfelt conversion of Abigail, who alone, of the central characters, has accepted a functional religious faith. Barabas the Jew, as much as Ferneze the Christian, is willing to cover his greed and guilt under the profession of religion, a religion with no inherent belief in a deity as far as we can see. It is ironic that, as a group, the Moslem Turks are the least anxious to use religion as an easy excuse. They admit that wealth, not love of God, motivates their actions, and they move without façades toward their goal. In the cases of Barabas and Ferneze, we must consider the distance between their professions of faith and their violent actions.

Marlowe helps the playgoer make this adjustment by creating the fable of Barabas as a partial parody of the Book of Job. Both Job and Barabas are brought from great wealth to comparative poverty and back to wealth again. Like Job, Barabas has three supposed friends who counsel him in his adversity. After Barabas has been relieved of his money, the first Jew advises him to "be patient" (I.402), and when Barabas does not reveal the proper patience, he tells him more specifically: "yet brother *Barabas* remember *Iob*" (413). However, this is a topic upon which Barabas has some unconventional thoughts:

> What tell you me of *Iob?* I wot his wealth
> Was written thus: he had seuen thousand sheepe,
> Three thousand Camels, and two hundred yoake
> Of labouring Oxen, and fiue hundred
> Shee Asses: but for euery one of those,
> Had they beene valued at indifferent rate,
> I had at home, and in mine Argosie
> And other ships that came from *Egypt* last,
> As much as would haue bought his beasts and him,
> And yet haue kept enough to liue vpon;
> So that not he, but I may curse the day,[13]
> Thy fatall birth-day, forlorne *Barabas;*
> And henceforth wish for an eternall night.   (I.414-26)

"Valued at indifferent rate" Job's losses are nothing compared

---

[13] Cf. Job 3:1ff.

to Barabas's, but the system of values which allows this judgment is completely inverted. First, and most obviously, when a man loses everything, it matters little how much or how little that everything is. This is one of Lear's realizations, but so egotistical is Barabas that he refuses to acknowledge that another may suffer as much or more than he. Second, Barabas treats the loss purely in material terms; he does not mention Job's children who are killed in a storm (Job 1:18). For Job, the loss is seen as a spiritual crisis; for Barabas, it is a matter of commercial mathematics. Barabas's omission of Job's lost children is further ironic when, in the course of the action, he poisons Abigail. Job's children die while they are feasting – "eating, and drinking wine" (Job 1:18) – and so will Abigail; but her father will not mourn her passing.

Far from being a patient Job, Barabas is known for his unrestrained anger, his quickness to curse and to revenge. The course of villainy that he follows is the obverse of patient suffering. Unlike Job who refuses to curse and die (Job 2:9-10), Barabas ends his life in the cauldron – a symbol of hell – shouting: "Dye life, flye soule, tongue curse thy fill and dye" (V.2373). The playgoer familiar with biblical story can hardly miss the allusions to Job, and the effect of the references is to set up a positive picture against which to judge Barabas. We are openly invited to compare the Book of Job with the negative, parodic world built by the playwright. The inversion of the biblical is, of course, also suggested in Barabas's name, since it is the same as the thief's who was released that Christ might be crucified. One might further wish to toy with an implied contrast between Christ's death on the cross with its overtones of universal salvation and Barabas's death in the fiery cauldron which saves only a few Turks from a similar fate. It is Marlowe's method to suggest such comparisons; the playwright's use of biblical story allows us to interpret with some degree of accuracy what our attitude toward Barabas should be and how far he is from any genuine religious faith.

One way to bring together some of the various thematic strands of the play is to explore the imaginative significance of Barabas's notoriously haunting question and answer: "Fornication? but

that was in another Country: / And besides, the Wench is dead"
(IV.1550-51). Twentieth-century artists have picked out this
brief passage as a gem with infinite facets. Eliot's "Portrait of a
Lady" uses it as an epigraph. Hemingway's title "In Another
Country" is taken from Marlowe, and Hemingway again plays
with the passage in *The Sun Also Rises*.[14] But the critics have not
seriously tried to explain why this passage – in context ironic to
the point of comedy – is so effective.

First, I would like to suggest that part of the power is in the
phrase Hemingway took as a title: "in another Country" opens
a vista of years in which to see Barabas's actions. Although the
play begins with a panoramic vision of Mediterranean commerce,
we have noticed that the action takes place entirely on Malta,
in one city and its immediate environs. There is an emphasis on
walls and fortifications, and walls not only exclude, they confine and enclose. Out of this increasingly stuffy and constricted
atmosphere comes Barabas's allusion to another country and to a
time past in which he was interested in the love of a girl.

But this sudden opening of a vista is only the smallest part of the
effect, for what haunts us most is the contrast between what we
feel behind the lines – a sense of human loss and suffering – and
the callousness of Barabas's attitude – "and besides, the Wench
is dead". For one thing, we realize that the actual dead girl is
his own daughter, not an unknown lady in another country.
The lines are further complicated by the knowledge that Barabas
is fully aware that the two friars are speaking of his present guilt:
"She has confest, and we are both vndone; / My bosome in[ti]-
mates, *but I must dissemble*" (IV.1555-56). Acting the role of an
innocent, he admits that he may have been guilty in another
country, at another time. The playgoer assumes that this previous
fornication is a complete pretense, another façade to cover his
actual crimes, and that he has chosen a sexual crime because the
lecherous friars will consider it most venial.

---

[14] Ernest Hemingway, *The Sun Also Rises* (New York: Scribner's, 1954), p. 75:
"'That was in another country,' Bill says, 'And besides all the animals were
dead.'" Cf. James Baldwin, *Another Country* (New York: Dial, 1962), and Harry
Levin, "Marlowe Today", *TDR*, 8:4 (1964), 27.

But his statement also carries the suggestion that guilt is only relative, that what he has done elsewhere cannot affect him on Malta; it has no moral relevance on the island. Although the friars seem to accept this contention, it is strange logic for a moral being; and this is precisely the point. As a dramatic character, Barabas has no moral framework outside himself; his only values are personal and material. He has no sense of a moral continuity in which he and his fellow characters exist. For the playgoer, a moral framework is supplied by the dramatist through his allusions to Judeo-Christian myth, and thus we have a sense of a spiritual background in which the death of a former lover DOES matter and DOES have meaning. We feel something behind Barabas's lines that he himself is not allowed to recognize. Our insight is set over against his moral blindness.

Moreover, these lines reverberate with Barabas's earlier statements about his past life. To Ithamore, he makes a more detailed confession:

> Being young, I studied Physicke, and began
> To practise first vpon the *Italian*;
> There I enric[h]'d the Priests with burials,
> ...
> And after that was I an Engineere,
> And in the warres 'twixt *France* and *Germanie*,
> Vnder pretence of helping *Charles* the fifth,
> Slew friend and enemy with my stratagems.
> Then after that was I an Vsurer.   (II.946-48, 951-55)

And so he continues. Outrageous in cruelty, his early crimes are probably intended to be taken as another pretense, a test to see how Ithamore will react. Ithamore answers with an account of his own exploits, and in all likelihood, we should take this whole episode as black humor. Ithamore's trick of putting irritating powder on shrines so that he may watch the pilgrims who knelt there go home on crutches can be taken no more seriously than Barabas's boast that he allowed himself to be robbed so that he might witness the thieves in chains. As Barabas notes, they are "villaines both" (979), but because of their lack of serious intent at this point in the action, we can do little more than laugh at their inconsequential villainy. Later, after Barabas has had Abigail murdered, our reaction to his comic admission of fornication cannot be so pure. We may see the comedy, but we feel a wealth of complexity which hinders a genuinely comic response.

These glances at Barabas's fraudulent accounts of his former life point to the mixture of comedy and tragedy which characterizes this play as distinctly as *Faustus*. Barabas is indeed both comedian and villain, and while some critics have been disturbed by this mixture, it is an integral part of the Marlovian dramaturgy. Ithamore's comic references to Barabas's bottle-nose – "I worship your nose for this" (II.938) – are not anti-Semitic, but rather point to Barabas's dramatic ancestors. In Fulwell's *Like Will to Like*, Newfangle the Vice marvels at Lucifer's "big ... nose", and says that his dame calls him a "bottle-nosed knave".[15] Barabas descends from the serio-comic devils of earlier drama. Although we may not be able to appreciate his comic aspects when he sends Ithamore to poison Abigail, we cannot think of him as downright abhorrent when he plays with such vehemence and dexterity to deceive the lecherous and greedy friars. In his plot to murder Ithamore, Pilia Borza, and Bellamira, he justly unites comedian and villain, as he puts on his comic French accent and comes dancing in with his poisoned flowers. Comedy here becomes one of the façades of villainy.

But the juxtaposition of comedy and villainy is only one of the dualities which inform the play. *The Jew of Malta* is bifurcated, built on doubles – on double characters, duplicity, double actions: Barabas twice becomes rich, twice murders a child or surrogate child, apparently dies twice. On the imagistic and thematic levels, there is the contrast between light and dark, law and mercy, the many and the one, pretense and reality. Each of these dualities in turn becomes part of the basic conflict between good and evil.

---

15 Ulpian Fulwell, *Like Will to Like*, in W. Carew Hazlitt (ed.), *A Select Collection of Old English Plays* (London, 1874), III, 311: "This hole in thy fury didst thou disclose, / That now may a tent be put in, so big as thy nose. / This was, when my dame called thee bottle-nosed knave." Sanders (*The Dramatist and the Received Idea*, p. 38) sees the bottle-nose as part of "the ethnic stereotype of the Jew" used by Marlowe.

On the surface, there is the verbal allegiance to the virtues of mercy, self-sacrifice, and peace; but on the submerged level of Barabas's asides and soliloquies, there is the actual allegiance to evil, simply, one begins to feel, for its own sake. Marlowe's logic here is perfect. If virtue is aphoristically its own reward, then just as obviously vice, to the vicious, must be equally rewarding. In Marlowe's strangely inverted dramatic world – a world which mirrors our own so stringently – this ethical paradox is thoroughly explored. Beginning as an acquisitive Renaissance merchant, Barabas is destroyed – like Dido, Mortimer, the Guise, Tamburlaine, and Faustus before him – by the unnatural evil of which he has become a part. Evil is rewarded with evil.

IX

CODA: THE MARLOVIAN WORLD PICTURE

Marlowe's vision is of a world of human evil. He had no feeling for a brave new Renaissance world such as Shakespeare pictured in *The Tempest*, where evil becomes only a latent, not a living power. For him, evil was a vital, though destructive, force, and he looked at it not with the optimistic eyes of Shakespeare, but with the savage indignation of Swift. There is something to be said for the analogy between Marlowe and Swift. Both saw man's inhumanity to man with the severe eye of the moralist; they pictured this inhumanity with clarity and comedy; and, ironically, they have been accused of exhibiting those same vices which they consciously and thoroughly despised.

In Marlowe's dramatic world, evil is man-made, or at least gains force through man's willing consent. The desire to get beyond the finite world by unnatural means, the wish to attain the reasonably impossible lead to evil and to destruction. This egotistical grasping after infinity in defiance of universal law is the Marlovian equivalent of Original Sin. At the same time, Marlowe's anti-heroes have little concept of spiritual infinity. They desire their infinity only in material terms – in terms of physical love, of overwhelming power, of unsurpassed wealth.

There are certain irrevocable dynamics of this world of human evil. First, the good are materially much less powerful than the bad. Zenocrate gives herself to Tamburlaine; Abigail, a more obstinate creature of good, is poisoned. A Marlovian play does not end with the basically good overcoming the basically bad, but with evil conquering evil. Ferneze outwits Barabas; Lucifer carries Faustus to hell. One sees no possibility of a triumphant good in Marlowe's world. Second, although evil characters may be materially powerful, spiritually they degenerate as their power increases. Slightly evident in Mortimer, this degenerative process is a recurring technique after *1 Tamburlaine*. The implication is that evil affects one very much like a degenerative disease, causing a blindness to essential reality in the evil character. Third, following from this degeneration, evil is self-destructive. The evil returns on the inventor's head; it is reflexive. Tamburlaine is burned by his own internal fire; Faustus is torn by the devils he has called; Barabas boils to death in the cauldron he has prepared for Calymath. Thus, with all the material power and wealth, evil is essentially undesirable – uncreative and destructive. Ironically, evil is both triumphant and doomed.

There is a traditional basis for Marlowe's inverted world; the concept of the world turned upside down was a medieval commonplace. But Marlowe uses the concept with a difference: here the inverted world is a reflection of Renaissance society. From the injunctions against ambition and aspiration we find in Renaissance literature, we may gather how socially disruptive the 'aspiring mind' actually was. Modern historians have only confirmed that the Renaissance commentators were essentially correct. And Marlowe's plays mirror this new, acquisitive society.

Romantic critics might agree at this point, but they would insist that Marlowe's attitude toward ambition was positive, that he was preaching a gospel of aspiration. For them, Marlowe is attempting to say: this is the glorious conqueror Tamburlaine; go and do likewise. In contrast, the Marlowe whom we have seen through the plays is perfectly aware of the failings of 'aspiring minds', and if the playgoer is able to generalize from his dramatic experience, he will take away with him an understanding of the limitations of ambition. The meaning, in one way, is simple; the complexity lies in the working out – the verbal artistry, the intricate patterns of action, the balance of characters, the ironies.

But perhaps a final clarification of what I mean by 'social implications or reflections' is in order. One may wish to link *Dido* with Elizabeth's contemplated marriage to Alençon. Here, in the Renaissance political arena was Elizabeth, a queen without a mate, toying with the possibility of marrying a man whose destinies were tied up with those of another country. In taking the story of Dido from Virgil, Marlowe may well have been considering the parallels between epic story and contemporary politics. But to see Marlowe's play as allegorical and to carry this kind of identification to specifics is extremely misguided. Marlowe was not writing political allegories, but generally reflecting the social and political problems of his time. Rather than seeing his characters as reflections of individuals, we may look at them as types – queen, king, general, scientist, merchant – who engage in typical forms of evil. Marlowe was pointing to the faults of a society, not at the failings of particular people.[1]

But along with the continuing penchant for social reflection, there is a movement toward what Tucker Brooke called "one-man drama", the domination of the play by a central figure: Tamburlaine, Faustus, Barabas.[2] It is significant that the movement toward monodrama is also a movement toward a sharper focus on the evils of ambition and the aspiration to power and wealth. The emphasis on a single character allows the playwright to explore more fully 'the aspiring mind'. One may complain of a pasteboard Aeneas or a poorly motivated Queen Isabel, but with Tamburlaine such objections must disappear. Marlowe gives him more than a third of the lines in his two plays and allows him to speak at full volume. With Tamburlaine we get a total look at what ambition is truly like.

In one way, the movement of Marlovian drama is toward a play like *Hamlet*. But ideologically, Shakespeare's play could not be more different from those of his skeptical contemporary. Hamlet is not the embodiment of social or political evil. One of his problems is that he is unwilling, on the one hand, to accept easy answers and, on the other, to sell his soul to evil. He wishes – is

[1] See David Bevington, *Tudor Drama and Politics: A Critical Approach to Topical Meaning* (Cambridge, Mass.: Harvard University Press, 1968), p. 14. Bevington's view of Marlowe's political and social position (pp. 213-18) differs greatly from the one offered in the present study.

[2] Tucker Brooke ("The Renaissance", in: *A Literary History of England*, ed. by Albert C. Baugh [New York: Appleton-Century-Crofts, 1948], p. 518) saw Marlowe moving away from one-man drama.

commanded by his father – to purge the state AND to save his own moral integrity. There is no such moral scrupulosity found in the Marlovian hero. Marlowe's heroes look forward to Richard III and beyond him to Macbeth. Here is the true line of Marlowe: the tragedy of degeneration and damnation.

Marlovian tragedy retained its popularity in the seventeenth century. Heywood revived the *Jew of Malta* in 1633, and Marlowe's plays were generally in print. T. S. Eliot has suggested that Ben Jonson is the true heir of Marlowe, and Edward Partridge has pointed out that Jonson uses the technique of the inverted world, a technique which we have identified as Marlovian.[3] Although one would not like to conclude that Jonson consciously took the technique from Marlowe, still it is an essential feature of Marlovian drama which Jonson carried into the next century. One may also see elements of Marlowe in the plays of Tourneur, Marston, Webster, and Ford. Though scholars and critics have thoroughly investigated (and disputed) the probable influence of Shakespeare and Jonson on the seventeenth-century drama, the influence of Marlowe has received comparatively little attention.[4] Marlowe may not have affected the language of drama as thoroughly as the other two, but there is in early seventeenth-century drama a certain mixture of morality, socio-political concern, and dark humor which we have come to see as Marlovian.

In the Heroic Drama of the Restoration we see the last burgeoning of Marlowe's influence. Although it has become an unexamined commonplace that Marlowe was virtually forgotten by the last part of the seventeenth century, Edward Phillips could still call him in 1675 "a kind of second Shakespeare".[5] Surely in the grand bragging and the fantastic deeds of Almanzor and

---

[3] T. S. Eliot, *Essays on Elizabethan Drama*, p. 74, and Edward Partridge, *The Broken Compass: A Study of the Major Comedies of Ben Jonson* (New York: Columbia University Press, 1958), pp. 63-69.

[4] The chief study has been Tucker Brooke, "The Reputation of Christopher Marlowe", *Transactions of the Connecticut Academy of Arts and Sciences*, 25 (1922), 347-88.

[5] See, e.g., Irving Ribner, *TDR*, 8:4 (1964), 211-24, and Edward Phillips, *Theatrum Poetarum* (London, 1675), "The Modern Poets", p. 24. Cf. William Winstanley, *The Lives of the Most Famous English Poets* (London, 1687), p. 134.

his compeers we are witnessing the grandsons of Tamburlaine. Strangely enough, the end of the line of Marlowe may be marked by Nicholas Rowe's play named after the old hero.[6] In his literary career, Rowe obviously had his eye on the Elizabethans, and like Marlowe, he translated Lucan's *Pharsalia*. But his Tamerlane is utterly un-Marlovian. In Rowe's play, Tamerlane is held up as a humanistic ideal, and it should not surprise us that Rowe's ultimate source is Du Bec's history. The Marlovian aspiration for the impossible is gone, and gone with it are those elements of exuberance and comedy, irony and moral insight which we have found in the dramatic world of Christopher Marlowe.

---

[6] Nicholas Rowe, *Tamerlane: A Tragedy* (London, 1702). In the Preface to his *Tamerlane the Great: A Tragedy* (London, 1681), Charles Saunders claims: "I never heard of any Play on the same Subject, untill my own was Acted, neither have I since seen it, though it hath been told me, there is a Cock-Pit Play, going under the name of the *Scythian Shepherd*, or *Tamberlain the Great*, which how good it is, any one may Judge by its obscurity." If Saunders had not seen a copy, as he asserts, it is strange that he adopts the Marlovian spelling *Tamberlain* when his usual form is *Tamerlane*. Saunders protests a bit too much.

BIBLIOGRAPHY

Adams, Joseph Q., "The *Massacre at Paris* Leaf", *Library*, 14 (1934), 447-69.

Adams, Thomas, *Diseases of the Soule* (London, 1616), STC 109.

Agrippa, Henry Cornelius, *Of the Vanitie and Vncertaintie of Artes and Sciences*, trans. by James Sanford (London, 1569), STC 204.

Allen, Don Cameron, *Doubt's Boundless Sea: Skepticism and Faith in the Renaissance* (Baltimore: John Hopkins Press, 1964).

——, "Marlowe's *Dido* and the Tradition", *Essays on Shakespeare and Elizabethan Drama in Honor of Hardin Craig*, ed. by Richard Hosley (Columbia: University of Missouri Press, 1962), 55-68.

Allott, Robert, *Wits Theater of the Little World* (London, 1599), STC 382.

Anonymous, *The Conduct and Character of Count Nicholas Serini ... with his Parallels Scanderbeg & Tamberlain* (London, 1664).

——, *The Contre-Guyse* (London, 1589), STC 12506.

——, *An Excellent Discovrse vpon the Now Present Estate of France*. See Hurault, Michel.

——, *An Historicall Discovrse, or rather a Tragicall Historie of the Citie of Antwerpe* (London, 1586), STC 691.

——, *The Historie of the Damnable Life and Deserued Death of Doctor Iohn Fausten* (London, 1592), STC 10711.

——, *The Historie of the Damnable Life and Deserved Death of Doctor John Faustus*, ed. by William Rose (Notre Dame: University of Notre Dame Press, 1963).

——, *Martine Mar-Sixtus*. See W., R.

——, *The Restorer of the French Estate* (London, 1589), STC 11289.

——, *Two Guides to a Good Life* (London, 1604), STC 12466.

Ariosto, Ludovico, *Orlando Furioso in English Heroical Verse*, trans. by John Harington (London, 1591), STC 746.

Babb, Howard S., "*Policy* in Marlowe's *The Jew of Malta*", *ELH*, 24 (1957), 85-94.

Bakeless, John, *The Tragicall History of Christopher Marlowe* (Cambridge: Harvard University Press, 1942).

Baker, Donald, "Ovid and Faustus: The *Noctis Equi*", *Classical Journal*, 55 (1959), 126-28.

Baldwin, James, *Another Country* (New York: Dial, 1962).

Barckley, Sir Richard, *A Discovrse of the Felicitie of Man* (London, 1598), STC 1381.

Batman, Stephen, *Batman Vppon Bartholome, his Booke De Proprietatibus Rerum* (London, 1582), STC 1538.

Battenhouse, Roy, *Marlowe's Tamburlaine: A Study in Renaissance Moral Philosophy* (Nashville: Vanderbilt University Press, 1964).

Beard, Thomas, *The Theatre of Gods Iudgements* (London, 1597), STC 1659.

Bevington, David, *Tudor Drama and Politics: A Critical Approach to Topical Meaning* (Cambridge: Harvard University Press, 1968).

The Bible, Translated according to the Ebrew and Greeke (London, 1586), Geneva version, STC 2145.

Blissett, William, "Caesar and Satan", *JHI*, 18 (1957), 221-32.

——, "Lucan's Caesar and the Elizabethan Villain", *SP*, 53 (1956), 553-75.

Boaistruau, Pierre, *Theatrum Mundi*, trans. by John Alday (London, 1574), STC 3169.

Boas, Frederick, *Christopher Marlowe: A Biographical and Critical Study* (Oxford: Clarendon, 1940).

Bodin, Jean, *The Six Bookes of a Commonweale*, trans. by Richard Knolles (London, 1606), STC 3193.

Brodwin, Leonora Leet, "*Edward II:* Marlowe's Culminating Treatment of Love", *ELH*, 31 (1964), 139-55.

Brooke, C. F. Tucker, "On the Date of the First Edition of Marlowe's *Edward II*", *MLN*, 24 (1909), 71-73.

——, "The Renaissance", *A Literary History of England*, ed. by Albert C. Baugh (New York: Appleton-Century-Crofts, 1948).

——, "The Reputation of Christopher Marlowe", *Transactions of the Connecticut Academy of Arts and Sciences*, 25 (1922), 347-408.

Bruce, J. Douglas, "The Three Days' Tournament Motif in Marlowe's *Tamburlaine*", *MLN*, 24 (1909), 257-58.

Bruno, Giordano, *The Heroic Frenzies*, trans. by Paul Eugene Memmo (Chapel Hill: University of North Carolina Press, 1964).

Byshop, John, *Beavtifull Blossomes* (London, 1577), STC 3091.

Calvin, John, *Sermons of Master Iohn Caluin, Vpon the Booke of Iob*, trans. by Arthur Golding (London, 1574), STC 4444.

Cambini, Andrea, *Tvvo Very Notable Commentaries*, trans. by John Shute (London, 1562), STC 4470.

Cavendish, George, "Life and Death of Thomas Wolsey", *The Renaissance in England*, ed. by Hyder Edward Rollins and Herschel Baker (Boston: Heath, 1954).

Caxton, William (trans.), *The Boke Intituled Eracles* (London, 1481), STC 13175.

Chambers, Edmund K., *The Elizabethan Stage*, rev. ed., 4 vols. (Oxford: Clarendon, 1951).

Chaucer, Geoffrey, *Troilus and Criseyde*, ed. by Robert K. Root (Princeton: Princeton University Press, 1926).

Cockcroft, Robert, "Emblematic Irony: Some Possible Significances of Tamburlaine's Chariot", *Renaissance and Modern Studies*, 12 (1968), 33-55.

Coignet, Matthieu, *Politiqve Discovrses Vpon Trveth and Lying* (London, 1586), STC 5486.

Cole, Douglas, *Suffering and Evil in the Plays of Christopher Marlowe* (Princeton: Princeton University Press, 1962).

Collier, John Payne, *The History of English Dramatic Poetry to the Time of Shakespeare: and Annals of the Stage to the Restoration* (London, 1879).

Colynet, Antony, *The True History of the Ciuill VVarres of France* (London, 1591), STC 5590.

Crane, Ronald S., *The Languages of Criticism and the Structure of Poetry* (Toronto: University of Toronto Press, 1953).

Curio, Coelius, *A Notable History of the Saracens*, trans. by Thomas Newton (London, 1575), STC 6129.

Curtius, Ernst Robert, *European Literature and the Latin Middle Ages*, trans. by Willard Trask (New York: Harper, 1963).

Cutts, John P., "Dido, Queen of Carthage", *N&Q*, 5 (1958), 371-74.

——, "The Ultimate Source of Tamburlaine's White, Red, Black and Death?", *N&Q*, 5 (1958), 146-47.

Danchin, F. -C., "Études critiques sur Christophe Marlowe", *Revue germanique*, 8 (1912), 23-33.

Dent, R.W., "Marlowe, Spenser, Donne, Shakespeare – and Joseph Wybarne", *Renaissance Quarterly*, 22 (1969), 360-62.

Dick, Hugh, "*Tamburlaine* Sources Once More", *SP*, 46 (1949), 154-66.

Dickinson, Gladys (ed.), *The Instructions sur le Faict de la Guerre of Raymond de Beccarie de Pavie* (University of London: Athlone Press, 1954).

Du Bec-Crespin, Jean, *Histoire du grand Tamerlanes, ov sont descrits les rencontres, escarmouches, batailles ... tirée des monumens antiques des Arabes* (Lyons, 1602).

——, *The Historie of the Great Emperovr Tamerlan. VVherein are expressed, encounters, skirmishes, battels, ... Drawen from the auncient Monuments of the Arabians*, trans. by H. M. (London, 1597), STC 7263.

——, *The Historie of Tamerlan the Great Taken out of Alhacent*, by Lord de Sainctyon, trans. by D'Assigny (London, 1679).

——, *The History of the Life of Tamerlane the Great*, trans. and ed. by Lyonell Vane (London, 1782).

Dunseath, Thomas K., *Spenser's Allegory of Justice in Book Five of The Faerie Queene* (Princeton: Princeton University Press, 1968).

Eccles, Mark, "Marlowe in Kentish Tradition", *N&Q*, 169 (1935), 20-23,39-41, 58-61, 134-35.

Eliot, T. S., *Essays on Elizabethan Drama* (1932; rpt. New York: Harcourt, 1956).

Empson, William, "Two Proper Crimes", *Nation*, 163 (1946), 444-45.

Esler, Anthony, *The Aspiring Mind of the Elizabethan Younger Generation* (Durham, N. C.: Duke University Press, 1966).

Estienne, Henri, *A Mervaylous Discourse vpon the Life, Deedes, and Behauiours of Katherine de Medicis* (?Heydelberge, 1575), STC 10550.

Fanta, Christopher G., *Marlowe's "Agonists": An Approach to the Ambiguity of His Plays* (Cambridge: Harvard University Press, 1970).

Fenne, Thomas, *Fennes Frutes* (London, 1590), STC 10763.

Feyrabendius, Sigismundus (ed.), *Historia Rervmin [sic] Oriente Gestarvm ab exordio mvndi et orbe condito ad nostra haec vsqve tempora* (Frankfort, 1587).

[Francus, Demetrius], *Tvvo Very Notable Commentaries*, trans. by John Shute (London, 1562), STC 4470.

Freeman, Arthur, *Thomas Kyd: Facts and Problems* (Oxford: Oxford University Press, 1967).

Frye, Northrop, *Anatomy of Criticism: Four Essays* (New York: Atheneum, 1968).

Fulwell, Ulpian, *Like Will to Like*, in: *A Select Collection of Old English Plays*, ed. by W. Carew Hazlitt, Vol. III (London, 1874).

Gardner, Helen, "The Second Part of *Tamburlaine the Great*", *MLR*, 37 (1942), 18-24.

Gates, Geffrey, *The Defence of Militarie Profession* (London, 1579), STC 11683.

Gibbons, Brian, "Unstable Proteus: Marlowe's *The Tragedy of Dido Queen of Carthage*", *Christopher Marlowe*, ed. by Brian Morris (New York: Hill and Wang, 1969), 27-46.

Golding, Arthur (trans.), *The Life of the Most Godly ... Iasper Colignie Shatilion*. See Serres, Jean de.

Greene, Robert, *The Lyfe and Complete Works in Prose and Verse of Robert Greene*, ed. by Alexander B. Grosart, 15 vols. (Huth Library, 1881-86).

——, *Mamillia: A Mirrour or Looking-glasse for the Ladies of Englande* (London, 1583), STC 12269.

H., R., *The Arraignement of the VVhole Creatvre* (London, 1631), STC 13069.

Harbage, Alfred, *As They Liked It: A Study of Shakespeare's Moral Artistry* (New York: Harper, 1961).

Hartsock, Mildred, "The Complexity of *Julius Caesar*", *PMLA*, 81 (1966), 56-62.

Harvey, Gabriel, *Gabriel Harvey's Marginalia*, ed. by G. C. Moore Smith (Stratford: Shakespeare Head Press, 1913).

Hemingway, Ernest, *The Sun Also Rises* (New York: Scribner's, 1954).

Henslowe, Philip, *Henslowe's Diary*, ed. by R. A. Foakes and R. T. Rickert (Cambridge: Cambridge University Press, 1961).

Herford, C. H., and A. Wagner, "The Sources of Marlowe's *Tamburlaine*", *Academy*, 24 (1883), 265-66.

Holinshed, Raphael, *The Laste Volume of the Chronicles of England, Scotlande, and Ireland* (London, 1577), Vol. II, STC 13568b.

Hookham, Hilda, *Tamburlaine the Conqueror* (London: Hodder and Stoughton, 1962).

[Hotman, François], *A True and Plaine Report of the Furious Outrages of Fraunce*, by Ernest Varamvnd (?Striveling, Scotland, 1573), STC 13847.

Hunter, G. K., "*Henry IV* and the Elizabethan Two-Part Play", *RES*, 5 (1954), 236-48.

——, "The Theology of Marlowe's *The Jew of Malta*", *JWCI*, 27 (1964), 211-40.

[Hurault, Michel], *A Discourse vpon the Present Estate of France*, trans. by E. Aggas (London, 1588), STC 14004.

——, *An Excellent Discovrse vpon the Now Present Estate of France* (London, 1592), STC 14005.

Iue, Paul, *Instructions for the Warres*, trans. from Raymond de Beccaria (London, 1589), STC 1708.5.

——, *The Practise of Fortification: Instructions for the Warres* (London, 1589), STC 14289.

John of Salisbury, *The Statesman's Book of John of Salisbury: Being the Fourth, Fifth, and Sixth Books, and Selections from the Seventh and Eighth Books of the Policraticus*, trans. by John Dickinson (New York: Knopf, 1927).

Kesler, Charlotte, "The Importance of the Comic Tradition of English Drama in the Interpretation of Marlowe's *Doctor Faustus*", Unpublished Dissertation (Missouri, 1954).

Kimbrough, Robert, "*1 Tamburlaine*: A Speaking Picture in a Tragic Glass", *RenD*, 7 (1964), 20-34.

Knights, Lionel C., *Drama and Society in the Age of Jonson* (Harmondsworth: Penguin, 1962).

Knoll, Robert, *Christopher Marlowe* (= *TEAS* 74) (New York: Twayne, 1969).

Knolles, Richard, *The Generall Historie of the Turkes* (London, 1603), STC 15051.

Knox, Bernard M. W., "The Serpent and the Flame: The Imagery of the Second Book of the *Aeneid*", *AJP*, 71 (1950), 379-400.

Kocher, Paul, *Christopher Marlowe: A Study of His Thought, Learning, and Character* (Chapel Hill: University of North Carolina Press, 1946).

——, "Contemporary Pamphlet Backgrounds for Marlowe's *The Massacre at Paris*", *MLQ*, 8 (1947), 151-73, 309-18.

——, "François Hotman and Marlowe's *The Massacre at Paris*", *PMLA*, 56 (1941), 349-68.

Langbaine, Gerard, *An Account of the English Dramatick Poets* (Oxford, 1691).

La Primaudaye, Pierre de, *The French Academie* (London, 1586), STC 15233.

Le Roy, Loys, *Of the Interchangeable Covrse, or Variety of Things*, trans. by R. A. (London, 1594), STC 15488.

L'Espine, Jean de, *A Very Excellent and Learned Discovrse, Touching the Tranquilitie and Contention of the Minde* (Cambridge, 1592), STC 15516.

Levin, Harry, "Marlowe Today", *TDR*, 8:4 (1964), 22-31.

——, *The Overreacher: A Study of Christopher Marlowe* (Cambridge: Harvard University Press, 1952).

Lonicero, Philippo, *Chronicorvm Tvrcicorvm* ... (Frankfort, 1578).

Lopez de Gomara, Francisco, *The Pleasant Historie of the Conquest of the VVeast India* (London, 1578), STC 16807.

Lydgate, John, *The Avncient Historie and Onely Trewe and Syncere Cronicle of the Warres Betwixte the Grecians and the Troyans* (London, 1555), STC 5580.

Lyly, John, *Euphues*, in: *Elizabethan Prose Fiction*, ed. by Merritt Lawlis (New York: Odyssey, 1967).

Mahood, Molly M., *Poetry and Humanism* (London: Jonathan Cape, 1950).

Marlowe, Christopher, *The Works of Christopher Marlowe*, ed. by C. F. Tucker Brooke (Oxford: Oxford University Press, 1910).

——, *The Works of Christopher Marlowe*, ed. by Alexander Dyce (London, 1858).

——, *The Plays of Christopher Marlowe*, ed. by Leo Kirschbaum (Cleveland: World, 1968).

——, *The Complete Plays of Christopher Marlowe*, ed. by Irving Ribner (New York: Odyssey, 1963).

——, *Christopher Marlowe: The Complete Plays*, ed. by J. B. Steane (Baltimore: Penguin, 1969).

——, *Dido Queen of Carthage and The Massacre at Paris*, ed. by H. J. Oliver (Cambridge: Harvard University Press, 1968).

——, *Marlowe's Doctor Faustus, 1604-1616: Parallel Texts*, ed. by W. W. Greg (Oxford: Clarendon, 1950).

——, *The Tragical History of the Life and Death of Doctor Faustus: A Conjectural Reconstruction*, ed. by W. W. Greg (Oxford: Clarendon, 1950).

——, *Edward II*, ed. by H. B. Charlton and R. D. Waller, revised by F. N. Lees (London: Methuen, 1955).

——, *Edward the Second*, ed. by W. W. Greg (Malone Society Rpts., 1925).

——, *Marlowe: Edward the Second*, ed. by Osborne W. Tancock (Oxford: Oxford University Press, 1879).

——, *The Jew of Malta and The Massacre at Paris*, ed. by H. S. Bennett (London: Methuen, 1931).

——, *The Jew of Malta*, ed. by Richard W. Van Fossen (Lincoln: University of Nebraska Press, 1964).

——, *Poems: Christopher Marlowe*, ed. by Millar MacLure (London: Methuen, 1968).

——, *Tamburlaine the Great in Two Parts*, ed. by Una Ellis-Fermor (New York: Dial, 1930).

——, *Tamburlaine the Great, Parts I and II*, ed. by John D. Jump (Lincoln: University of Nebraska Press, 1967).

Masinton, Charles G., *Christopher Marlowe's Tragic Vision: A Study in Damnation* (Athens: Ohio University Press, 1972).

Maxwell, J. C., "How Bad Is the Text of *The Jew of Malta?*", *MLR*, 48 (1953), 435-38.

Mexia, Pedro, *The Forest or Collection of Historyes*, trans. by Thomas Fortescue (London, 1576), STC 17850.

Mills, L. J., "The Meaning of *Edward II*", *MP*, 32 (1934-35), 11-31.

Montaigne, Michel Eyquem de, *Selected Essays of Montaigne in the Translation of John Florio*, ed. by Walter Kaiser (Boston: Houghton Mifflin, 1964).

——, *The Essayes*, trans. by John Florio (London, 1603), STC 18041.

Moore, Hale, "Gabriel Harvey's References to Marlowe", *SP*, 23 (1926), 337-57.

Mornay, Philippe de, *A Woorke Concerning the Trewnesse of the Christian Religion* (London, 1587), STC 18149.

Nashe, Thomas, *The Works of Thomas Nashe*, ed. by Ronald McKerrow, 5 vols. (London: A. H. Bullen, 1904-10).

Nicholay, Nicholas, *The Nauigations, Peregrinations and Voyages, Made into Turkie*, trans. by T. Washington (London, 1585), STC 18574.

Noguères, Henri, *The Massacre of Saint Bartholomew*, trans. by Claire Eliane Engel (New York: Macmillan, 1962).

Nosworthy, J. M., "The Marlowe Manuscript", *Library*, 26 (1945), 158-71.

O'Conner, John, "Another Human Footstool", *N&Q*, 2 (1955), 332.

Ornstein, Robert, "The Comic Synthesis in *Doctor Faustus*", *ELH*, 22 (1955), 165-72.

——, "Marlowe and God: The Tragic Theology of *Dr. Faustus*", *PMLA*, 83 (1968), 1378-85.

Oxinden, Henry, Notebooks, V.b. 100, Folger Shakespeare Library, Washington, D. C.

Panofsky, Erwin, *Studies in Iconology* (1939; rpt. New York: Harper, 1962).

Partridge, Edward, *The Broken Compass: A Study of the Major Comedies of Ben Jonson* (New York: Columbia University Press, 1958).

Peacham, Henry, *Minerva Britanna, 1612*, ed. by John Horden (Menston, Yorkshire: Scolar Press, 1969).

Pearce, T. M., "Evidence for Dating Marlowe's *Tragedy of Dido*", *Studies in the English Renaissance Drama in Memory of Karl Julius Holzknecht*, ed. by J. W. Bennett *et al.* (New York: New York University Press, 1959), 231-47.

——, "Tamburlaine's 'Discipline to His Three Sonnes': An Interpretation of *Tamburlaine, Part II*", *MLQ*, 15 (1954), 18-27.

Peele, George, *Edward I*, ed. by Frank Hook, in: *The Dramatic Works of George Peele*, Vol. II (New Haven: Yale University Press, 1961).

——, *The Battle of Alcazar*, ed. by John Yoklavich, in: *The Dramatic Works of George Peele*, Vol. II (New Haven: Yale University Press, 1967).

Phaer, Thomas, *The Whole. xii. Bookes of the AEneidos of Virgill* (London, 1573), STC 24801.

Phillips, Edward, *Theatrum Poetarum* (London, 1675).

Poirier, Michel, *Christopher Marlowe* (London: Chatto and Windus, 1951).

Preston, Thomas, *Cambises*, in: *Chief Pre-Shakespearean Dramas*, ed. by Joseph Q. Adams (Boston: Houghton Mifflin, 1924).

Procopius, *History of the Wars* (London: Heinemann, 1914).

Purchas, Samuel, *Pvrchas His Pilgrimes, Part II* (London, 1625), STC 20509.

Quinn, Michael, "The Freedom of Tamburlaine", *MLQ*, 21 (1960), 315-20.

Raleigh, Sir Walter, *The History of the World* (London, 1614), STC 20637.2.

Rastell, John, *The Pastime of People* (1529; London, 1811).

Reynolds, E. E., *Thomas More and Erasmus* (London: Burns and Oates, 1965).

Ribner, Irving, "Marlowe and the Critics", *TDR*, 8:4 (1964), 211-24.

Richards, Susan, "Marlowe's *Tamburlaine II:* A Drama of Death", *MLQ*, 26 (1965), 375-87.

Ricks, Christopher, "*Sejanus* and Dismemberment", *MLN*, 76 (1961), 301-08.

Robbins, Rossell Hope, *The Encyclopedia of Witchcraft and Demonology* (New York: Crown, 1959).

Rogers, David M., "Love and Honor in Marlowe's *Dido, Queen of Carthage*", *Greyfriar*, 6 (1963), 3-7.

Rousseau, G. S., "Marlowe's *Dido* and a Rhetoric of Love", *EM*, 19 (1968), 25-49.

Rowe, Nicholas, *Tamerlane: A Tragedy* (London, 1702).

Rowse, A. L., *The England of Elizabeth: The Structure of Society* (London: Macmillan, 1950).

Sanders, Wilbur, *The Dramatist and the Received Idea: Studies in the Plays of Marlowe & Shakespeare* (Cambridge: Cambridge University Press, 1968).

Saunders, Charles, *Tamerlane the Great: A Tragedy* (London, 1681).

Seaton, Ethel, "Fresh Sources for Marlowe", *RES*, 5 (1929), 385-401.

——, "Marlowe and His Authorities", *TLS* (16 June 1921), 388.

——, "Marlowe's Light Reading", *Elizabethan and Jacobean Studies Presented to Frank Percy Wilson* (Oxford: Oxford University Press, 1959), 17-35.

——, "Marlowe's Map", *E&S*, 10 (1924), 13-35.

Seneca, Lucius Annaeus, *The Work of that excellent Philosopher ... Seneca concerning Benefyting*, trans. by Arthur Golding (London, 1578), STC 22215.

Serres, Jean de, *The Fourth Parte of Cōmentaries of the Ciuill Warres in France* (London, 1576), STC 22243.

——, *The Lyfe of the Most Godly ... Iasper Colignie Shatilion*, trans. by Arthur Golding (London, 1576), STC 22248.

Shakespeare, William, *Macbeth*, ed. by Kenneth Muir (Cambridge: Harvard University Press, 1962).

——, *William Shakespeare: The Complete Works*, general ed. Alfred Harbage (Baltimore: Penguin, 1060).

Sidney, Sir Philip, *The Prose Works of Sir Philip Sidney*, ed. by Albert Feuillerat (Cambridge: Cambridge University Press, 1962).

Smith, G. C. Moore, *Gabriel Harvey's Marginalia*. See Harvey, Gabriel.

Smith, Hallett, *Elizabethan Poetry* (Cambridge: Harvard University Press, 1952).

Smith, Marion Bodwell, *Marlowe's Imagery and the Marlowe Canon* (Philadelphia, 1940).

Spenser, Edmund, *Faerie Queene*, ed. by J. C. Smith, in: *Poetical Works*, 3 vols. (Oxford: Oxford University Press, 1909).

Starnes, DeWitt T., and Ernest William Talbert, *Classical Myth and Legend in Renaissance Dictionaries* (Chapel Hill: University of North Carolina Press, 1955).

Steadman, John M., "Falstaff as Actaeon: A Dramatic Emblem", *SQ*, 14 (1963), 231-44.

Steane, J. B., *Marlowe: A Critical Study* (Cambridge: Cambridge University Press, 1964).

Stow, John, *Annales of England* (London, 1592), STC 23334.

——, *The Chronicles of England* (London, 1580), STC 23333.

Tayler, Edward William, *Nature and Art in Renaissance Literature* (New York: Columbia University Press, 1964).

Taylor, Robert T., "Maximinus and Tamburlaine", *N&Q*, 4 (1957), 417-18.

Vaughan, William, *The Golden-groue, Moralized in Three Bookes* (London, 1608), STC 24611.

Vigenere, Blaise de (trans.), *L'Histoire de la decadence de l'empire Grec, et establissement de celvy des Turcs ...* par Nicolas Chalcondyle [Chalkokondyles] (Paris, 1577).

Voegelin, Eric, "Das Timurbild der Humanisten", *Zeitschrift für öffentliches Recht*, XVII:5.

W., R., *Martine Mar-Sixtus* (London, 1592), STC 24913a.

Waddington, Raymond, "*Antony and Cleopatra:* 'What Venus did with Mars'", *Shakespeare Studies*, 2 (1966), 210-27.

Waith, Eugene, *The Herculean Hero in Marlowe, Chapman, Shakespeare and Dryden* (London: Chatto and Windus, 1962).

Wehling, Mary Mellen, "Marlowe's Mnemonic Nominology with Especial Reference to Tamburlaine", *MLN*, 73 (1958), 243-47.

Welsh, Robert Ford, *The Printing of the Early Editions of Marlowe's Plays* (Ann Arbor, Michigan: University Microfilms, 1964).

Whetstone, George, *The English Myrror* (London, 1586), STC 25336.

Whitney, Geffrey, *A Choice of Emblemes* (1586; rpt. New York: Benjamin Blom, 1967).

Wilson, Frank Percy, *Marlowe and the Early Shakespeare* (Oxford: Oxford University Press, 1953).

Wind, Edgar, *Pagan Mysteries in the Renaissance*, rev. ed. (London: Faber, 1968).

Winstanley, William, *The Lives of the Most Famous English Poets* (London, 1687).

Wyatt, Sir Thomas, *Collected Poems of Sir Thomas Wyatt*, ed. by Kenneth Muir (London: Routledge, 1949).

Wybarne, Joseph, *The New Age of Old Names* (London, 1609), STC 26055.

Zimansky, Curt, "Marlowe's *Faustus*: The Date Again", *PQ*, 41 (1962), 181-87.

INDEX